LES BROWN CHANGED OUR LIVES

77 Stories To Inspire You To Live Your Dreams

Dr Patrick Businge

Published by Greatness University Publishers
info@greatness-university.com
www.greatness-university.com

ISBN: 1999949498
ISBN-13: 9781999949495

DEDICATION

This book is dedicated to Mr Les Brown: the world's number one motivational speaker. For many years, he has helped people discover and walk their paths to greatness. May these stories, from the people who are saying 'Les Brown Changed Our Lives,' inspire you to live the rest of your life as the best of your life.

Dr Patrick Businge

CONTENTS

CONTENTS BY CONTRIBUTOR

CHAPTER 1: ACTION

CHAPTER 2: AUTHORS

CHAPTER 3: BUSINESS

CHAPTER 4: COACHING

CHAPTER 5: COMEBACK POWER

CHAPTER 6: COMPANIONSHIP

CHAPTER 7: EDUCATION

CHAPTER 8: ENCOUNTERS

CHAPTER 9: GREATNESS

CHAPTER 10: HEALTH

CHAPTER 11: KIDPRENEURS

CHAPTER 12: LEGACY

CHAPTER 13: MINDSET

CHAPTER 14: MOTIVATION

CHAPTER 15: PERSEVERANCE

CHAPTER 16: POWER

CHAPTER 17: RELIGION

CHAPTER 18: RISKING

CHAPTER 19: SPEAKING

CHAPTER 20: SUCCESS

CHAPTER 21: TRANSFORMATION

CHAPTER 22: UBUNTU

CHAPTER 23: VISION

CHAPTER 24: VOICE OF HOPE

ACKNOWLEDGMENTS

This book would have not been possible without the wisdom from God who has made it possible to bring it to fruition. A lot of thanks to Mr Les Brown for his inspiring speeches and online videos which are freely available to help people step into their greatness.

I cannot proceed without thanking Mrs Serena Brown Travis for her dedicated support during the writing of this book and for accepting to write its Foreword. It is with great joy that I extend my gratitude to over 100 people who sent me their stories and the 77 people who willingly shared them in this book. I was also fortunate to come to the attention of Jayson Gerald Nenis, Founder of Big Lake Visions in Muskegon, Michigan, USA who acted as my proofreader.

I am indebted to colleagues in the Les Brown Unlimited Team. It is because of their critical friendship and social and moral support that I have accomplished writing this long awaited book. Special applause to Antonio Smith Jr, the Founder of Plant Better University, who offered a listening ear and removed the roadblocks I was encountering along the way.

Special thanks to my family, relatives and friends for the gift of education. While my father Mr George Rusoke inspired my head, my mother Stella Rusoke ignited my heart. I cannot fail to thank my wife Mrs Julian Businge and my two little children for the patience and courtesy I received whilst writing this book.

FOREWORD

By

Serena Brown Travis

Serena Brown Travis

Daughter of Les Brown

SERENA BROWN TRAVIS

Before reading the Foreword, allow me to introduce to you Serena Brown Travis. She is an Ohio native and daughter of the legendary motivational speaker Les Brown. Since her and her family's life's work has been full of positivity, motivation, and inspiration; having small goals was frowned upon. While 'shooting for the moon to land among the stars', Serena earned her Bachelor of Arts degree from Hampton University and Masters in Marketing and Communication from Franklin University.

Serena is a bestselling author of five children's books focused on the tougher issues youngsters are facing such as homelessness, bullying, childhood hunger, and abandonment. With a unique and subtle approach, the stories in the Perfect Penny series will entertain, inspire, motivate, and teach compassion to its readers, a lesson that never gets old.

Outside of viewing the glass half full and acting as the Business Manager for Les Brown Enterprises and CEO of Les Brown Unlimited, Serena enjoys spending time as a volunteer for various non-profit organizations, running her popular food truck, and spending time with her husband and two daughters. I am so excited that Serena has taken time out of her busy schedule to write this Foreword.

Les Brown Changed My Life

As the youngest daughter of the legendary motivational speaker Les Brown, it is an honor to proudly say *Les Brown Changed My Life.*

I literally would not have life if it were not for the partnership between my mother and father. In addition to Les Brown changing my life, Les Brown gave me life. I am proud of the blood of greatness, grit, and determination flowing through my veins. However, instead of giving a lesson on biology and reproduction, it is easier for me to share my experiences on how Les Brown as my father changed me.

I've always known IT'S POSSIBLE. Not because of encouraging posters in schools or listening to more motivational speeches than I can count, I've known this because I've witnessed my father live it. My father, Les Brown lives, breathes, and moves in the spirit that any and everything is possible.

More often than not, parents operate in the *do as I say and not as I do* spirit. My father is a doer, a man who puts his money where his mouth is, who gives hope to the hopeless, and who fights for the ones who have lost the will to fight for themselves.

I've watched a selfless humanitarian empty his suitcase to someone in need of clothes, who will go out of his way to offer food to someone who is hungry, and will give his last dime away to those in need.

Les Brown changed my life because I've seen on multiple occasions his God-ordained gift of service overtake rational ideology to be a blessing to others. He is a man who demonstrates and practices faith on a whole new level. He's serious when he says "leap and grow your wings on the way down", he practices that principle to this day. He is determined to change minds, soften hearts, just to let the world know that in spite of your current circumstances and a grim diagnosis, IT'S POSSIBLE.

As my father, who aggressively pursued his career, our time spent together was minimal, however, the moments of laughter, talks, and fun will never leave my memory. Dad's three minute voicemails to sing me the Happy Birthday song or his occasional messages to encourage me to do well on a test that were motivational speeches are unforgettable. Les Brown changed my life by his example of love and compassion, grit and grace, and pleasant memories and moments.

As a source of inspiration, an advocate of education, and a proponent of independence, my father Les Brown made sure I would never experience some of his childhood pains; the mystery of not knowing your parents, he proudly claimed me November 1980. He made sure, unlike himself, I never went hungry, or without food or clothes, but more important than this, he became a father to hundreds of fatherless sons and daughters who now I have the pleasure of having brothers and sisters in love everywhere.

He is a brave man who I've watched snatch victory from the jaws of defeat again and again. He is a fearless man who I've watched never give up even with all odds stacked against him. He is a fighter, who told the attacks of cancer in his body to leave him to the work that God placed in him and to this day, my father Les Brown is an 18 year cancer conqueror.

Les Brown my business advisor, father, and friend changed my life. I now have the pleasure of inviting you to read the life changing stories in this book so that you may be inspired to pursue your greatness.

Love and Kindness,

Serena Brown Travis

INTRODUCTION

LES BROWN CHANGED OUR LIVES

77 stories to inspire you to live your dreams

Antonio Smith, Jr

Cheryl Du Plooy

Julian Businge

Michelle Watson

Ty Cohen

Dr Ruben West

Neil Huntley

Jayson Gerald

King Twitty

Elda Gjoka

Greg Walker

Lee Roberts

22

Who is Les Brown?

**World's Leading Motivational Speaker,
Master Storyteller, Bestselling Author,
and Television Personality
www.lesbrown.com**

24

Who is Les Brown?

As a renowned public speaker, author and television personality, Les Brown has risen to national prominence by delivering a high energy message which tells people how to shake off mediocrity and live up to their greatness. It is a message Les Brown has learned from his own life and one he is helping others apply to their lives.

Born a twin in low-income Liberty City in Miami, Florida, Les and his twin brother, Wes, were adopted when they were six weeks old by Mrs. Mamie Brown, a single woman who had very little education and financial means, but a very big heart. As a child his inattention to school work, his restless energy and the failure of his teachers to recognize his real potential resulted in him being mislabelled as a slow learner. The label and the stigma stayed with Les, damaging his self-esteem to such an extent that it took several years to overcome.

In 1989, Les Brown was the recipient of the National Speakers Association's highest honour: The Council of Peers Award of Excellence. In addition, he was selected as one of America's Top Five Speakers in 1992 by Toastmasters International.

In 1990, Les recorded his first in a series of speech presentations entitled 'You Deserve' with Les Brown. He was awarded a Chicago-area Emmy and became the leading fund-raising program of its kind for pledges to PBS stations nationwide.

Les Brown is not only an internationally recognized speaker but he is also the author of the highly acclaimed and successful book, 'Live Your Dreams', and former host of 'The Les Brown Show,' a nationally syndicated daily television talk show which focused on solutions rather than problems.

Les Brown is one of the America's leading authorities in understanding and stimulating human potential, utilizing powerful delivery and newly emerging insights to teach, inspire and channel people to new levels of achievement.

Les Brown Fans

27

What Les Brown Fans Are Saying

Listen, I was homeless and sleeping on the floor when your words of motivation kept my faith alive and now I'm thriving at life.

Adam

Les Brown coaching helped me to be a phenomenal speaker. I have witnessed the growth and I am taking my life to great new levels.

Alka Sharma
International Speaker and Fitness Coach
Toronto, Canada

One pack of Les Brown. You can do it Brother. Your first cassette tape inspired me. You went from poverty to State Legislator. I went from poverty and grew up on welfare. Today, I'm a State Legislator.

Carlos

You have helped me in so many ways in a short period of time. Such an inspiration and I thank you Mr. Brown. I consider you a Bread and Butter of mine for advice.

Daryl

My journey has been one of depression from having been bullied and numerous suicide attempts from a teen to an adult. I didn't think I would ever achieve anything due to the labels I was living with...My greatest moment was reading the Les Brown quote that would change my life, "Don't let other people's opinion of you become your reality!" That day I started living beyond my labels and now I'm ready to soar like an eagle. Thank you Les Brown for helping me to see my potential!

Dr Ira Roach III

I was at a dark moment in my life. I had just lost my dad and was trying to make sense of it. I discovered Les Brown and when he asked, 'In what you've done with your life thus far, is it giving you what you want?' I had to answer no, it hadn't. So Les Brown triggered a change in life. I dusted off my dream and have been working on it like a man possessed. I'm proud to say like a puzzle, all the pieces are coming together.

John Nowinsky
Founder of Creative Computer Concepts
Texas, USA

I have been asking what my purpose is for years. Mr. Brown, you helped me discover my purpose. Thank you.

Maria

Tell it like it is. Man you have changed our lives forever… And you should be proud of yourself. You have said as long as you have reached one… Then you have changed a community. Trust me, you have changed my life forever!!!

Mia

You're an incredible human being Les! Thank you so much for everything you've done for me and countless others. Your thought energy will always be with all of us!

Nick

Middle of the night here in Japan. I am remembering how you first touched me deeply starting decades ago. You are an important foundation of inspiration and common sense in a world of chaos.

Richard

I have spent years listening to Les Brown daily. As a housekeeper I could listen on my cell phone as I worked away for hours a day. When I heard the words "I'm the one", something shifted in me and I knew that it was time to live the life I deserved. In April 2018 I found the courage and got on a plane by myself and attended his training event. I arrived knowing nobody but I left having family. Today I am fulfilling a dream to build my business as a speaker, trainer and coach. Thank you Les Brown. I am the only one that can tell my story.

**Rachel Elizabeth Bell
Mother, Coach, and CEO of Don't You Dare Quit.
Ontario, Canada**

Mr. Les Brown helped me get over my fear by reminding me that I'm changing lives, not giving open heart surgery, so there's nothing to fear. To speak on purpose and always with a purpose. To never make a point without a story, and never tell a story without making a point. My life changed when he said, 'What if you die today and the ghost of the goals and dreams come back and ask 'why did we have to die with you?' What will you tell them?'

**Ron Lewis Jr,
The comeback kid from the 1.3 to the PhD
Florida, USA**

I was in deep depression 6 months ago. Lost all hope on life. Somehow God lead me to your YouTube channel. I'm completely changed now, full of hope. Thank you.

Samuel

Les Brown Changed Our Lives

CONTRIBUTORS

Philly Gifo Matsepa, South Africa

PJ Douglas, USA

Pog Thanee, Thailand

Rachael Krasny, USA

Reginald L Russell, USA

Gil Evans, USA

Greg Walker, USA

Hannah Zemzam, UK

Hector Luis Cruz, USA

Herman Thystere, Congo- Brazaville

Julian Businge, UK

Keidi Awadu, USA

Kevin Miguel Langford, USA

Lee Roberts, UK

Lehlohonolo Mazindo, South Africa

Sandra Pelletier, Dominican Republic

Selsabil Hamrouni, Tunisia

Serena Brown Travis, USA

Shermanda Anderson-Ramsay, USA

Simone Tessari, Guatemala

Stella Businge, UK

Steve Mcmenamin, Australia

Terrance Stafford, USA

Tommy Pichardo, USA

Toni Thompson, USA

Dexter Patterson, USA

Carolina Lanfair, USA

Charles and Nadia Antony, USA

Cheryl du Plooy, South Africa

David Hall, USA

David Lubuurwa, USA

Jayson Gerald Nenis, USA

Jean Edouard Brutus, Haiti

Joanne Louise Kavanagh, Ireland

Jonathan Nicholas, USA

Jorge Alejandro Valdez, USA

Michelle Watson, UK

Milton Sithole, Zimbabwe

Neil Huntley, UK

Nikki Garcia, USA

Paul Kenny, Australia

Rich Fontaine, USA

Richard Shokane, Brunei

Rogers Mbaziira, Uganda

Ronnette Hopgood, USA

Samuel Gerson Andrisse, Belgium

Ty Cohen, USA

Tyler Jamal Smith, USA

Umana Anieka, Nigeria

Vastine East, USA

Vi Nedd-Jackman, USA

Veronika Sam, UK

Dr. Ira Roach III, USA

Dr. Patrick Businge, UK

Dr. Ruben West, USA

Elda Gjoka, Albania

Felix Kawawa, Nigeria

Inna Joy Martin-Carter, USA

Inspiring Vanessa, UK

Ires Alliston, USA

Jacek Salek, Netherlands

Jane Chicoyne, Canada

Manuel Shipwood

Levan Adams, USA

Lucy Sabiiti, Uganda

Lynnette Richardson, USA

Maria-Lewis Ramadane, USA

Michael J Callum Esq, UK

Anonymous, Earth

Alka Sharma, Canada

Antionette Blake, USA

Antonio Smith Jr, USA

Benjamin Hinton, USA

Vinette Hoffman Jackson, UK

Wilken Dorcilien, USA

Wishum Gregory, USA

Benjovi Benson, Turkey

Fred O Juma, UK

A Walk Through The Chapters

Do you want to change your life? Do you want to create a better version of yourself? Are you looking for new ways to win? If you have answered YES to any of these questions, then this book is for you. As you read this book, you will discover how Les Brown has inspired people to do exactly what you wish to accomplish. As a member of the Les Brown Unlimited Team, I have witnessed my life blossom to a Bestselling Author, Founder of Greatness University, International Speaker, Book Creation Mentor, Greatness Researcher and won an award for Authentic Leadership. Based on what I know, I can proudly say that Les Brown has changed my life. Here is a brief overview of the chapters in this book.

Your action

As you read Chapter 1, don't be the person who misses out on opportunities because you take too long to take action on what you have read. As you read the stories therein, allow your life to soar to new heights, just as mine did while I wrote it. Be the kind of person that takes action so that your life will be more meaningful and purpose driven. This is what Ty Cohen from North Carolina, USA did when he 'stole' a copy of Les Brown's book *Live Your Dreams* from the back of his dad's car. After reaching its final page, Ty was able to make a transition from immanent death to immediate success. It's by taking action that Shermanda Anderson-Ramsay from Florida, USA, while bedridden, take the unwavering decision to join the Les Brown Unlimited Team … It's by taking action that David Lubuuwa from Massachusetts, USA created his greatest life as a human rights activist and broadcaster. Finally, after listening to Les Brown saying that greatness is the least sold commodity, I created Greatness University: the world's first institution dedicated to researching and monetising greatness in people, organisations and businesses.

Your book

The great American poet, singer, and civil rights activist Maya Angelou said, 'There is nothing more painful than an "Untold Story" buried in your soul'. I believe you have a great story. That story within you is waiting for you to write it down and share it with the world. In Chapter 2, you will read examples of stories from Lehlohonolo Mazinda from South Africa, Fred O. Juma and Dr Patrick Businge from England, UK. These stories have the power to shift minds, mend broken hearts and transform the world.

Your business

Chapter 3 is for you if you want to win big in business. In this chapter, you will discover why the Big Dreamer Greg Walker from Ohio, USA has come to the conclusion that you are too big to dream small. In this chapter, you will reflect on how Gil Evans from Ohio, USA managed to turn his failure into success. In this chapter, you will journey with Jean Edouard Brutus from Haiti and find a way to win in the USA.

Your coach

Les Brown says, 'There are winners and there are losers and there are people who have not discovered how to win. And all they need is some coaching. All they need is some help and assistance — just a little support'. As you know, when you learn from the best how to win, you increase your chances of doing your best. Chapter 4 gives you examples of people like Chef Keidi Awadu from Nevada, USA; Pog Thanee from Thailand, and Alka Sharma from Toronto, Canada who have become winners because of the coaching and mentoring from Les Brown. As you read this chapter, you might be attracted to doing what Les Brown does. Your next step is to join the Les Brown Unlimited Team. In joining this team, you will have doors opened for you in avenues of life that you never imagined.

Your comeback power

Have you ever been in a situation where you felt powerless? How did you bounce back? Chapter 5 is full of examples of people who have exercised their comeback power. This power has led Cheryl du Plooy from South Africa to create 'Hooked on Life'. This power has allowed Michael J Callum, Esq from England, UK to fight for his dreams. This power has allowed Joanne Kavanagh from Ireland to become unstoppable. This power has become the key for Milton Sithole from Zimbabwe to get unstuck.

Your network

When it comes to the people we associate with, there is no shortage of sayings, proverbs and statements. One African proverb says, 'Birds of the same feather flock together'. Another goes, 'Show me your friends and I will show you who you are'. The President of the United States of America Donald Trump says, 'If you hang around with losers you become a loser'. Porter Gale titled her book, 'Your Network is Your Net Worth'. Chapter 6 contains stories from people who have made Les Brown their companion and they include: Manuel Shipwood; Antionette Blake and Dr. Ira Roach III from Delaware, USA; and Sandra Pelletier from the Dominican Republic It is my hope that by the end of this chapter, you would have discovered how Les Brown can be your companion too in your journey through life.

Your education

Les Brown is a master storyteller and he has educated millions of people through stories. Chapter 7 contains stories from: Vastine East from Texas, USA; Amy Jane Chicoyne from Ontario, Canada; and Levan Adams from Michigan, USA. These great people have learnt from Les Brown's stories and changed their lives. They are a testament that education can be the difference between success and failure.

Your possibilities

I think that this excerpt from Les Brown's speech is all we need to set the scene for the stories in chapter 8, *'So what is that something? When you've got an idea you want to move on. You might not have the money, you might not have the education, you might not have the support or the resources you need. What is that something that can keep us going, that will enable us to act on our dream? What's one of those keys that will begin to help us to discover the secrets to our dream? Here's what I want you to repeat after me please with power and conviction, say:* **'It's Possible'**. *It's all I want you to do when you look at your dream, just say to yourself every day: It's possible. Just say that every day to yourself: It's possible'.* My advice as you read the story of Michelle Watson and Vinette Hoffman Jackson from England, UK; and Herman

Thystere from Congo-Brazaville, remember to say to yourself, *'It's Possible'*.

Your greatness

Chapter 9 is about greatness. Failure, pain, disappointment, struggle, are steps to greatness. Greatness is about following where these steps are leading us in life. Nelson Mandela said, "Sometimes, it falls upon a generation to be great. You can be that great generation. Let your greatness blossom." You are going to discover how Maria-Lewis Ramadane from Virginia, USA; Hannah Zemzam from England, UK; and another anonymous writer are examples of this great generation. I leave you with this final thought from Les Brown to accompany you as you read, "If you do what is easy, your life will be hard. If you do what is hard, your life will be easy". My question to you is: what are you currently doing?

Your health

Just a thought: how much will your bill be if you were to pay or every hour you are alive?. In Chapter 10, you will read stories from Dexter Patterson from Wisconsin, USA and Paul Kelly from Tasmania, Australia who have come to the realisation that their health is their wealth and how Les Brown has accompanied them to regain this wealth when it all seemed lost.

Your creativity

Approximately a third of the world population has been touched by the message of Jesus Christ. In Matthew 18, his disciples came to him and asked, 'Who, then, is the greatest in the kingdom of heaven?' In response, Jesus called a little child and said, 'Truly I tell you, unless you change and become like little children, you will never enter the kingdom of heaven'. From this story, I think that if we want to step into our greatness, we have to become like little children. Little children are open-minded, creative, and above willing to risk to get what they want. Chapter 11 contains stories from Inspiring Vanessa and Stella Businge from England, UK who are stepping into their greatness. I invite you to read and be inspired by their journey.

Your legacy

Do you believe in ghosts? Take time to read this reflection from Les Brown and let me know your answer afterwards: *'So, I say that your life is worth finding, what it is that you are supposed to do. Imagine if you will, being on your death bed and standing around your bed are the ghosts of the dreams, the ideas, the abilities, the talents, given to you by life but you, for whatever reason, you never pursued those dreams, you never acted on those ideas, and you never used those gifts. You never used those talents, and there they are staring at you as you are lying on your bed, with large angry eyes, saying: 'We came to you, and only you could have given us life, and now we must die with you forever'.* I can already guess your answer. Now, my question to you is: If you died today, how will future generations know that your life was worth living? In chapter 12, we are going to discover how Nikki Garcia from New Mexico, USA and Carolina Lanfair from California, USA have made marks not on their bodies but on this great universe.

After decades of research on achievement and success, the World-renowned Stanford University psychologist Carol Dweck discovered a ground-breaking idea about the power of our mindset. In her book 'Mindset', Carol Dweck explains why it's not just our abilities and talent that bring us success but whether we approach them with a fixed or growth mindset. With a growth mindset, we can achieve far beyond our horizons in any area. Chapter 13 is a clear testimony on the extent to which the enabling words of Les Brown have allowed Elda Gjoka from Tirana, Albania; Kevin Miguel from North Carolina, USA; and an anonymous writer to be successful in spite of their circumstances.

Allow me to introduce chapter 14 with this reflection from Les Brown taken from his famous keynote speech 'You Gotta be Hungry': *When would a baby walk? It will walk when it walks. That's when it will walk. Les, when will you be known nationally as the motivator? I will be known when I am known. That's when I'll be known. Don't get caught up in — well, I've tried it four or five times and things didn't work out. If there's something that you want and you're hungry for it, you've got to do whatever is necessary until and when you give the best you can and that's not enough, you must do what is required. And don't give up on yourself.*

Effectively, the hunger within us sustains our motivation. This chapter contains stories of people whose deep hunger has allowed them, like the babies, to persist and succeed. Reginald L Russell from Arizona, USA has had the motivation to go before he is ready. Julian Businge share's how she has transitioned from her comfort zone to chasing her dreams. Jorge Alexandro Valdez has moved from being broken to breakthrough.

Your mindset

Before you read this chapter on how people have persevered amidst the violent storms of life, I would like to share with you this reflection I received from Les Brown on 18th January 2018. *I believe…If you fall, land on your back; if you can look up, you can get up because…**YOU STILL HAVE A DREAM!** I believe…A setback is a set up for a comeback; but YOU won't give up because…**YOU STILL HAVE A DREAM!** I believe... Life has a way of bruising and bending you; yet you refuse to break, WHY? **YOU STILL HAVE A DREAM!** Never give up, quit, or throw in the towel…KEEP DREAMING and PURSUE IT.* So, my advice to you is not to choose to be a permanent victim of fear in your life. Read these stories from Toni Thompson from California, USA; Steve Mcmenamin from Victoria, Australia; and Veronika Sam from England, UK who have stood to life and its challenges. Like them, you have got what it takes to find a way to win and get a message from misery. I look forward to you becoming an example of a person who believes like us that, 'I will persevere until I succeed'.

Your power

In her book 'A Return to Love', Marianne Williamson wrote, 'Our deepest fear is not that we are inadequate. Our deepest fear is that we are powerful beyond measure'. As you read chapter 16 on power, I would like you to reflect on this question: What is my power? Tyler Jamal Smith from Florida, USA and Philly Figo Matsepa from South Africa will be a testimony for you to turn to your deepest fear and get the courage to turn your tragedy into triumph and your test into a testimony. I leave you with the words of Nelson Mandela, 'There is no passion to be found playing small in settling for a life that is less than the one you are capable of living'.

Your faith

While religion is the number one cause of conflict in the world, it is also the number one cause of peace. At the heart of any religion is faith: from the Latin word 'fidere' which means to trust.   Life is full of examples of people who have lived by faith in extraordinary ways: Mother Teresa, Nelson Mandela, Martin Luther King, Dietrich Bonhoeffer, and many others. Life is also full of people who have lived by faith in ordinary ways: our parents, siblings, neighbours, etc. In my case, faith is one of the treasures I got from my parents when they walked to their dreams with great determination and unwavering hope. This taught me that I can achieve my dreams if I lived from a place of faith. As you read chapter 17, you will discover people with faith. It is this faith that has led Charles and Nadia Anthony from Texas, USA to move from prison to the pulpit. It is faith that has allowed Umana Anieka from Nigeria to journey from himself to God. It is faith that has made Felix Kawawa from Nigeria move from loss to wealth. It is my hope that their faith will take you to another hemisphere with a different time zone where your dreams are possible.

Your risk appetite

In January 2018, I sent an email to Les Brown and started collecting stories of people whose lives had been changed by him. When one of the women who was not even a relative of Les Brown got my Facebook invitation to share her story in my book, her reply was, 'You have stolen my idea. I have had it for many years. If you touch it, I will sue you'. Where did I get the courage to continue after this unexpected response? Of course you can easily guess: it is from Les Brown. He says, *'You wanna become a risk-taker. You wanna raise the bar on yourself. Most people won't do that. See most people engage in low-life living, low-risk living...If you're not willing to risk, you cannot grow. And if you cannot grow, you cannot become your best. And if you cannot become your best, you can't be happy. And if you can't be happy, then what else is there?'* As I wanted to do what I loved, I became a risk taker. Had I continued living a low-risk life, you would not be reading this book. As you read chapter 18, you will discover how Rachael Krasny from Florida, USA made a transition from living a life as a victim to being victorious. Like Rich Fontaine from Florida, USA, you will learn to follow your heart and take risks so that you discover your treasure. Like Tommy Pichardo, you will take every step to give up your treasured possession to get what you want.

Your story

In chapter 19, you will read stories from people who have been transformed by the way Les Brown tells his story. As you read Dr Ruben West's story and Jacek Salek's story, you will discover Les Brown's three key principles of storytelling. As you read David Hall's story, you will discover how Les Brown's voice gave him the power to change his perception and led him to sharing his story given to him through life's experiences in Iraq, Afghanistan and the USA. As you read Ires Alliston's story and Wilken Dorcilien's story, you will learn how she rose above her circumstances, discovered her powerful voice and went on to become an international speaker. If, after reading these stories, you feel that it is time for you to unleash the story buried within your soul, get in touch. I believe that the world is waiting to hear your story. I am looking forward to helping you share your story and change the world.

Your success

I attribute most of my success to education. I have always had a hunger for education. It is because of this hunger that I invested a lot of money to the point of gaining 7 university qualifications from 7 universities. In chapter 20, you will encounter 5 examples of people who have been hungry for knowledge and how their hunger led them to success: Lee Roberts and Neil Huntley from England, UK; Benjamin Hinton from Pennsylvania, USA; Benjovi Benson from Turkey; and an anonymous writer from Zambia. If they have been successful against all odds, why not you? At the end of this Chapter, my wish for you is that you gain all the knowledge you need to make the rest of your life the best of your life.

Your transformation

Like butterflies, we too undergo visible and invisible transformation in our life time. While we look towards some of the transformations, we hate to think about or go through some others. We consider them to be tough times in our lives. Thanks to people like the American televangelist, motivational speaker, and author Robert Schuller who encourage us by their words, 'Tough times never last, but tough people do!' The 5 stories you will read in chapter 21 are examples of people who have gone through profound moments of transformation. Like the beautiful butterflies, you can hardly tell the tough times they have gone through. While Antonio T. Smith, Jr in

Texas, USA has been able to move from being homeless to a millionaire, PJ Douglas has made a transition from crime to commitment. While an anonymous writer has moved from drugs to dreams, Hector Luiz Cruz can be perceived as the Les Brown of Rhode Island, Inna Joy Martin-Carter is confidently marching to her destiny. They all testify that what has helped them to go through tough times and become the tough people they are today is Les Brown.

Your Ubuntu

Chapter 22 is about Ubuntu. You might be wondering and asking, what is *Ubuntu*? Ubuntu is an African word that is difficult to render into any other language. Despite this being the case, Ubuntu is Africa's greatest gift to the world. It refers to the African belief that our humanity is intricately linked and we all belong to a bundle of life. Through these stories, Les Brown is seen as a man with *Ubuntu.*   After having a house fire and still wearing the same clothes after the fire, Les Brown took Wishum Gregory aka King Twitty from New York to the Beltway Plaza Mall and bought him 7 suits, 10 shirts and 14 ties. As he went through marital problems, Samuel Gerson Andrisse from Belgium discovered Les Brown and came to the conclusion that Les Brown was like a brother telling him what to do. As you read chapter 22, you will discover other stories from Selsabil Hamrouni from Tunisia and Simone Tessari from Guatemala how Les Brown has manifested his Ubuntu in the words of the people who have experienced these life defining moments.

Your vision

In Proverbs 29:18, it is written, 'Where there is no vision, the people perish'. For me this means that if you don't have a vision for your life, you are at risk of having a premature death. Having vision is essential to having a long and fulfilled life. In my book '7 Steps to Greatness', I consider **V.I.S.I.O.N** to be the 5th step to greatness. The acronym **V.I.S.I.O.N** stands for: **V**isualise, **I**nside the mind, **S**enses, **I**magine, **O**vercome obstacles, **N**o fear. To help you remember this, I urge you to learn this sentence: I Visualise Inside my mind with my Senses and I Imagine Overcoming obstacles with No fear. Let us now read stories from Lucy Sabiiti from Uganda, Ronnette Hopgood from Wisconsin, USA and Lynnette Richardson from Virginia, USA on how Les Brown inspired her daughter to get more from life.

Your hope

In my bestselling book '7 Steps to Greatness', I write about the shortage of hope as one of the biggest challenges facing our world today. In this powerful final chapter, you will discover how Les Brown's voice gave hope to people. By increasing the size of her hope, Vi Nedd-Jackman from Illinois, USA was able to move from the valley to the mountain top. As he faced life's challenges, Les Brown's voice woke up Richard Shokane from Brunei from the deep sleep of helplessness, depression and came to the conclusion that Les Brown's voice is God's voice. As he tuned in on Les Brown for the first time, Jayson Gerald Nenis from Michigan heard, "Most people have done all that they are ever going to do. They raise a family, they earn a living, and then they die!" These words led him to the realisation that there are so many lives that have no drive, no direction, and people who are not really living in their life! As he did not want to be like them, Les Brown's voice set him on the journey of looking for more from life. Listening from The Sunshine State of Florida, Terrance Stafford had a great epiphany when he heard Les Brown talk about changing your mindset and using all that is inside of you to manifest it to your reality.

As you read this final chapter, be open to the possibility that you might be failing to reach your greatness not because of the place you are born and not because of your career, gender or race. You might be failing because of the size of your hope. My question to you is - what is the size of your hope? Are you ready to measure the size of your hope? Are you willing to increase the size of your hope? What are you willing to do or change after reading this book so that you increase your hope? I leave you with the words I heard from Pope Francis while in Rome in 2017, 'Hope does not disappoint. Hope is sure. Be men and women of hope'.

CHAPTER 1: ACTION

What do you do...when...?

As you lay on your hospital bed, what do you do when you hear the doctors saying, 'you have a couple of years to live'? As you walk in a city car park, what do you do when you are hit by a vehicle and you are severely injured? As a teenager suffering from depression, loneliness and hopelessness in Africa, what do you do when you hear a stranger saying, 'It's possible?' As an entrepreneur looking to take your business to the next level, what do you do when you hear your coach saying, 'everyday, people are sold everything except one thing- greatness?

As you read this chapter, you will discover the answers to these questions. First, you will learn that it is possible to turn immanent death to immediate success. Second, you will recognise that when things go wrong, you have the power to turn your life's lemons into lemonades. Third, you will understand that when you have big dreams, it is possible to turn your depression and hopelessness into unparalleled activism. Fourth and last, you will resolve and accept that there is no perfect time to start your own business and admit what Les Brown says that anything worth doing is worth doing badly.

From Immanent Death to Success
Ty Cohen
North Carolina, USA

Internet Marketer, Business Consultant, Personal
Development Coach, and Radio Personality
www.KindleCashFlow.com

From immanent death to success

We start our journey discovery by moving to Raleigh in North Carolina, USA where we meet Ty Cohen. Ty is an internationally renowned internet marketer, business consultant, personal development coach, speaker, former morning talk show host, and radio personality. He is a bestselling author and creator of over a dozen best-selling books, software programs, directories and products. Over the last 11 years, Ty has taught thousands of individuals how to successfully market, promote and sell their products and services online using his free system which he makes available at KindleCashFlow.com. In his story, you will discover how he turned his life's obstacles into financial opportunities that will enable you to reach your personal and business goals.

I did not know I was poor

My life did not start out as a success. In fact my life started out just the opposite. I was born in one of the nation's most crime ridden and notorious housing projects, Father Panik Village, located in Bridgeport, Connecticut. I grew up extremely poor but we did not know that we were poor because everyone else around us was poor. I did not have anything else to compare to. So, it wasn't until I got my first job at 14 when I was working at the police station for two months and later at the Walgreens' Pharmacy for about 9 years that I realized that I was poor. Not only was I poor but I was very poor. I realized this when my boss who was an awesome guy invited us for a party at his house. He had a nice house with a big garden and a swimming pool. Whenever I would go to his house, I would notice how nice it was. I would then go back to my home and neighborhood and I would say, 'this is different'. This is not going to be where I live for the rest of my life. I was able to compare and contrast the lifestyles that people lived in. This soon became one of the pivotal points in my life.

I expected my life to end at anytime

Not only did I grow up extremely poor, but I also grew up with the chronic and life threatening disease, sickle cell anaemia: a disease that is passed down from generation to generation if both parents have the trait or if one has the trait and the other has the disease. I had 7 siblings growing up, of which my older sister and I got the disease. There were times when I would go into a sickle cell anaemia crisis (a painful episode that can inflict excruciating pain in any part of the body) for hours, weeks and even months. This was not a pretty thing to grow up with. As a kid from the age of 7, I knew that I was different from other kids because I had it. I had to avoid certain things including extreme weather conditions and swimming in cold water. Though I didn't know I was poor, I knew I was different because things like playing football and swimming I was not able to do or else I would end up in the hospital for days, weeks or months. So, I had a very sheltered childhood. This taught me that although life comes with obstacles, there is always a way to get around them especially with determination, will power and a Never Give Up attitude. It may sound weird, but growing up poor and having sickle cell anaemia are literally two of the best things that have ever happened to me.

Unfortunately, my older sister Gwen, who also had sickle cell anaemia died early. She was just in her twenties when she passed. I too thought that I would die very young. I remember one time after being sick and in Yale New Haven Hospital for weeks on end, I was lying in my hospital bed. Just outside of my hospital room door, I overheard one of the doctors tell my mother, in a matter of fact tone, 'Mrs. Cohen, you should not expect your son to live past the age of 17 years old. This disease will kill him'. As a 12 year old, I couldn't believe it. I was thinking, 'this is my fate now'. I was thinking, 'You mean I have just a few more years to live? At the ripe young age of 12, death would become my reality?' This was devastating to me.

With this in mind, I had nothing to live for. Either I would die young from the disease that just took my sister's life or in the streets of the ghetto that I lived in, like my peers. Either way at this point in my life, an early death was inevitable for me, because I believed this to be true, I started living a fast and reckless life of loving guns, robbing people, associating with gang members and dealing drugs. I started living expecting my life to end at any time. Yet, soon something unexpected would change my life forever.

I stole Les Brown's book

One day, I was riding with my dad in the back of his car and he had a book by Les Brown. The title of the book was 'Live Your Dreams'. I loved reading. My mother would always bring me comic books and books about science and history whenever I went to the hospital but this was the first time I had ever saw something in the personal development genre. And nevertheless, coming from someone that looked like me! What I read in that book, the first few paragraphs alone, was the beginning of my personal power being ignited! After reading it for a few minutes, I literally fell in love with what Les Brown was saying. So much so that at the end of our car ride I did what any 17 year old would do… I stole the book from my dad's car :-). This was one of the most proud moments in my life. No, not stealing the book, but rather being awoken to the message that it contained. I stayed awake that entire night, late into the early morning reading it from cover to cover… All 260 pages! As I turned each page I would read passages that read 'You have greatness within you… Don't let your current circumstances become your reality…' I was totally mesmerised and intrigued by these words because I had never heard them before. Reading this I was saying to myself, 'This is incredible...' But more importantly, luckily for me, I totally believed it and at this point I said to myself, regardless of all of the obstacles, this is the reason I am still here.

This same year I had lost 6 of my friends who had been killed in the streets, most on the East side of Bridgeport where I lived, others had gone to jail and as this was happening all around me I started to reflect on my life. I was 17. I was still working at Walgreen's. I was just about to be promoted to assistant manager. After reading Les Brown's book, I was so determined to totally change things and use the challenges that were surrounding me, as fuel to propel me to the next level of my life. I was also determined to help anyone around me that was willing to make that change, including family members and friends. As a result, I was able to change the perspective of a lot of people just by changing myself.

Accept fate or create the life you want

I now believe that life is what you make it. Either you accept the fate that was handed to you or you make an unwavering decision to create the one you want. After creating millions of dollars in sales and successfully working with thousands of clients from across the globe, I decided to take my expertise global and I have consulted with thousands of individuals and businesses around the world. I help them find that missing piece that would allow them to create lasting success in both business and life. I have created a formula for success that has helped me to accomplish more in less than a decade than most people do in an entire lifetime including:

- Speaking at marketing and business events around the world
- Authoring several best-selling books and audio programs
- Hosting a hugely successful morning talk show
- Appearing on numerous television and radio shows and within countless news publications
- Working with some of the biggest names in online and personal development industry
- Using my Kindle Cash Flow program to show thousands of people how to create a recurring income stream online.

Today I am living my dream life alongside my wife and four children. From me to each of you, I wish you much success and remember, 'Either you accept the fate that was handed to you or you make an unwavering decision to create the one you want'. For more information, visit www.KindleCashFlow.com

Standing Tall Inside Myself
Shermanda Anderson-Ramsay
Florida, USA

Speaker, Author, and CEO at Jax Business Pros
"The Vision Birthing Doula"
www.shermanda.com

Standing Tall Inside Myself

We now journey in Florida: the state where Les Brown was born. Approximately 70 miles from Miami is Jacksonville: a large city in Northeast Florida where the St. John River meets the Atlantic Ocean. You will be astounded by its many bridges, lovely beaches, and of course the NFL Team 'The Jacksonville Jaguars', amongst other great things. Here we meet Shermanda Anderson-Ramsay: A mother, Author, Business Owner, Certified Speaker, Founding Member of the Les Brown Institute, Corporate Trainer at the Maximum Potential Institute, Coach, Singer, and Ordained Minister. Shermanda is a very gifted and creative person and she is ready to share her story with you in the Sunshine State.

Bedridden at the time, I pressed forth to join the Les Brown Institute when everything surrounding my situation said this is not the time. Well, I pushed away the doubt and grabbed a hold of life, beyond my then current state, and became a founding member of the institute. Since that time, I have written 5 books. I published one book, "Love Inspired Living" in September 2017. I have a 30 day devotional book being released in the Spring of 2018. I have also written 2 children's books, waiting for illustrations to be done, and one eBook ready to be published, while yet working on a curriculum and more books.

You see, when life happened I could have easily given up, but giving up is not in my DNA. In this process of life, I realized this: Life Didn't Happen To Me in May of 2015, when I was hit by a vehicle as a pedestrian walking in a parking lot. In actuality, Life Happened For Me. Yes, I had to stop my business and job because of it, for a while, and still I'm in the healing process and yet have many challenges. But, I was afforded the opportunity to spend time with God, and learn how to create new roads of living, that are ultimately creating jobs for other people with disabilities. I have secured businesses, contracts, bids, services and much more from my healing bed. The DNA in me is greatness and birthing vision and dreams is my name regardless of what state I'm in because I'm fearfully and wonderfully made in the image of God.

Creating my greatest life

Les Brown's motivational speeches and books on 'Living Your Best Life,' 'It's Not Over Until I Win', and hearing from him day in and day out say, 'You have greatness within you' and 'That's my story and I'm sticking to it'. Hahaaa, that smile has helped me to dig deep within me and rise to the greatness within from our creator. I have been able to create the greatest life from inside out while hit by life's circumstances and seated in this wheelchair. I'm standing up tall inside myself and there is nothing too hard for me to accomplish. There is only an expectancy of even greater things, as we know that later shall be greater as a promise. From walking one day to using a cane, to a wheelchair to now working my way in a walker, it's only time before I'm running again. But the beauty is I'm yielded to the process and standing up and running inside victoriously.

My family forever

The Les Brown Maximum Achievement Team (LBMAT) now Les Brown Unlimited Team (LBUT) is my family forever. Becoming a founding member of this team connected me to my tribe: the hearts of those who walk to the same beat of greatness. This connection also led me to know and join the members of the Train The Trainer (TTT) organization/certification at the Maximum Potential Institute, as well as host various speaker events with teammates from these amazing organizations on an on-going basis to bring greatness to the world. I just went Zip-Lining for the first time, which though a dream, I never thought would come true due to the accident. Through a team building exercise, my TTT team members pulled me up the line; while I was securely strapped to a line; and all together they pulled me up. A to do-list dream was accomplished and became a reality. Les Brown has been instrumental in directing me to an even greater life and as I yield all I am, even the more to God, I'm living an amazing, winning life.

From Possible to Hunger to Action
David Lubuurwa
Massachusetts, USA

Human Rights Activist, Global Influencer and Broadcaster

From Possible to Hunger to Action

In Massachusetts, USA, we meet David Lubuurwa: a 22 year old born and raised in Uganda. Despite being in his early twenties, people think that he is in his 30s because of how he dresses, talks and thinks. People who listen to him admire his commanding voice and ask: Where does David get all this from? His simple answer is: from The Great Les Brown. Here is his story from being nobody in the streets of Uganda's capital Kampala to being a global influencer, broadcaster and human rights activist.

Les Brown, thank you for coming into my life and transforming it. Whenever I listen to you, I don't just stop there. I imitate you. I act like you. This is how I have built my life. This is how I have constructed my business empire. You have taken me from nobody to a great influencer and broadcaster. I would not be the person I am today without you. I know that you will keep inspiring me to become a better version of myself every day. I listen to your speech 'It's possible' every day, whenever I am doing my rehearsals for broadcasting, before giving a public speech or directing TV shows.

You have taught me that I don't have to be great to get started but I have to start to be great. I have done exactly that. You have told me that most people operate out of their personal history, out of their memory, from the things they have done, things they have experienced, things they have seen, and things that they have observed. You have inspired me to operate from a larger vision of myself. You want me to see myself doing what I want to do, experience what I want to experience, have what I want to have, do what gives my life meaning and value. I now operate out of my imagination not my memory because whenever I look where I want to go, I say to myself 'It's possible'.

The first time I listened to your speech 'It's possible', I was depressed. Being a teenager in Africa with limited access to the internet, I sacrificed what I had to download it. I learnt it and did what you told me. I also remember that this was the time when some of my siblings had deserted me as if I was not part of their family. I may not fully explain to you what happened but what I can say is that it wasn't a good time in my life. You were there for me as a best friend. I had to download lots of your videos and I could hear you in my sleep saying: 'David, live your dreams not your fears. David have no fear'. I learnt a lot from you. I developed deep hunger to succeed in life no matter what.

'You gotta be hungry'

I remember before I joined the media world, I feared to appear on TV or Radio. I always told this to my friends with whom I run an online TV station called BUE TV. I would ask myself: what I am going to tell the public on a weekly basis? One morning in 2016 I was driving to work and playing on my phone 'The best way to be successful on YouTube'. Suddenly came your voice "You gotta be hungry!" I intently listened to your story on how you became a disk jockey. You said,

> I told Mr. Washington I wanted to become a disc jockey. Someone asked me to tell the story. And he said, 'Les Brown', he said, 'if you want to do anything worthwhile in life you've got to be hungry.' And so I started working to develop myself. He said, 'I want you to practice every day

being a disc jockey'. I said, 'But I don't have any job.'

Now he said it doesn't matter. He said that it's better to be prepared for an opportunity and not have one than to have an opportunity and not be prepared. So every day I was working to develop myself and that's what you must do. And as I was working to develop myself, I applied for a job as a disc jockey, WMBF, Miami Beach. I went to a guy named Milton Butterball. I said, 'How you doing, Mr. Butterball? I'd like to get a job as a disc jockey.' He looked at me and said, 'Do you have any broadcast background?' I said, 'No sir, I don't.' 'Do you have any journalism background?' I said, 'No sir, I don't.' He said, 'We don't have any jobs available.' I said, 'Yes sir.' I went back to Mr. Washington and I told him, he said, 'Don't take it personally'. He said most people are so negative they will have to say 'no' seven times before they say yes. He said go back again. So I went back again. I said, 'How you doing Mr. Butterball? My name is Les Brown.' He said, 'I know what your name is. What do you want?' I said, 'I like to know whether or not you have any jobs as disc jockey, sir?' He said, 'Didn't I just tell you yesterday we didn't have any jobs?' I said, 'Yes sir, but I don't know whether or not somebody got laid off or somebody was fired, sir.' He said, 'No one was laid off or fired. Now get on out of here.' I came back the next day: 'Hello Mr. Butterball, how are you?' He said, 'Fine. What do you want now?' I said, 'I'd like to know whether or not you got any job, sir?' 'Didn't I tell you the last two days we didn't have any jobs?' I said, 'Yes sir, but I don't know whether or not somebody got sick or somebody died, sir.' He said, 'No one got sick or died. Don't come back here' and threw me out again.

I came back the next day like I was seeing him for the first time and said, 'Hello, Mr. Butterball, how are you?' He looked at me with rage. He said, 'Go get me some coffee.' I said, 'Yes sir.' And I went to get him some coffee. After a while I would give their lunch and dinner and I would go into control rooms and take the disc jockeys their food and I would not leave until they would ask me to leave. Then they started trusting me to pick up entertainers that came to town, entertainers like The Four Tops and the Temptations and Diana Ross and The Supremes. I would drive them all over Miami Beach in the disc jockey's big long Cadillacs. I didn't have any driver's license but I was driving like I had some.

And one day, one Saturday afternoon while I was at the radio station, a guy named Rock was drinking while he was on the air. I was the only one there, looking at him through the control room windows, walking back and forth, young, ready and hungry. I was saying, 'Drink Rock, drink. Drink rock', I'd go and get him some more if he'd asked me to. Pretty soon the phone rang and it was the general manager. And I answered the phone, I said, 'Hello?' He said, 'Les, this is Mr. Klein.' I said I know. He said,

'Rock can't finish his program.' I said I know. He said, 'Would you call one of the other DJs in?' I said yes sir. I hung the phone up. I said now he must be thinking I'm crazy. I called my mom and my girlfriend Cassandra, and said, 'You all turn up the radio and come out on the front porch, I'm about to come on the air.' I waited for about 20 minutes and I called him back, I said, 'Mr. Klein, I can't find nobody.' He said, 'Young boy, do you know how to work the controls?' I said, 'Yes sir.' He said, 'Go in there and sit down there.' I said, 'Yes sir.' I couldn't wait to get behind those controls. I put on an old Stevie Wonder record called Fingertips. I sat down behind that turntable. I said, 'Look out, this is me, LB, Triple P — Les Brown, Your Platter Playing Poppa. There were none before me and there will be none after me. Therefore, that makes me the one and only. Young and single and love to mingle. Certified, bona fide, indubitably qualified to bring you satisfaction, a whole lot of action. Look out, baby, I'm your lo-o-ove man." I was hungry. I was hungry. You gotta be hungry. You gotta be hungry.

I now listen to this speech almost every week as it reminds me that every day is a new day with new ideas and opportunities. Once an opportunity comes, I have to take it using the fastest means possible. My shows are becoming popular. I am also getting new friends who, I think if I had remained behind closed doors just mourning how the world is not fair, I wouldn't have made. Though I may not be in a position to put together all things, I have learnt from you to believe in myself. I have become a very influential person not only to my colleagues but to the communities I go to.

'The courage to act'

I really didn't want to share this story with you but let me do it today. In 2013 before I became a human rights activist, I used to think the world is ok with bad things that happen in it and it's a part of human nature. I would read about gay people being killed and disowned by their families. I would talk to girls who had been raped. I would meet women who had been abused by their husbands. I would feel powerless. When I finished my final year in high school in Uganda, I felt powerless to make any change. I knew that people in Uganda looked at teenagers as having no say. Others were being used by those in power to pass on their agenda. This bothered me a lot and I started looking for ideas on how to start up a movement that would at least reduce the number of victims of abuse, rape, and violence.

One day while at the American Embassy Public Library, I read your book 'Live Your Dreams'. You and your twin brother grew up on the tough streets of Miami's Liberty City after being adopted at the age of six weeks by Mamie Brown, a single woman with a big heart. You still call yourself Mamie's baby boy. You graduated from high school although you had been mistakenly labeled mentally retarded in school. You built yourself a successful career with no radio training. You became a community leader and were eventually elected to three full terms in the Ohio State Legislature. Along the way, you developed hunger for reading and self-improvement that led to your speaking career. Today you spend your time with your children and family and giving about 200 speeches a year which focus on helping people find ways to overcome the obstacles they face in their own lives. After reading your story, I started believing that I have the power to change my life because you had changed yours. You created a bridge between what I wanted and what I can actually do.

Since reading your story, I have not moved back on the issues of human rights advocacy, reading and speaking so that I can change our society. I also learnt that it doesn't require me to be part of a group to fight for the right cause but rather using the skills I have to create change. I have learnt that I need not to be a girl to stop forced marriages, I don't have be raped to advocate against rape, I don't have to be gay to stand up for LGBTQ rights. Continuously watching your videos and reading your books has allowed me to get rid of fear, excuses and laziness.

To cut my story short, I am always disappointed when I read some of the comments people post on Facebook. People speak against your work and what comes into my mind is: Do people really know how many people you have talked to who had lost hope and then regained it? Do people know what achievements I personally I have got in the last 6 six years since I started reading your books? Do they know how many people have talked to me just because I got advice from your books and videos? Do people really know that my wealth has been greatly achieved because I don't take for granted what you remind me when you say, David: 'honor your dreams', 'develop strong relationships with successful people', and 'honor your commitment'?

Les Brown Changed Our Lives

Let me give you some of the things I have done in the last 6 years since I listened to you and read your books. First, I have become a very knowledgeable and payable motivational speaker. Second, I have set up a farm of animals and chickens in Uganda. Third, I have set up a non-governmental organization with colleagues called KUENDEREZA Africa with the aim of helping the youth in Uganda and later in Africa to get rid of poverty and low self-esteem. Fourth, I started a TV and audio online network (BUE TV) Based in Boston, Massachusetts USA. Fifth, I am a TV presenter and a moderator on local and international panels. I would like to end with the message from a lady who watched one of my Facebook Lives. She wrote: 'You inspire me to be the best version of myself. I look up to you. I feel that more people should strive to have the strength and passion that you exemplify in everyday life. You may be stubborn at points but when you really need help, you let others in, which shows strength in itself. I have never been more proud to know someone and to call someone my role model. You have taught me so many things and I want to thank you. Thank you for inspiring me in life. Thank you for making me want to be a better person'. Without you, Les Brown, in my life, I wouldn't have made this impact in this lady's life. Thank you for leading me from it's possible to hunger and to action. I will forever be grateful.

Yours,

David Lubuurwa.

Creating Greatness University
Dr. Patrick Businge
England, UK

Founder of Greatness University
www.greatness-university.com

Creating Greatness University

In Summer 2017, my wife and I were hungry to achieve our dream of becoming international speakers and coaches. Our deep hunger put us on a journey from London in England to Fort Lauderdale in Florida. We were going to start a life changing mentorship programme with Les Brown - the world's number one motivational speaker – at his institute: The Les Brown Institute.

When we reached the Doubletree by Hilton Hotel in Deerfield Beach, Fort Lauderdale: the venue where the Certification was to take place, we discovered that we just had seeing missed Les Brown during the meet and greet session. The next day, Les Brown came to the stage. As I listened to Les Brown speak, at one point he said, 'we are sold everything except one product: greatness'. He went on to say, 'You have something special, you have greatness within you'. He then added, 'The graveyard is the richest place on earth, because it is here that you will find all the hopes and dreams that were never fulfilled, the books that were never written, the songs that were never sung, the inventions that were never shared, the cures that were never discovered, all because someone was too afraid to take that first step, keep with the problem, or determined to carry out their dream'.

As I listened to Les Brown speaking, his message quickly travelled from my heart and dwelt in my heart. This triggered an inner conversation with myself. Here is how it went: 'Many people are born and live without knowing that they have a great treasure in them: greatness. They end up dying without ever living to their full potential because they are not aware of their greatness. What if I made a business that sold greatness to people? This will surely help them discover their greatness and live a great life'. This conversation effected a change in me that was beyond my wildest dreams.

My intention of coming to the Certification in Florida was not to start a business but to learn how to become a better speaker. At the end of the certification, I left with a business and a great product to sell. Indeed, Les Brown changed my life by because he led me to my heart. It is here I discovered the product that I was to speak about, write about, help people discover, and sell in my business. Upon my return to England, I created Greatness University.

Today, Greatness University prides itself as the world's first institution dedicated to researching and monetising greatness. At Greatness University, we believe that greatness leaves clues. We are therefore committed to helping people tap into their greatness faster and easily than they can ever imagine. We do this by researching greatness in individuals, organizations, businesses, and other spheres of life. We help people create their own personal economies by monetising their greatness. We guide people on the best ways to create a lasting legacy. Remember, legacy is not what we give to the people we love but what we leave in them.

At Greatness University, we partner with like-minded people to unlock greatness around the world. We offer online courses, run face to face training, give one to one mentoring, and organize boot camps in our areas of expertise worldwide including helping people discover, write about, publish, and monetise their greatness. We look forward to working with you and walking the path to greatness together.

CHAPTER 2: AUTHORS

There is a book within you

Where is the richest place on earth? At this point in time, you might be thinking of USA, China, Buckingham Place or the White House. Here is the response from Les Brown,

> The graveyard is the richest place on earth, because it is here that you will find all the hopes and dreams that were never fulfilled, the books that were never written, the songs that were never sung, the inventions that were never shared, the cures that were never discovered, all because someone was too afraid to take that first step, keep with the problem, or determined to carry out their dream.

What a surprising response! When I first read this quote, I asked myself: what am I going to do differently so that I do not take all the riches with me to my grave? This created urgency in me to write the book within me. Here are some stories on how people made marks, not on their bodies but, on the world by becoming authors.

A Winning Character
Fred O. Juma
England, UK

Author, Educator and Philanthropist

Dr Patrick Businge

A Winning Character

In the mazy streets of London, we are going to search for Mwalimu Fred Juma. Mwalimu is a Swahili word that means teacher. Mwalimu Fred Juma's story is entangled with nearly a decade of educating students in the South East of London. He moved from Kenya to the UK to study in 2003. Upon completion of his undergraduate studies at Middlesex University in London, he enrolled on a Post-Graduate Certificate in Education (PGCE) program at Oxford Brookes University and earned his Qualified Teacher Status in 2008. He is now a published author of *A Winning Character.* Let us read what happened.

The quest for my purpose

In 2008, I was very much transfixed to my job and hardly had a chance to do anything else. However in 2011, I was becoming clearly dissatisfied with the direction my life was taking and the excessive pressure from my job. I took some time off and in 2011 I enrolled for a master's program at Heythrop College, University of London. In 2012 I began reflecting deeply about my own life work; as clearly, I didn't think that teaching Religious Studies in secondary schools was what I was meant to do 'until death do us part'. I immersed myself in a process of deep self-reflection; and pondered, surely there must be more to my life's purpose. This quest has led me to various mentors, self-help books, seminars and wider motivational literature.

Les Brown, 'Mwalimu, you gotta be hungry'

In the last five years, there has been one voice that has been constant in my life: the voice of the phenomenal speaker Les Brown. In fact this voice has been so tremendous in my life that when my son was born 3 years ago, my wife and I named him Lesley.

When I started out as a classroom teacher nearly a decade ago, my sense of self-belief in doing anything else other than carrying on as a classroom teacher was almost null and void. In fact, outwardly I was saying to myself, "Yes, I am meant to live my dream, to become a best-selling author, to become a world class motivational speaker and gain financial freedom." However, deep down me, I seriously doubted if I could achieve any of these things.

In 2013, I watched Les Brown's YouTube recording for the first time and had a glimpse of that transformational powerful voice. Les Brown's message resonated with the deepest part of my being. I felt something was happening in my inner self. I just knew that it was no longer business as usual. The very first speech I watched was "You Gotta be Hungry Les Brown Greatest speech". I just knew that life was not going to be the same again. I immersed myself in a process of self-development. Back then, I made one clear decision that I was going to become a successful author of numerous books. I didn't know how I was going to do this, but I held a firm belief that I was called to accomplish this, my life's mission. A year later, I began writing the manuscript of my first book *A Winning Character*. After a few months, I stopped writing and mainly due to lack of self-belief and low self-esteem in my ability as a writer.

Inner critic, 'Fred, be realistic'

My inner critic would surface particularly during difficult times and ask me, 'Fred what makes you think the world needs a book from you? There are so many accomplished and world class bestselling authors out there. What makes you think anyone will consider reading your book? Why will anybody care when there are thousands of books out there from prolific bestselling authors? Get real, this is a waste of time! Why not consider doing something that will earn you money more quickly? My inner conversation summoned me, 'Fred, have you forgotten, you are currently holding a hectic job teaching at a comprehensive secondary school and hardly have any time to write? How are you going to make it work without risking your job? Be realistic, you can't even afford the publishing fees!!! Look, you are walking to work, you don't even have a cheap car for a start; you are begging for lifts and hopping on buses to make ends meet!'

The critic within would remind me often of all the things I lacked. With all these thrashings, I would end up not only with lack of general confidence, but also a weakened self-image and dwindling self-belief in my ability to set and reach my goals, particularly the goal of writing my first book. This went on for years. Many times, I felt great pressure and discouragement. I even abandoned writing for several months and came close to dumping the whole project for good. I was always aware that I could easily be influenced by negative voices - particularly from my inner critic. I needed to programme my mind to avoid being automatically programmed by my life's circumstances. I had several tough conversations and encounters with my critic within.

Les Brown, 'Mwalimu, it's possible'

However, there was something else - It was like something greater than me that kept this dream alive, encouraged me all the way through, and kept telling me not to give up. I always had the awareness that I seriously needed to build up my self-image as well as my self-belief. Consequently, I listened to and watched lots of motivational recordings on YouTube. I vividly remember the invaluable advice I received from at least a dozen world class inspirational people and motivational speakers.

In 2015 I picked up this project of writing *A Winning Character* seriously, at the time I intensified listening to the phenomenal Les Browns' recordings on YouTube. I particularly listened to hundreds of hours of recordings. I listened repeatedly to the extent that I began completing Les Brown's sentences. It was as though Les Brown was right there in my room whispering these positive messages into my ear.

- Fred, it is possible…
- You don't have to be great to get started, but you have to get started to be great…
- There is greatness within you…
- It is not over until you win…
- Other people's opinion of you do not have to become your reality…
- Live out of your imagination instead of out of your memory…
- It is better to be prepared for an opportunity and not have one than to have one and not be prepared…

- To be successful, you must be willing to do the things today others won't do in order to have the things tomorrow others won't have…
- Shoot for the moon, because even if you miss, you'll land among the stars…

Inner critic, 'Mwalimu, you are a winner'

I can confidently say that indeed Les Brown changed my life. He did overturn that little negative voice that was bringing me to my knees. My first book *A Winning Character* was published in July 2017. I wrote this on the books' acknowledgement section: "Also, I want to thank my legendary role model and mentor, Les Brown, who continues to sow seeds of greatness in my mind through his life changing motivational messages." My life is evolving today, and my sense of self-belief is on upward curve as a result of engaging with these great motivational messages. I will continue to ride on the shoulders of giants like Les Brown as I march towards my life's purpose, happiness and fulfillment.

Les Brown, 'Mwalimu, write your book because it was given to you'

In my particular goal of writing my book, I was greatly inspired by this advice from Les Brown along the lines of; 'Write your book even if no one publishes your book, write your book because it was given to you.' Ultimately, this leads me to this vital lesson, irrespective of the kind of goal you have set for yourself, be it a health or fitness goal, a financial or business goal, a work goal, a family goal, a social goal or an academic goal. For whatever goal that you have set for yourself, never stop marching towards your dream because of lack of validation from other people. Go ahead, do that which you have been given to accomplish by God or higher power. Eventually, you will be pleased that you had the guts to swim against the trend and do that which you were put on earth to do.

I did seriously worry if anyone would bother reading my book. Those worries were completely unfounded as every day I am receiving awesome feedback from my readers. Guess what would have happened had I given up the goal of writing my book? All my readers and future readers would have been denied this opportunity. Follow your greatness and do that which you were put here on earth to accomplish.

7 Steps to Greatness

After finishing 5 years of intense PhD study at Exeter University, I had a great thirst to change the world. I had lots of ideas of what I could do but I was a bit indecisive. It is at this point that I came to know Les Brown. One night in 2015 as I was surfing on the internet and I landed on a video clip of Les Brown. In this video clip he said to me , 'You have something special, you have greatness within you'. This clicked with what I was aspiring for: do something special with my life that the world would be proud of. I said to myself, I must meet this man. I looked for his conferences around the world but I couldn't see any events.

As I continued searching, I landed on a website that started off the journey of change in me. This website gave me the opportunity not only to see Les Brown but partner with him. However, this came at a financial cost that I was not prepared for. At this moment, I remembered what one of my business mentors had told me, 'when you get an opportunity, say yes and then work on the how later'. I immediately called the Les Brown Institute and enrolled using my credit cards. One month later, my wife too enrolled. Since then, my life and that of my wife has been transformed in ways that we could ever imagine. When I reflect on my life now, I can clearly see that Les Brown has been three things to me: mentor, midwife, motivator.

Mentor

I have studied in 7 universities and obtained 7 University degrees. While this formal education allowed me to study other people, places, events and ideas, Les Brown put me on a journey to study myself. I become the object and subject of study and some of my findings are found in my bestselling book, *7 Steps to Greatness: The Masterplan to Take Your Life, Studies, Career and Business to the Next Level.* In this book, I chart the journey to finding my greatness in 7 steps:

i)   Find Yourself
ii)   Discover Your Purpose
iii) Dream While Awake
iv)   Develop STAR Goals
v)   See with VISION
vi)   Network with Great PEOPLE
vii) Take Massive ACTION.

Before meeting Les Brown, I was like the two boys in Africa that were playing with stones in Africa that Les Brown talks about. When the explorers saw the stones which were diamonds, they asked the boys to give them the stones in exchange for sweets. Had the boys known stones were expensive diamonds, they would have not given them up. Les has helped me discover the diamond that I had in my hands and was not using it. Once I discovered this diamond, I gained clarity and became unstoppable in my pursuit for greatness.

Midwife

Les Brown helped me to deliver the dreams I had. I was not born in the greatness of Great Britain but in the poverty of Uganda. While in Uganda, I also lived in war but I did not let war live in me. I remember we had just finished our dinner in the back courtyard under the light of the moon. Like every other night, we were getting ready to sleep. Suddenly, there was noise and gunshots outside. With my parents and two elder brothers, we left our house by the back gate and ran into the banana plantation and spent there the night. When we came back in the morning, part of our house was destroyed, my parent's shop had been burgled, and my primary school had been turned into an army barracks. I remember my family and many other people travelling in a refugee truck being displaced to another country. That was the start of a life without school, living in a new village and a time to dream.

When I met Les Brown, he stretched me to dream further as he told me that 'Most people fail in life not because they aim too high and miss, but because they aim too low and hit'. It is because of Les Brown's skills as a midwife that I have been able to write 5 books in 5 months and create my personal economy.

Motivator

Finally, Les Brown has motivated me to leave my comfort zone and venture into uncharted territories. Without this motivation, you wouldn't be reading this book as I have had insurmountable challenges to overcome in order to write and publish this book for you. I remember in January 2018, I sent an email to Les Brown and started collecting stories of people whose lives had been changed by him. When one of the women who was not even a relative of Les Brown got my Facebook invitation to share her story in my book, her reply was, 'You have stolen my idea. I have had it for many years. If you touch it, I will sue you'.

Where did I get the motivation to continue after this unexpected response? Of course you can easily guess: it is from Les Brown. He says, 'You wanna become a risk-taker. You wanna raise the bar on yourself. Most people won't do that. See most people engage in low-life living, low-risk living...If you're not willing to risk, you cannot grow. And if you cannot grow, you cannot become your best. And if you cannot become your best, you can't be happy. And if you can't be happy, then what else is there?'

Thank you Les Brown for helping me step into my greatness.

Think or Shrink
Lehlohonolo Mazindo aka Mr. Mazzz
South Africa

Author, Speaker and Registered Counsellor
www.lehlohonolomazinda.co.za

Think or Shrink

I first heard of Les Brown when I attended a business breakfast seminar in my former city of residence - Welkom, Free State, South Africa. It was around 2014, and I was sinking in depression (diagnosed with Major Depressive Disorder with Psychotic Symptoms). I was a highly esteemed Marriage Counsellor and Speaker in town, and I was doing weekly radio talks on marriage and relationships; but I was going through a divorce. It was a humiliating experience; devastating to the core - especially to hear people talk about how much of a hypocrite I was to tell people how to build their marriages while I was walking out on my own. Local pastors gave strict orders to their congregants never to attend my seminars or listen to me because the spirit of divorce in me would rub off on them. At that time, I had completed a manuscript on marriage titled, *Together Till the End: A Blueprint for Successful Marriage*. I wanted to delete it because I felt disqualified to empower people's marriages when I couldn't make mine work.

During the Q and A session at the breakfast seminar, I asked how I can continue to empower people's marriages while I couldn't keep mine together. The speaker replied telling me about Les Brown - how his marriage fell apart and yet he continued to empower the world with his motivational talks. After the seminar I went to watch Les Brown's YouTube videos, and since then, I've been listening to him on a daily basis. How he narrates his stories found a way into the parts of my heart I never thought could ever be reached, not even by the preacher.

His openness and vulnerability keeps on winning my heart. Not only do I connect with his words as a speaker; I also connect with him as a person. Mrs. Mamie Brown's Baby Boy's talks have become my daily prescription to date. Out of his talks, the story that changed my life is that of his day at school when Mr. Washington requested him to do something for him on the board; and he told him, "I can't do it sir, I'm labelled educable mentally retarded. And I'm DT sir - Dumb Twin". Then Mr. Washington came to him from behind his desk, looked him in the eyes and said, "Don't you ever say that! Someone's opinion of you does not have to become your reality!" And that interrupted his thinking and aligned him to a life of greatness. Ever since I heard that story, I began to create my own reality - separate from people's opinions; a reality that defined who I really am instead of what people thought I was. Now I have a breakthrough in most of the things I do; and I can safely say I am living my dream.

As a result of Mr. Brown's influence, I published the book I so desperately wanted to delete, and I published another one afterwards - titled Think or Shrink: Explore Your Mind to Expand Your Life. I owe it to Les Brown to do for others what he has done for me for as long as I live. That's my story, and I'm sticking to it!!!

Dr Patrick Businge

CHAPTER 3: BUSINESS

'You gotta be hungry'

Starting and running a business is not for the faint hearted. In the words of Les Brown, 'You gotta be hungry' to start a business. In the words of Steve Jobs, 'You have to stay hungry' to stay in business.

In this Chapter, you will read the story of Greg Walker, the Big Dreamer from Ohio, USA. Greg learnt from Les Brown that he was too big to dream small. He shares his story so that you are able to see him as an example of a person who did not wait to be great to start his business but had to start to be great.

In this Chapter, you will read the story of Gil Evans from Ohio, USA. After working for a family business for approximately 10 years, he was asked to leave. At this point in his life, he felt defeated and depressed. As he laid on the couch and hid from the world, he heard Les Brown telling him, 'You gotta be hungry!' In Gil's story, you will discover how he turned his failure into hunger and believed it's not over until he wins.

In this Chapter, you will explore how Jean Edouard Brutus originally from Haiti, has found a way to win in the USA. He is a living example of a person who has had business failures, looked up, got up and chased after his dreams. It is my hope that by the end of these stories, you will have the power to dream big, turn your failure into hunger, and find a way to win.

You Are Too Big To Dream Small
Greg Walker
Ohio, USA

Bestselling Author, Entrepreneur and Speaker
www.greginspires.com

The Big Dreamer

Columbus in Ohio State, USA is where we meet Greg Walker: The Big Dreamer. He is the Best-Selling Author of 'Dream To Grow Rich' and a sought after speaker. He has spoken to Fortune 500 Companies as well as to professional athletes. He was born and raised on the south side of Columbus, Ohio. He is the only one of fifteen children to ever graduate from High School. Greg says he was living in a drug infested, alcoholic, and a domestic violence environment. This changed when Greg met Les Brown/ His story will help you overcome obstacles and inspire you to dream big.

You are too big to dream small

I grew up in Columbus, Ohio. As a child, I grew up all my life hearing about two things: Ohio State Football Team and the Great Les Brown: Mamie Brown's baby boy. I came to meet Les Brown because, being among the few white kids in the neighborhood, we used to listen to a black radio station called WVKL. Here Les Brown had a Monday night program called 'Blue Monday' where he would play soulful slow music and it was so beautiful to my ears.

What touched me and connected me with Les Brown was that we had a similar story. He had 6 brothers and sisters when his mum adopted him and I had 13 brothers and sisters. Looking at Les Brown's story who as adopted and was labelled EMR, people did not believe in him. I too had that background where people did not believe in me. I came from a family of failures. I was always teased and labeled as a slow learner. I was asked to drop out of high school on my very first day just because my twelve siblings had dropped out before me.

I refused and people called me a big dreamer. They thought I wasn't going to make it but I proved them wrong because I had learned from Les Brown that I was too big to dream small. I refused to drop out and graduated from high school because of Les Brown and another loving teacher who believed in me. I went on and attended the University of Florida where I pursued my dreams even though everyone around me laughed and called me "The Big Dreamer".

Discover your God given gift

Les Brown told me what we all have a God given gift and we should let the world see that gift. Imagine, I did not know this until I was 48 years old when I joined Toastmasters. Mike Williams, a mentor to Les Brown, came to where I was speaking and he too taught me things that took me to the next level. He became my mentor and taught me the same techniques that he taught Les Brown when they were young and hungry at WKVL Radio. I used the same lessons that Mike Williams taught Les Brown and Les Brown taught me those lessons.

This unrivalled coaching changed my mindset and I was able to discover my gifts. I became a successful entrepreneur and now I own three National Franchises including Subway Sandwiches and a Master Developer of one of them. I also have a speaking and coaching business called Greg Inspires Worldwide LLC. I was voted Business Person of the Year and I have become an Award Winning National Motivational Speaker at the age of forty-eight.

Dream to grow rich

Les Brown wrote the foreword for my book: *Dream to Grow Rich: How to Dream, Grind and Hustle, Your Way to Success.* This book became a number one bestselling book. In this book, I tell my story on how I grew up where Les Brown grew up: Columbus, Ohio, an environment filled with drugs, alcohol and violence. I write about my dream to grow rich and how, despite people trying to pull me down, I grinded and hustled to become the person I am today. I truly believe that success is for everyone who is willing to dream, grind and hustle and it doesn't matter where you start, as long as you start. It is because of my big dreams that I now travel the world speaking on motivation, personal development and leadership.

I leave you my some of my favorite quotations from Les Brown that have allowed me to dream big: 'If you get knocked down, land on your back because if you can look up you can get up' and 'a setup is a setting for a comeback'. I also leave you with one of my quotes that I always tell people, 'we are all too big to dream small'. So, don't live life with regret. Live full, live your dreams, and die empty.

From Failure to Hunger
Gil Evans
Ohio, USA

**Business Coach, Restaurant Consultant and
Leadership Speaker
www.chefgilevans.com**

Dr Patrick Businge

From Failure to Hunger

From Columbus, Ohio we move to Toledo in Ohio where we meet Gil Evans: a dedicated husband, father, and motivational speaker. Gil has spent much of his life in Toledo where he lives happily with his beautiful wife, Jennifer, and their three dogs. When he isn't building up his brand and taking social media by storm, Gil enjoys all that Toledo has to offer: one of the top 10 zoo's in America, the Toledo Museum of Art, Triple-A baseball team the Mud Hens, and the breath-taking views of Lake Erie.

While Gil has accomplished many things in his life, the journey has not been without struggle. There has been loss and lessons learned along the way, all of which has prepared him to live out his passions for inspiring and advising others to be their best selves. He is ready to tell his story from failure to hunger.

In the late 1980s, I was a manager for a large chain of restaurants. I was in my twenties, my self-esteem couldn't get any lower, and I considered myself to be a failure. I was a manager, and a leader, but I lacked the confidence to be in control. One day my district manager sat me down and he said that my performance was the worst he had ever encountered. He said that he wanted to help me by enrolling me in some classes that would improve my self-image and management skills. I knew that if I failed this opportunity, nothing more could be done for me.

Previous to this position, I had worked 10 years with a family owned business that I loved and worked tirelessly for. When the family's son returned from college, I was fired. I could not be fired again. After speaking with my district manager, I went home. I felt defeated. For two days, I laid on the couch: unmoving, depressed, and hiding from the world. On the second night at around 3:00 A.M, I was absently listening to a late night program on PBS, Public Broadcasting System, playing on the television. My attention was suddenly drawn to a man speaking. He had an amazing voice and laugh that showed his vitality. He said, "You gotta be hungry!" These words resonated in my head. Immediately, I sat up and pledged the money needed to get the inspirational videos of this man. I even recorded the television broadcast onto a VHS so that I could continue to watch the show until my own tapes were delivered. It became my lifeline.

I was hungry when I first applied for the manager position. Doubt and nerves crept in and I failed my first interview. But, I was hungry! This wasn't going hold me back. I went to the library, studied like crazy, read books on self-esteem, and I got the job. My failure after that was letting the fire die out. I had the ability to be hungry, but I didn't realize how important it was to "stay hungry." The incredible man speaking on PBS that night was Les Brown. He woke me up. He made me want to fight and aspire to be great again. "You gotta be hungry!" All it took were those words to lift my spirit. Not only did I start performing well, I was also able to take our bottom-ranking store to the top of the 260 stores in the company!

After creating so much success within that business and finding my own personal strength, I decided it was time to venture out. Eventually, I migrated to Columbus, Ohio where a dream of mine would come true. Les Brown was going to be speaking at a local church. I was going to be in the same room as the man that saved my life. At the end of his unforgettable speech, Brown held a book signing at the front of the church. I was able to personally thank the man that forever changed my life and to this day his book "Live Your Dreams" is one of my most prized possessions. Now, my greatest joy in life is spreading hope and inspiration, like Les Brown provided me and so many others. Every day, I post two Vlogs to help people stay motivated and "stay hungry." Today, I have two Vlogs that I do daily in hopes to return to the world what Les did for me. I hope this helps you. I am now a business coach, restaurant consultant and Ohio's Inspirational Leadership Speaker.

Finding a Way to Win
Jean Edouard Brutus
Haiti

CEO at Boston Healthcare Services LLC
Bostonhealthcareservices.com

Finding a Way to Win

I grew up in Haiti, and I came from a divorced family. I am the youngest of 5 boys, and like most children from third world countries, I grew up lacking most of the basic necessities including food and adequate schooling. My parents did the best they could to be good providers but not much was possible in a poor country with plenty of political problems as well as economic chaos.

I came to the USA in April 1990 when I was 16 years old, with the dream of creating a better life, like most immigrants. I enrolled in high school to continue my education, I landed my first job when I was 17 years old and I managed to always make sure I had a job. I was all alone in a new country. My father had passed away and my mother back home was paralyzed and required daily care that we could not afford when I was in Haiti. So, my motivation to keep working was like that of Les Brown, because my mother and brothers in Haiti were depending on me for money. I could not afford to get into any trouble with the law because I had to maintain a job so that I could take care of my mother.

After high school, I drove a cab for a few years until I realized that my calling was in healthcare. I enrolled in college to pursue a career in nursing. I obtained a bachelor's degree in nursing in 2002, and quickly began working. I have worked in multiple different areas and departments in healthcare. I quickly discovered that my passion was to be my own boss and run my own business. In 2004, I started my first business which was a learning center. This failed miserably for lack of knowledge and experience. I lost thousands of dollars, and that was money that I earned with hard labor. But, I did not get discouraged. In 2005, I started my second business, which was a staffing agency. I had a little bit of experience, this time around, so I made some money, but still I failed miserably for lack of knowledge on how to keep the business going. The second business failed so bad that my wife and I ended up owing a lot of tax money to the Inland Revenue Service (IRS). After that last episode, I parked, and decided that I would not try to go into business and put my family through this ever again.

In 2012, a friend of mine introduced me to a CD of Les Brown motivation. The more I listened, the more I wanted to listen and the stronger I got mentally, and spiritually. I began to set goals for myself; I began to work harder toward those goals. As time went by and I continued to listen, I picked up the courage to believe that I could be successful in business. Well, in 2014, I made the decision to try again. As I listened to Les Brown, I became more disciplined and focused to get the success that I was aiming for. Well, to make a long story short, today my wife and I own and operate a learning center called Boston Healthcare Institute. We have been in business for the past 3 years and we are going strong. We also own and operate Boston Healthcare Services, LLC a home care company that is developing and taking shape, and looks very promising financially. We are also launching a Staffing Agency, called Boston Healthcare Staffing.

My wife and I are going back in time to fix the failures of the past, thanks to you, Les Brown. So, keep on preaching Les, you are changing lives. Thanks to you Les, I have been spreading motivational messages on the radio since 2014. My dream now is to meet you someday soon. You are a real inspiration and a true American Hero for saving and changing lives. GOD BLESS YOU.

CHAPTER 4: COACHING

Learn to Win at Les Brown Unlimited

Les Brown says, 'There are winners and there are losers and there are people who have not discovered how to win. And all they need is some coaching. All they need is some help and assistance — just a little support'. As you know, when you learn from the best, you increase your chances of doing your best. If speaking is your passion, you can't leave the results to chance. A missed opportunity can mean the difference between mediocrity and greatness.

This chapter gives you examples of people who have become winners because of the coaching and mentoring from Les Brown. As you read this chapter, you might be attracted to doing what Les Brown does. Your next step is to join the Les Brown Unlimited Team. In joining this team, you will have doors opened for you in avenues of life that you never imagined. Here is a word from Serena Brown, the CEO of Les Brown Unlimited:

> Les Brown Unlimited is committed. Our success is defined by you, your progress, and your growth as you influence others. We only want people who are seriously serious to making the world a better place. We only attract those who are ready to expand outside of their comfort zones. And we are proud to serve those who gladly serve others, because we know the greatest among you will be your servant. This is a selfless business with true sacrifices and rewards that will live forever...the results include hope, inspiration, and audiences left telling you, "Your words helped to change my life. Thank you."

Baba Les Brown and Life Coaching
Keidi Awadu
Nevada, USA

Broadcaster, Healthy Lifestyle Coach and Author
www.LivingSuperFood.com

Baba Les Brown and Life Coaching

We now travel to Las Vegas, Nevada. Here we meet the Celebrity Chef Keidi Awadu. Chef Keidi is also a broadcaster, a healthy lifestyle coach, and an award winning author. He has written over 33 books including *Living Superfood Recipes (Vol's 1 & 2)*, *Living Superfood Longevity* and *Living Super in Paradise: Creating Space for Perfect Health*. You might have heard that what happens in Vegas stays in Vegas. According to Chef Keidi, what happens in Vegas is too great to stay in Vegas. He is going to break the rules and share his journey of growth with Les Brown.

I have had the opportunity to get to know Les Brown increasingly over the past ten years. I've come to refer to him as "Baba," an African term of endearment for older men, equating to "Father" or "Uncle." Les Brown and I share the same hometown of Columbus, Ohio. As such we have developed several common values, outlooks, and senses of perceiving the world. As well, my partner Terri has worked in Baba's office over many years as well as working on other projects together. We're proud to say that Les Brown's voice is heard in our household every week via telephone.

Much of my life with Baba is centred around the deep set of studies into healthy living, disease resistance and healing, as well as optimizing conditions within our lives by which we can each be *Living in Super Paradise*, through creating space within our lives for perfect health. My background includes authoring nearly three dozen books, traveling internationally on an annual basis, speaking at conferences around the world and developing a nutrition-based disease-prevention and holistic healing system called Living

Superfood (www.LivingSuperFood.com). Over decades of pursuit of these health-related biomedical studies, I have managed to accrue a few notable credentials including that of an award-winning raw vegan chef, numerous community awards, as well as college-level credentials in childhood nutrition and public health policies.

Baba Les has been one of the most inspiring life coaches that has helped me to shape my focus and personal discipline to achieve along this pathway. I further teach, inspire and mentor others to become effective teachers of holistic health and optimized physical well-being. I always emphasize just how important it is to bring the right guides into our lives and to study at the highest level that we can access accurate information which supports our *Massive Transforming Purpose (MTP)* in life.

There are just so many life coaches that one can access in this modern era. When it comes to natural living, the whole-foods lifestyle, escaping the impact of toxic stressors, and actively pursuing quality life extension, there are some great coaching sources available. Conversely, I've observed that there is also an excess of bad coaching out here competing for our attention. Because I've been in this lifestyle for so long, it is not difficult for me to recognize the difference between good and bad information that is passing for life coaching and health counseling. I have a mantra that I use on the front or back page of nearly all my books which reads "Cutting edge research to serve an emerging leadership," – I teach the teachers.

Taking on such a responsibility of teaching those who are instructing this holistic lifestyle is a tremendous responsibility. It requires many hours a week of verifying that one's fundamental ideas are based on sound science and can be verified by anyone who would bring their healthy scepticism to the issue at hand. While we should welcome healthy scepticism, it can also deviate into an excess of negative opinions about the beliefs and teachings of others. It is a fine line between being an effective critic and being a narcissist, convinced that they are the only one worthy of being an influence.

A quality life coach must constantly be prepared to teach the neophyte. We should expect that one day the student will become an even more-effective teacher than their Master. To become a master teacher worthy of serving as a life coach, it is necessary that one's expertise be authentic. The unwelcome news is that there are just too many inauthentic consultants crowding the market. How can you assure that you are not investing time, money and your health in such bad life coaching? We must have standards and Baba Les Brown has set the standard high so that we may live the rest of our lives the best of our lives.

It's Not Over Until I Win
Pog Thanee
Thailand

It's Not Over Until I Win

Before I came to know of Les Brown, I had just left my job because my boss changed my role from marketing to sales. I did not want to do this. After a few weeks without a job, I started asking myself various questions- Who am I? What do I want to be? What is my passion? In the process of asking and researching these questions, I found a man who is a motivator on YouTube.

I started from one clips to ten clips. I liked his tone of voice, metaphors, jokes, hand movements, and quotes. His name was Les Brown, who has fought life and never given up. As I watched his videos, one quote pierced my heart, 'It's not over until I win'. This quote made my heart beat so fast and created more power inside me. After listening to Les Brown, I have embarked on a journey of personal development. I have learned from many motivational speakers, including Tony Robbins and Jim Rohn. My life has started to grow by using their techniques.

My dream is to change people's lives by transforming them into happy and wealthy individuals. I want to be a life coach and every time I think about my big dream, tears run through my eyes. That's right, even now as I write. I am now an NLP Practitioner. I have already changed more than ten people's lives. They have their own business and are living happy lives. Thank you, Les Brown. One day I will be at your seminar. It is not over until I win.

My Best Coach in the World
Alka Sharma
Toronto, Canada

International Speaker and Fitness Coach
www.alkastotalfitness.com

My Best Coach in the World

We now travel to Markham: a city in the Regional Municipality of York within the Greater Toronto Area of Southern Ontario, Canada. It is located approximately 30 km northeast of downtown Toronto. Many tourists love to come to Markham as it is a hidden treasure and a must see. Here we meet Alka Sharma: the CEO of Alka's Total Fitness. Fitness has always been part of Alka's life and she is a great believer in heathy living and motivating others to lead healthier lives. Here is her story.

Les Brown started changing my life last year in 2017. I was at a seminar in Toronto and my friend was talking to Les Brown via Skype. I was immediately captivated by his powerful voice. I knew there and then that I had to meet him. Immediately, I went to the back of the room and I signed up for his one on one coaching. A couple of weeks after, I got a phone call from Les Brown telling me that he is going to fly me down to Cleveland, Ohio for one on one coaching. It was a GREAT feeling. This gets better when, a couple of months later, he picks me up from the airport. Oh my God! I saw Les Brown walking towards me and his car is waiting for me. I have never had a greater feeling than this. From this moment on, life is great being connected to him.

I am so glad to have Les Brown as my coach. He is the best in the world when it comes to telling your story. When he is coaching me to tell my story, I am always amazed by his inner genius to transform my story within a very short space of time and experience it as if he was there when things were happening to me. Following his principle, 'never make a point without telling a story and never tell a story without making a point' is very powerful. I have witnessed growth in myself when I am speaking and applying it. I cherish what I have learned from him.

Les Brown has even motivated me to do things that I have never imagined. For instance, one day I was at my studio and I got a phone call. It was Les Brown, OMG! I was excited and I said to myself, 'Les is calling me…I wonder for what?' When I took the phone call, Les Brown said, 'Alka, if you want to be the best speaker in the world, you need to come to Florida and be at the Institute'. Wow! I couldn't believe how my ranking just got higher. So I called up the Les Brown Institute and spoke to one of the staff members there. The year after, I came to Florida and I was astounded by the Les Brown Team. It is because of Les Brown and the Les Brown Institute that I am able to speak both nationally and internationally.

Dr Patrick Businge

CHAPTER 5: COMEBACK POWER

There is Comeback Power in You

Have you ever been in a situation where you felt powerless? How did you bounce back? Here is a story about Les Brown's comeback power taken from his speech 'It's Possible'.

Well, I was working, I kept saying it's possible, they got other speakers on this program. I can be on that program too. I kept telling myself, I got all fired up. And I was calling in every day, every day. And the lady finally said, 'Mr. Brown, I tell you what! We want you to come in and talk to our sales executive. You've got the kind of fire and guts that they want that will motivate them. And let me tell you something else. We want you to bring your motivational tapes. You're going to need at least $50,000 worth of tapes. Is that right? Yes because they want to keep that drive alive'.

I said, 'All right. I'll call a guy to duplicate my tape'. I said, 'Don, how you doing? This is Les. Let me tell you, I've got a major speaking engagement. Man, it's the speakers' dream. I need over $50,000 worth of product'. He said, 'Les, you don't have that kind of credit'. I said. 'I know but Don, I can sell that. Just right after the speaking engagement, I'll give you your money in four days'. He said, 'Are you sure, Les?' I said, 'Yes, but I got a major speaking engagement and they told me to do it.' He said, 'Man, that's a bit odd. Let me talk with the lady with you'. I said, 'Hold on just a minute, man'.

I called the lady back. 'Hello, Evelyn, how are you doing? This is Les Brown. I got Don on the phone. What did you say? Do I have the speaking engagement?' 'Yes, you do.' 'And what else do you suggest?' 'Les, our people, they buy a lot of tapes, your tapes are very popular among them. I'm saying bring at least $50,000 worth of tapes, Les. You'll sell everything you've got and more.' 'I said, 'Did you hear that Don?' He said, 'Yes.' I said, 'Now, if anybody else has to make a decision, are you the final person?' She said, 'I'm the final person. I will send you the contract. I want you'. I said, 'Did you hear that, Don?' I said, 'Oh ye of little faith!'

Well, he duplicated tapes. One week passed by, I'm checking her mail every day. No contract. I said, 'Come on Murphy, don't start on that. Come on, man. Give me a break, come on'. I'd talk to myself. I don't want to call him right now. Two weeks passed by, Murphy said, 'Don't you think you ought to call?' I said, OK. I called her and say, 'Hello, this is Les Brown calling'. 'How you doing, Les?' I said fine. I said, 'Evelyn hasn't sent my contract out yet. Any additional information you need?' 'So Les, you haven't heard?' I said no. 'Evelyn died. How soon she died!' I said, 'Did she say anything about me?'

When I got home I was so wiped out. And Murphy was in the house waiting for me. Murphy said, 'Is it possible you want to listen to some of your tapes?' Well, ladies and gentlemen here is what I had to do. I had to begin to focus on what was the solution, that this was not the only place that I'll be able to sell those products. And as I began to challenge myself and got in help and support and some other input, I eventually did, it took longer. But it was challenging but I did it. Repeat after me please. No matter how bad it is, or how bad it gets, I'm going to make it. I'm going to make it. It is not over until I win!

Wow! What an experience! This Chapter offers testimonies of people who have exercised their comeback power like Les Brown. Reading the story of Cheryl du Plooy from South Africa, you will discover how, despite being called a whore by her mother, being abused by the people she thought loved her, and despite what she calls a 'filthy past', she stayed hooked on life. Reading the story of Michael J Callum, you will discover how Les Brown was the only person to pull him out of where he was to where he wanted to be. Reading the story of Milton Sithole, you will realise how he tapped into his comeback power after imagining the ghosts of his dreams looking at him with large angry eyes and saying, 'we came to you, only you could have given us life, and now we must die with you forever'. As you read this chapter, ask yourself this question: if I died today, what dreams, what talents, what gifts, what ideas would die with me?

Hooked on Life
Cheryl Du Plooy
South Africa

Founder of Hooked on Life

Hooked on Life

South Africa is one of the most beautiful countries in the world. It has approximately 11 official languages and hosted the 2010 FIFA World Cup. The Table Mountain in Cape Town is believed to be one of the oldest mountains in the world and one of the planet's 12 main energy centres, radiating magnetic, electric or spiritual energy. Some countries have deserts, some have subtropical forests, right? South Africa has deserts, wetlands, grasslands, bush, subtropical forests, mountains and escarpments. South Africa's water is rated as the 3rd best in the world for being safe and ready to drink. Water is not all there is to drink in this thirsty country.

South Africa's Cape wine lands have around 560 wineries and 4400 primary producers. Included in the Cape wine lands region is Route 62, considered the longest wine route in the world. Can you think of any other place in the world where two Nobel Peace Prize winners lived on the same street? Both Nelson Mandela and Archbishop Desmond Tutu had houses on Vilakazi Street in Soweto. It is in this great country that we meet Cheryl, a survivor of drug addictions. She is now on a journey to becoming a speaker and a coach. She has a non-profit organisation called "Hooked On Life" where she aspires to be the voice for those who suffer in silence.

My mother called me a whore

Phew, where do I start? I am 33 years old. I live in South Africa. I have never travelled. I was brought up in a house where my father drank from the morning till late. He would come home drunk and then physically abuse my mother, me and my 2 brothers. I am the oldest. I had a very depressed mother who called me a whore since the age of 5. I never really understood why, until I found out much later that my dad had affairs with multiple women. Then I remembered that my dad use to take me with when he saw some of them and then told me it was for work. So then it made sense why my mother called me my father's whore daughter.

Addicted to drugs at 13

As I grew older, I started to hide behind my fears by being a tom boy and very big mouthed and pretty soon I got involved with the wrong friends. At a tender age of 13, I met a guy who I fell in love with. I started using drugs with him and at the age of 16 I fell pregnant. Can you imagine my mother's response? 'Yeah I told you she is a whore'. I got married at 18 and moved in with my husband and our 8 month old baby. For that next 10 years I kept on using drugs for 5 years. I almost lost my child who later had 8 brain surgeries.

Divorced and remarried

Lust, porn addiction, drugs and alcohol had me down to my knees when I finally decided to get a divorce. Two years later, I married again. A loving man and I gained another daughter who had lost her mother due to malaria. Since then, I honestly can't say that we have had a bad life. I recovered from drugs and have been clean for almost 10 years now. I am very grateful for that. I have been a house wife all my life. I did not finish school and I don't have any university degree. The belief system that was printed into me was that a mother should stay at home and take care of children.

The father I never had

About a year ago, I was on Facebook one morning in April 2017 when I came across a live video of Warren Ryan. I signed up to one of his online coaching programs for 30 days. And in that 30 days, he shared so much value with us that my mind was blown away. He said one morning that if we want inspiration, we must listen to audios such as Les Brown and other speakers. So that's exactly what I did. And since then, I have been addicted to listening to audios. Mr. Les Brown is like the father I wished to have. He taught me to never give up, and that I have greatness within me. He told me that I am in control of creating my own destiny. He taught me to feel the fear and do it anyway. The truth he speaks and the stories he tells gives me fuel to know that it is possible for me to live my dreams.

Filthy past, spotless future

I now know that it doesn't matter how filthy my past was, that my future is still spotless. Les Brown has helped me to love myself again and in return others are loving me more. I am so grateful to have the privilege of listening to Les Brown in the mornings. I believe we all have a story, and I would love to be a speaker one day. I have a mission and a purpose for my life. I know that now.

Inspired and motivated

I recently started a nonprofit organization and an aquaponic business. Who would have thought this was possible for me: a teenage drug addicted mother who didn't even finish school with no university degree or experience? I have listened to Les Brown with my heart. 'Don't let someone's opinion of you become your reality'. Now here I am feeling inspired and motivated to create something beautiful and to love people. I had to forgive a lot of people but most importantly I forgave myself. It is because of Les Brown that I am a new person and loving life. If you see Mr. Les Brown, please give him a hug from me and tell him Cheryl from South Africa says thank you and God bless you.

Dr Patrick Businge

Fight For Your Dreams
Michael J Callum, Esq
England, UK

Fight For Your Dreams

I come from a family, where for 3 generations, we have produced preachers. So, growing up as a young boy, I was never afraid of talking to new people. I learnt to embrace both the spotlight and the anonymous shadows with humility. My patience has been tested, and that's the fun. I have had anger management issues as a teenager. With time, a combination of parental advice, university experience and 14 years as a bouncer have all prepared me to be able to control it. When you find a way to control a force, you teach that to others also looking for freedom. That is what my purpose is.

After a tough and unexpected break-up, I found myself at rock bottom. I quickly realised that as a talented young man I was not exempt from feeling rejected and worthless. After hitting rock bottom, my journey back started with a friend of mine, Beefy, advising me to listen to positive affirmations every day from people like Les Brown, Zig Ziglar, Tony Robbins, Eric Thomas, TD Jakes, and others. After trawling the internet for so long and listening to many voices, one speaker stood out for me. It was Les Brown that touched me personally. The first time I listened to him he said…

> Now let me tell you something, ladies and gentlemen. What will reasons do, Les? Nietzsche said if you know the 'why' for doing you can endure almost any 'how'. What do you mean by that? If you know why you're doing something when the hard times come and they're going to come, when the disappointments and rejections come and they're going to come by the truckloads, your reasons will

be your rod and staff to comfort to pick you up. Once again I got a saying on one of my tapes: if life knocks you down, try and land on your back, because if you can look up you can get up. Let your reasons get you back up.

Hearing this message started my journey from the rock bottom I had hit. It started my rehabilitation. As if it was planned, at the same time my dad sent me a video clip to watch. On opening it, I found it was Les Brown. I saw this as a confirmation that Les Brown was the person to pull me out of where I was to where I wanted to be. It has now become my routine to listen to his motivational speeches every day. He has become part of my daily ritual: I wake up, I pray, I do my pushups, and I listen to Les Brown.

There is something in his story that his belief in himself when the world says he's not capable that I definitely relate. I was born with cataracts. I developed glaucoma at the age of 15. In 2012, I became photo-phobic. There are times if it is not one thing, it is another. Listening to Les Brown, made me appreciate my life and the gifts I have. He has reminded me that I have something special: there is greatness within me. He has reminded me that before I was born, I ran a race with 40 other million sperms and the greatness within me made me a winner. Indeed he has been the Yoda to my Luke Skywalker. Considering, I have never met the man, his quotes are etched on my heart and I share them with you: "If life knocks you down, try and land on your back, because if you can look up you can get up". "Yes, you CAN!" "You have greatness within you!"

Because of Les Brown, I have been able to get up and find my purpose and live my dreams. I now work as a Qualified

Teacher in the UK and I have been doing this for the past 3 years. Though my teaching career is challenging, I can truly say that I love what I do. At this point in time, I believe what I do is my purpose in life. I'm not into teaching for the money, believe it! I do what I do because it is worth it. Les Brown says, 'nobody is going to bring it to you on a silver platter and say: 'Here's your dream manifested'. No, it's hard. Yes, it's hard. It's difficult, yes right and it's worth it'. It is hard to live your dreams. It is hard to go through the challenges of life. One thing I am certain about is that your dream is worth fighting for'. This is what I have discovered in my work as a teacher: there is something uniquely empowering and ironically humbling about inspiring and motivating young people to do well in life. This is what Les Brown has done for me and I am paying back.

I Stopped at Les Brown and Became Unstoppable
By Joanne Louise Kavanagh
Dublin, Ireland

Les Brown Certified Speaker and Law of Attraction Coach
www.joannekavanagh.com

Have you ever felt that you couldn't speak about feeling, sad, lost, Depressed? Have you ever felt that people might judge you or not understand you? Well I have felt those things since I was a child. Depression, anxiety and mental illness have had a significant thread running through my family lineage.

My Grandfather on my father's side was incarcerated in a mental institute aged 40 suffering from depression, delusions and paranoia. He never came home. His youngest child was only a baby. My father became the man of the house. My grandmother, walked into the sea and drowned. Her body was washed up and a year later found in Scotland. It was thought that she had been suffering from depression, which she kept hidden.

My father also suffered mental illness through depression, which was also hidden. He used alcohol to deal with his issues being afraid to talk about it and I'm sure his father's incarceration was a factor in his own silence. He died aged 57 from a massive heart attack (a broken heart in my opinion). *Emotions kept hidden.*

When my eldest brother had just turned 13, he was diagnosed with a mental illness, schizophrenia. He made many attempts to end his life and in 1991, a year to the month that my mother passed away he did end his life by drowning himself in Dublin's river Liffey.

There have been many times in my own life when I have felt lost. I have felt depressed, I have felt like giving up. Then something inside me would scream NO, NO, NO. YOU MUST BREAK THE SPELL, YOU MUST BE STRONG, YOU MUST BE UNSTOPPABLE. I told myself; I would not be silenced. I vowed that SOMEDAY I would help others to overcome their mental 'sickness' and try to change the taboo of how mental illness is viewed in Ireland as mental weakness.

My journey begins

I began to look for people to motivate me in my life. I found books and I began to read and soak up every word on the pages I read. It felt like food for the soul. *You can Heal Your Life* by Louise Hay, *The Power of Positive Thinking* by Vincent Norman Peale, and so many more. One day when I was feeling very low inside I recall hearing a man's voice on the TV. I stopped what I was doing and I sat down and listened. His name was Dr Robert Shuler, a minister from Garden Grove, California. He was speaking from the Crystal Cathedral. The story of how he built his church was so amazing to me and fascinating. I made it my business to record Dr Shuler every week and listen to his inspirational messages. This was the beginning of my journey to find my greatest self. I remember hearing him speak about Dr Norman Vincent Peale and how he would say, "YOU HAVE SOMETHING SPECIAL IN YOU, YOU HAVE GREATNESS IN YOU", "DON'T ALLOW YOUR NEGATIVE THOUGHTS TO HOLD YOU BACK'.

Wow, I found those words so powerful, and he also used a quote which I later found out was Les Brown's quote. "SHOOT FOR THE MOON BECAUSE EVEN IF YOU MISS YOU'LL LAND AMONG THE STARS". Les Brown was so influenced by Dr Norman Vincent Peale. He dreamed of speaking on the same stage as him and it happened for him and this was when he learned that Dr

Norman Vincent Peale used his quote; shoot for the moon, to end all his speeches. Little did I know when I was listening to Robert Schuler and reading Vincent Normans book, that it would lead me to my greatest influencer and the person who has changed my life forever, Mr Les Brown.

The Hour of Power

So, here I was on my quest and hungry; for more food for the soul. The World Wide Web was in its infancy, so I relied on books. I couldn't get enough of them. I had books for breakfast, dinner and tea. I made contact with the Crystal Cathedral in Garden Grove, California and I asked quite blatantly if I could be a guest and sing on the show. I was asked to send a demo of my voice, which I did. I was contacted by a lady who introduced herself as Dr Schuler's personal assistant. This was it. I was so excited by the prospect of singing on the Hour of Power. I was then contacted by the daughter of his personal assistant who was so happy to be making friends with an Irish girl as she was engaged to be married to an Irish boy and she was learning to do Irish dancing. We became pen friends and spent months writing to each other.

I arranged to travel to America, and then something happened. I discovered I was pregnant and the doctor said I couldn't travel for over 3 months. I thought the opportunity was lost. But I couldn't get Les Brown's shoot for the moon quote out of my head. I decided to revisit my plan to sing on the Hour of Power. My doctor gave the window of one month to travel, as by this stage I was almost 7 months pregnant. My friend in America encouraged me to come so I booked my flights and I was on my way to being a guest singer on the Hour of Power…. so I thought.

Hit on the blind side

Les Brown talks about how we can get hit on the 'blind side' and how things can go wrong, just like when he lost his house because he didn't do a title search, and when all his products and contacts were stolen, and when his girlfriend secretly found a new partner while he was out on the road trying to make it as a speaker.

Well that is what happened to me. The night before I was leaving to go to California, I tried to call my friend; and her brother answered the phone. Her mother spoke with me on the phone as well, but both of them were very vague. When I arrived, I was supposed to meet her family and all her friends. Instead she was stone walling me and I had no idea why. "Why would she do this to me, what had changed?' In my panic, I booked a hotel and I decided to go ahead with my plan to sing on the Hour of Power. "When life knocks you down land on your back, because if you can look up you can get up"- Les Brown.

Arriving in Los Angeles Airport alone and pregnant was a very scary experience. No one turned up to greet me. That was one of the loneliest times of my life. I was so upset, I cried. Then a voice inside me said, "Stop crying, be strong, trust your higher self, after all your higher self is what sent you on this journey". I thought of a Louise Hay affirmation I had read 'All is well in my world'. I repeated this over and over again and I felt better and stronger inside.

I didn't get to see my friend the whole time I was in Orange County. I did visit the Crystal Cathedral and experience from the audience the amazing voice of Dr Robert Schuler and his son Robert Junior. I never got to sing there but as I think about it now, it's like one degree of separation. Think about how close I was to Les Brown due to Robert Schuler knowing his shoot for the moon quote. This trip was a catalytic part of my new life journey. It would be many more years before I would actually get to meet Les Brown.

An Angel is born

Unlike Les Brown's entrance into the world - born in an abandoned building on a cold floor, my daughter arrived 2 months after my trip to Orange County, healthy and safe into the arms of a loving mother and extended family. We had a roof over our heads, we were not rich but we were not poor. She was the best thing that ever happened to me, a blessing, a child who would motivate me to strive to be my greatest self I could ever be. That was it, the bar was set, I had work to do. I embarked on a ten-year journey of study and learning and became a professional psychotherapist for children, adolescents and adults. I was going to help people to heal from mental illness, I was going to serve, but I still needed a mentor and I didn't know where to find such a person.

Fast forward, 2006, we move into a new home with the man I was to marry. Not long into our life there something happened, he had a personality change and became; depressed, angry, aggressive and abusive. I tried to make it work and help him to get some help but he would not listen to me. I pleaded with him to hear how this was affecting me and my daughter but he just couldn't hear me.

We fled the home leaving everything behind just before Christmas my daughter and I, and our two dogs, Scotty and Shadow. We were homeless for three months. In 2007, I found a new home for us. I had to take out a mortgage to buy it and then the property crash happened. I lost everything: all the equity I had was gone into the big black hole in the Irish economy. I struggled so hard for the next ten years, robbing Peter to pay Paul, borrowing money from friends and family and not being able to pay it back when I said I would. BUT I BELIEVED IN MYSELF. I knew there was greatness in me. Les Brown's quote 'Shoot for the moon' rang through my ears constantly. I had listened to every motivational speaker going, Louise Hay, Jim Rohn, Tony Robins, Bob Proctor, Dr Joseph Murphy, however I still felt so lost.

One day I prayed to my higher self, something I did from time to time. I recall that day; it was the 13th of January, a cold wintery day. I was feeling so lost and felt like giving up on my dreams because it just felt like I was trying so hard for years and nothing was happening. 'Please, please give me a sign as to where I go from here. What do you want me to do in the world? Send me a mentor, someone who can help me find my true purpose. I got a message, almost instantly, a thought, which said, go to your computer and go straight to YouTube. I did that and in the auto play there was a picture of Rocky Balboa.

I clicked on it and it was a voice I had never heard before, it was Les Brown. He was speaking to me, he was telling me that to give up is not an option. 'YOU HAVE THE

POWER IN YOU TO DO MORE THAN YOU CAN IMAGINE, TO MAKE A DIFFERENCE IN OUR CHILDREN, TO MAKE A DIFFERENCE IN OUR PLANET'. He told me 'you are never too old to learn and you're never too young to teach'.

It felt like I was being touched by God, this was real and I was going to listen to every word he said. I went searching for more Les Brown material and I made a library of his talks. I turned off the radio and the TV and began to listen to him every chance I got. I felt so uplifted and so happy that at last I knew where I was going, I was home. My life was going to change, I could feel it stronger than anything.

Les Brown Institute

One day I was listening to a recorded radio interview with Les Brown as a guest and he announced 'I want to train over a million speakers'. He gave out his email address and as I hurried to write it down with my eyebrow pencil, because I couldn't find a pen in my panic. I felt a rush of excitement, fear, panic and hope.

That was the beginning of the most amazing journey of my life. Les Brown had just offered to change my life. I was so overjoyed to join the Les Brown Institute and community. I am on my way to becoming a certified speaker trained by the world's most inspirational, caring, giving teacher, Mr Les Brown. Little did I know all those years ago when I was in my 20's, when I was so lost, and heard the words 'Shoot for the moon because even if you miss you will land on the stars', that I would ever get to stand beside and be affiliated with Les Brown. The man who changed my life, forever.

Getting Unstuck
Milton Sithole
Zimbabwe

Founder of Yatie Yatie Productions, PVT LTD
www.yatieyatieproductions.com

Getting Unstuck

We now travel to Bulawayo. It is located on the South Western part of Zimbabwe's Capital Harare at 475 km. It is a hub of cultural diversity where many people meet. Bulawayo is vibrant with a variety of music from traditional to classic-contemporary. It is the hub of the country's industry and being the second Capital city of Zimbabwe, it provides a gateway to Botswana, Zambia, Namibia and South Africa. The original location of Bulawayo is historical in that it was the last residence of the founder of the Ndebele Kingdom, King Mzilikazi. Here we meet Milton Sithole who share his story on how he got unstuck.

Hungry for success

Have you ever heard of the phrase there is a time and a season for everything under the sun? That is not something you want to hear when your life is going offside and you are in need of a breakthrough. That is how I felt in the past year and a half. In 2016 my company, Yatie Yatie Productions, hosted our first International Gospel Concert with an acclaimed award winning gospel singer. The concert was self-funded, we had no sponsors. It's a difficult thing to get or find sponsors for gospel acts in Bulawayo, Zimbabwe where I come from. I did not however let that stop me, as I was hungry for success and to create platforms for the local gospel acts to be able to share the stage with an International gospel sensation.

The shock of my life came when I could not solicit support from my church to paste concert posters in all our churches in Bulawayo and announcement on the podium. One would think that after many years of service in the church, such an endeavor would make the church leaders proud and happy. This affected our ticket sales and attendance because the gospel singer had a strong following in the church.

Bitter and wounded soldier

Needless to say, I was left a bitter and wounded soldier. I was tempted to leave the church but my wife said, 'Baby don't pack your bags yet maybe God has a lesson for us in all of this'. Though I stayed, my level of commitment deteriorated. Though I was attending church services, my heart was not fully there. I was angry as I lost over $4000 USD which was meant to refurbish our home. As I was in debt after that concert my zeal, focus, and hunger for success had died. I was screwed up. I needed an adrenaline boost.

My healing began in May 2017 when I got the opportunity to be a content contributor in radio as a host and producer of Thinking Blueprint and Operation of Life (TBOL) on www.the1873fm. The 1873 FM gives individual voices to be heard on matters that promote an inclusive, progressive and prosperous Africa. My motivational show was aired every Sunday from 12-3PM CAT. During this show, my goal was to inspire people to find their life's purpose and to live their dreams no matter their disappointments. As part of my ritual, I would play some motivational talks by the world's most renowned motivational people before I interviewed the guest of the day.

Spoke to the very core of my being

On the Sunday of 9th July 2017, I had an interview with Tinda: a Christian Rap Artist from Bulawayo, Zimbabwe. Before interviewing him, I played a clip of which I had no idea who the speaker was. To my big surprise, this speaker stood out for me. He spoke to the very core of my being. He spoke to my heart. He spoke with so much power and conviction. The speaker said,

> If you don't know why you are hear, I encourage you to find out what your purpose is here. What is the meaning of your life? What would be different? Have you ever asked yourself that question? And most people they go to their graves with their greatness still in them. What if you lived your whole life only to discover that it was wrong? We have all taken time just to stop and reflect many times when we hear what's happening in the news or read the newspapers, where is all of this leading to? What's going on here?

> And so I think that now more than ever we must begin to look at what are the things that we can do, that would put us on some firm footing in life, that will enable us to do some things and use some powers that we have, that many of us go through life never ever discovering that we have those things going for us. And part of that I believe is knowing what it is your life's work. What it is that gives your life a sense of meaning and purpose? See if you know what your life work is. I encourage you to start working on it.

If you can't do it all at one time do just a little bit of it, and if you don't know what it is that you showed up to do, if you don't know why you are here, I encourage you to find out what your purpose is here. What is the meaning of your life because once you find that, it puts you in your power place...

85% of the American public according to recent studies are going to jobs that they hate, working on jobs that do not challenge them, they get sick thinking about going, because see when you go to a job and you already know how far you can go, you can already see that proverbial glass ceiling. See when you are going someplace and you know how much you are going to make, you already know how far you are going to go. You are in a dead end position. It erodes yourself esteem. It lowers your sense of yourself. It creates an inner turmoil. It creates an emptiness in you.

So, I say that your life is worth finding, what it is that you are supposed to do. Imagine if you being on your death bed and standing around your bed the ghosts of the dreams, the ideas, the abilities, the talents, given to you by life but you, for whatever reason, you never pursued those dreams, you never acted on those ideas, and you never used those gifts. You never used those talents, and there they are starting at you as you are lying on your bed, with large angry eyes, saying we came to you only you could have given us life, and now we must die with you forever.

And the question is: if you died today, what dreams, what talents, what abilities, what gifts, what ideas would die with you?

Oh my God, who is this man and where has he been all this while? Had I heard these words a year ago, my life would be different. He challenged me and from this day forth, I didn't want to be haunted by the ghosts of my talents. This message encouraged me to not give up on my dreams, talents, skills and abilities. I was busy fussing about who had or had not done what for me such that I had lost sight of who I was, what I had, and what I was supposed to do with my life.

Getting unstuck

Les helped me to get unstuck. My hunger for success, my desire to help other people, and my thirst to serve the Lord was ignited by the message from his heart to my heart. He opened my eyes and I resolved to help other people with my story and use my voice to empower other people too.

I had started giving free talks in schools but I was not doing enough. I needed training and mentorship and who better qualified to mentor me in this journey other than the world number one motivational speaker, who speaks from the heart. The legendary Les Brown, because if you want to be great, you must get trained by the best.

I found out how I could be a part of his team, and I am now a member of the Les Brown Unlimited Team since December 2017. It is a commitment I made to myself to be a lifelong leaner and I am committed to my commitment. Never in a million years would I have thought I would be a part of a collaborative and achievement driven like-minded individuals all dedicated to achieving success in the professional speaking, training, and coaching industry.

Inspired by Les Brown's love for his adopted mother, I am dedicated to do all that I can to provide for my family. As an only child raised by a single mother, I somehow was not comfortable being a mama's boy but after hearing Les Brown's story, I can safely say this is Milton Sithole aka Miltn Millionz Mabo's baby boy. I am my mother's child and I am proud of it. My mother Sibongile Sithole is one of the most hard working, and resilient woman I know. She is one Lady who makes something out of nothing. I would one day like to honor her with a dream vacation or a cruise because she deserves it. She has always been there for me.

My mother is that sort of person who loves unconditionally and I feel some relatives picked that about her and have very often taken advantage of her kindness. She is my rock and pillar and if I was to choose a mother I would still pick her, she acts as my father also. My father left us when I was 5 years old for South Africa and he never came back. That affected me so much growing up. Hence, I vowed to be a different father to my children, I pledged to be always there and to be accountable and take responsibility for my family because I saw how that affected me. I was angry with my father for not being there for me I had no face to direct my anger to. I was stuck in anger for 33 years. Till I heard the message getting unstuck by Les Brown. In spite of all that has happened in your life just know that you matter; no flatter, go ahead and live your passion and dream.

CHAPTER 6: COMPANIONSHIP

P.E.O.P.L.E©

When it comes to the people we associate with, there is no shortage of sayings, proverbs and statements. One African proverb says, 'Birds of the same feather flock together'. Another goes, 'Show me your friends and I will show you who you are'. The President of the United States of America, Donald Trump says, 'If you hang around with losers you become a loser'. Porter Gale titled her book, 'Your Network is Your Net Worth'.

Having lived these truths, I included P.E.O.P.L.E© as the 6th step in my book '7 Steps to Greatness'. I believe that if you want to step into your greatness, you have to surround yourself with great P.E.O.P.L.E©. You might be asking: How do I know who the great P.E.O.P.L.E© are? Here is my simple answer: Great people are P.E.O.P.L.E© who are:

- **P**urposeful

- **E**ncouraging

- **O**pportunity experts

- **P**roductive

- **L**ive full

- **E**xemplary

If you want to be great, take time and evaluate the people you associate with using this model. It is my hope that by the end of this chapter, you would have discovered how Les Brown has been a great P.E.O.P.L.E to many people.

The Courage To Be Who You Are
Manuel Shipwood

International Speaker and Coach
www.manuelshipwood.com

The Courage To Be Who You Are

Manuel Shipwood is a coach, author, and speaker. He is not local to any place as he lives and works internationally. His mission is to help people discover their purpose and live it. He shares with you how to develop the courage to be who you are.

"You have greatness within you!"

Words so powerful that the amazing Les Brown uses them many times during a talk. Words so important that everybody should hear them on a regular basis. As a coach I meet people with a lack of self-esteem, self-confidence, a lack of vision and motivation on a daily basis. Two key beliefs are the most common in all of them: "I am not enough" and "I am only worth to be loved IF ...xyz." - Sentences I thought I was over with but apparently some parts still resided in me.

One day I discovered an audiobook on the internet, called "The Power of Purpose" which was a recording of Les Brown's speeches about "How to create the life you always wanted" as Nightingale Conant put it. It came to me after quitting a job which no longer served me and grew me. A job in which I couldn't see enough meaning or impact anymore. After that I became a Life and Business Coach and wanted to support people. There was just one thing that I was hearing in my head: "Am I good enough? Who am I, to stand up and tell everybody what to do? Shall I really walk that path? Maybe I can sit and watch what happens?!" Sitting and watching doesn't bring success. It did neither to bring clients or education to quiet the question: "Am I good enough?"

"Tired, exhausted and frustrated"

I had found my purpose but didn't have the power to walk my talk anymore. I was tired, exhausted, frustrated. Why? About 10 years earlier I started a media and communications agency and was very successful, serving top corporations like AUDI, Linde Gas, BMW, Fujitsu and many others with state of the art multimedia and internet products, some of them trailblazing stuff back then, that everybody was proud of. I was thriving, bought a new car, and I had great relationships. I loved life.

Eventually that changed: I was working overtime, cleaning up the mess of others, understanding that the products I was working on had no meaningful impact for what was important to me and the world at that moment and that there must be more out there. I asked myself: is THIS really is the most valuable and meaningful thing I could do with my precious life, energy and time? The answer was very clear, which started a big shift. But obviously I waited for too long to just "switch" from what I was doing. I did not have a burn-out like many others around me, including good friends. But I knew that I pulled the emergency break only very close before the impact.

"Make a step"

It took a long while to heal and recharge. Among others, Les Brown was one of the first who came to me to fire up those engines again with his amazingly powerful voice, sometimes "shouting" at me to MAKE A STEP. It was pure energy flowing into my ears, right into my heart. The reason wasn't only his eloquence but rather the energetic, authentic passion he radiates naturally. He absolutely was born to do exactly what he did. And I asked myself the question: What about ME? What am I born to do? What did I come for? What will people recognize in me that one could feel, that I was born to do exactly this or that?

I cannot remember how many times I listened to his recordings but let me say, he was a faithful companion at my side, on a journey, filled with gritting my teeth, tears, stumbling, falling, and standing up again. A journey of healing, growing, and surrendering to who I am meant to be and working accordingly. Here is one of Les Brown's quotes that effected a change in me:

> What would your life be like, if you decided to become courageous? … If you did what you felt in your heart? ... Courage comes from a French word which means "of the heart" ... It takes courage to live! ...The courage to love yourself... THE COURAGE TO BE WHO YOU ARE!! ... Courage is about what feels, at that moment, right for YOU! ...What feels right in your HEART!

Today, I'm not only an extremely happy coach, I also help people to find THEIR purpose in life with my coaching program "The PURPOSE System" and the add-on "RISE & SHINE as a purpose driven entrepreneur" for the newly self-employed. I love to motivate people and I'm even coaching other coaches on how to be a great coach. I love to share my message. I'm living my dream. I'm living my purpose.

If you would like me to help you do the same, go to **www.findyourpurpose.today** where, over a period of 6 months, you will learn how to apply "The PURPOSE System™". During a period of 6 months, you will take a journey towards discovering your full potential and living the life you are really meant for. Once you have found your purpose, you will integrate it into your life using my resources at **www.RISEandSHINE.coach**. It fills me with gratitude that people tell me that they see, hear and feel that I was born to do what I do. Thank you, Les!

My Travel Companion
Antionette Blake
Delaware, USA

Social Media Strategist, Educator and Speaker
www.ablakeenterprises.com

My Travel Companion

We now travel to Delaware where we meet Antionette Blake. She is a multi-award winning Social Media Strategist, Educator and Speaker. She is popularly known as the 'Delaware Blogger'. She hosts a weekly Podcast titled 'Social Media Sunday with the Delaware Blogger' on Sundays at 6:00 PM EST on BlogTalkRadio. She is the CEO of ABlake Enterprises: a Social Media Management & Consulting Company that works with businesses on strategies to help them broaden their brand and expand their online exposure. She has been featured in Women's Day, Parade Magazine, and the September edition of Delaware Today Magazine as one of the '36 Most Intriguing Delawareans'. Here is her story.

In 1983, I started my career in Corporate America with IBM after graduating from Delaware State College. I received my Bachelors of Science Degree in Elementary Education and taught for a year. During this time, I felt I had experience in being a "motivational speaker" even if my audience was comprised of 6-7-year-olds! However, it wasn't until I became a secretary for IBM at "New Manager's School" in Armonk, NY, that I became intrigued with true professional motivational speakers; Lewis Timberlake, was my favorite, that was until I heard Mr. Les Brown speak.

Not only was I intrigued that Mr. Les Brown was a Motivational Speaker, but that he was also an African American Motivational Speaker, a rarity at the time. Throughout my 32+ year career, I would listen to his tapes, YouTube Videos or read his books and was proud that at one time he even had a television program, albeit briefly. Recently I started listening to him again. I remember how proud my grandmother was when she told me he was getting married to Gladys Knight in her hometown of Canton, NC, even though I never confirmed this to be true (the location not the marriage to Gladys).

Here I am many years later, the founder of ABlake Enterprises Social Media Management & Consulting and getting ready to transition from Corporate America to a full-time Encore Entrepreneur. I start every morning reading scriptures then listening to Les Brown during my 1 and a half hour commute which further energizes me to pursue my passion. I often share some of his anecdotes when giving presentations to other business owners and think of 'Mamie Brown's Baby Boy' yelling in my ear, 'You've got to be HUNGRY' and that sir, I am! Hungry even more so at the age of 56, to be successful in my next phase of life as an educator of Blogging and Social Media. Thank you for giving me an opportunity to share my story.

162

Keep The Faith
Sandra Pelletier
Dominican Republic

Keep the Faith

We are now going to the beautiful island of the Dominican Republic. We are going to meet Sandra who has lived in this lovely island rich of natural beauty and unrivalled history. The Dominican Republic has exceptional places to visit including Santo Domingo: its capital where Sandra lives. There are beaches, beautiful mountains, excellent food and the locals are very friendly and will always make you feel like at home. Here is her story.

I started following Les Brown less than a year ago. I have found him to be an excellent human being. There are so many situations in my life when I am lost and I need someone to help me to find my way and help me stay strong. When I get the chance to read his Facebook posts and listen to his voice, his words touch me so deep. Les Brown gives me encouraging messages about faith, love, trust, and relationships. Some of my favourite words from him are:

- Listen to yourself, the voice that is in your heart, not your head, it will lead you to your goal
- Forgive yourself for your faults and your mistakes and move on
- Perfection does not exist, you can always do better and you can always grow
- Life is a fight for territory, once you stop fighting, what you do not want automatically takes over
- Keep the faith.

It is because of Les Brown that I now have faith in myself and in my purpose in life. I have learned to be grateful with everything that I have. I am able to keep moving forward and going for what I want from life. My life has changed in positive ways. My father passed away one month ago, my mom almost 6 years ago. This is not the best thing to happen to me! I just feel grateful for the time in life that I spent with my parents. They gave to me so much love. They gave me education. They gave me a home.

I am glad that I started following Les Brown because losing my father was so hard. It is because of Les Brown that I have been able to go through this tough time successfully. Les Brown has told me to keep my faith and I am fighting for my dreams every day.

Living Beyond My Labels
Dr. Ira Roach III
Delaware, USA

Living Beyond My Labels

In 2015, after years of searching for ways of becoming the best version of myself, I came across a story of a man that was a self-made millionaire. His name was Daniel Ally and I dropped an email in the contact information and to my surprise, he called me. We spoke for about 30 minutes and he asked me all types of questions but one question was clear, 'Do you want to become a millionaire?' His disclaimer was that he would only work with me if my mindset was together. He said, "You have to change your mentality in order to change your reality." He also asked me, "Ira, if you are who everyone says that you are, who will be you?" I enrolled in his six month program but I didn't follow all of the action steps we went over. I was still afraid of success.

Longing for a better version of me

In October 2017, I made the greatest decision in my life. Yes, I earned degrees from an Associates in Early Childhood to a Doctorate in Christian Education, but I still knew that I could become a better version of me. I have raised four awesome kids, mentored hundreds of young absent fatherless boys, assisted numerous non-profit organizations, acted in the gospel circuit and local community stages but I needed more. I have been an ordained minister since the age of 26 and have been pastoring since 2004 but I have never felt as if this was my only calling and stage to inspire people.

I joined the Les Brown Unlimited Team because I wanted to surround myself with a new village, that believed in me, that would hold me accountable for the action steps in becoming the best version of myself and that would support and teach me how to tell my story. The Les Brown Team has done this and much more. I remember signing on, going through the orientation and then taking my first course which was *Speak Your Way to Unlimited Wealth.* I thought wow, its him Les Brown!

I completed this first course in two days! I was so excited and then the Facebook page actually had people congratulating me for joining the team! When you have never had this type of experience with a village and new community. It was mind blowing. Now I feel like all of the knowledge and action steps that I will attempt can help me reach my destiny. I realized that I really could find my purpose through this training.

The next awesome component was my Strategic Business Launch (SBL) team and led by Alisa Arvind. It was an experience that I will forever hold dear to my heart. The greatest part of all was that I would get to meet my team at the Certification in April 2018. Luis, Michelle, Rhazia, Valerie, Printella and Ires made up the DREAM TEAM. We had a Monday night call at 7:00pm (Eastern time) and I looked forward to the knowledge and encouragement that I would receive from this call. One night, it was only three of us on the call: Alisa, Rhazia and myself. These women drilled me and brought some ideas out of me that I didn't realize were within me. God allowed me to be on that call by myself to receive and be imparted in by these two women. My life has changed. My mindset has changed. My money is changing.

Statistics show: 98% of people don't achieve their goals, only 6% achieve their childhood dreams, and 53% of young Americans give up on their dreams. How do these statistics measure in my world? I too was not achieving my dreams, not reaching my goals and had given up. The amount of years I spent taking classes, attending seminars and even paying for a coach didn't seem to have helped me.

I attempted suicide numerous times

My world changed when I entered middle school because it was there I learned about my unique ability to make others happy. However, it also made others upset so much so that the bullying began. I was called sissies, queers and dumb boy. This continued until I discovered that I could fight and then I got out of control. I tried to hurt people because I was hurt.

My self-esteem was low and I never felt good enough from my teen years to my twenties. I was wearing the labels that people had given me over the years and it did not make me love myself. I gave up my hopes, dreams and aspirations. I did receive a Life Coach Certification after six months, but I did not implement what I learnt. I attempted suicide numerous times because I did not want to be on earth if I was only this stupid, queer, weak and poor person. Every time it seemed as though my moment was here, it would be taken away but some circumstance beyond my control.

I connected with a fellow Les Brown Unlimited sister by the name of Davina Carter back in October of 2017. She gave me some pointers on how to best utilize the program and how she was expanding her reach through her efforts in speaking and coaching. Mr. Antonio Smith Jr was a wealth of help. I did not know who this man was, but he was my go to guy for about three months before the

Certification event. He set me up to be able to view all of the Les Brown courses and then said, "Get your plane ticket and don't worry about your monthly payment, see you in April at the certification."

I saw this advertised but somehow received the wrong message. I was under the impression that I would have to pay the amount of the registration and I said to myself I can't afford this. I'm going to be broke after this and I cannot afford this. I had once again come so close to finally reaching a place that I know would change my life and boom in my face, finances would not allow me to get there.

I had already enlisted a roommate named Luis Zamora, my friend from the SBL group so I am thinking aww man this just my life story. I was talking to Davina and she was preparing to go and I happened to tell her that I was not going this time. She asked me why and I told her because I don't have the registration money, hotel fees and for a plane ticket. She gave me the best news I have heard in a long time. She told me that because I was a member of the Les Brown Unlimited, we did not have to register. I let out the greatest shout that I could muster up in my belly. So I bought my plane ticket and gave Luis the price of the hotel and told my family that I was on my way to Les Brown Certification event.

Discovering my power voice

My immediate family really did not know who he was and how important this was to me, but my close friends and colleagues were excited!   I got to the certification met my

SBL group members who were in attendance and celebrated with my new village! I discovered my Power voice that weekend and I have taken the tools that I received and this time I have implemented.

I realized what Les Brown says, "Don't let other people's opinion of you, become your reality." I have learned that I am bigger than labels and anyone's opinion. Since being a part of this village, I have joined a web series and its announced that I was nominated for a best actor award. I came home after the certification and gained three clients. I have a definite date for an exit strategy from my 9-5 job. I have enrolled with a branding and marketing coach who is my sister in the Les Brown Unlimited family and I was booked for my very first break out session workshop on the 18th of May in Richmond Virginia. My latest book project may or may not be in publication when this is released but its titled, *Daddy Knows Best: What Every Boy Needs From His Dad.* This book is about helping absent fathers to understand that they too are bigger than their labels and it's not too late to live their dreams.

Thank you Les Brown for your wisdom, integrity and story. It has changed my life forever.

CHAPTER 7: EDUCATION

Educate Yourself and Become Unstoppable

I was not born in the greatness of Great Britain where education is free. I was born in the poverty of Uganda where education was paid for. My parents believed education was my only ticket out of poverty and as a result, worked day and night to make their dreams become true. Though they still struggled to get fees so that my siblings and I received a good education, they did not let their struggles become their benchmark.

I vividly remember when my father got into debt due to paying our school fees. One of the people whom he had borrowed money from took legal action and he was imprisoned. After two weeks in a prison cell, one of our family friends gave money to him so that he could use it to buy his freedom from prison. But as it was the start of the new school term and I had to go to school, he chose to stay in prison so that I could have the money to pay off my school fees. My father sacrificed his freedom so that I received education. Allow me to ask you one question: Are you ready to sacrifice all that you have for your education?

Les Brown is a master storyteller and he has educated millions of people through stories. Here are some of the stories from people who have learnt from Les Brown's stories and changed their lives. They are a testament that education can be the difference between success and failure.

You Don't Have to be Great to Get Started
Vastine East
Texas, USA

You Don't Have to be Great to Get Started
Vastine East
Texas, USA

"I'm honored!"

I live in Texas in the large coastal city of Houston, where the summers are hot, winters are cold, food is sweet and the people are great! I am honored to say a few words about my respect for Mr. Les Brown! Wow!!! I'm honored! Thank you Dr. Businge!

"You don't have to be great to get started, but you have to get started to be great."

It was after I read that quote by Les Brown, then reading it repeatedly, did I finally realize, I had procrastinated long enough. I had deliberately found ways to keep my ship safely anchored in the harbor of life! Those words after they finally soaked in, forced me to question why God allowed me to be here, forced me to re-evaluate my life and then I determined it was time to hoist my anchor and head out to open waters!

For years, I listened to Les Brown give his message on audio tapes. I had watched him on YouTube and television tell his story! I was drawn to his honesty and his passion to reach people just like me. If I had failed to seriously consider his teachings, I would have continued to live the life of Walter Mitty! Continuing to live my life in quiet desperation! His motivational teachings helped me understand the proverb, "calm seas don't make a great sailor."

I was a caterpillar, afraid to emerge from my cocoon. Overcome with doubts to take wings and fly to heights I only dreamed about in silence. Growing up was unpleasant at times. I was often labelled as a shy child, I felt I could never come up the accolades laid on my brothers! I always wanted to do great things. Silently competing with my brothers. Always wanting to receive the accolades I felt my brothers received when we were growing up from family and community!

After public school, I studied drafting as my major at The University of Houston. I eventually began my career as a Civil Structural Designer for Brown & Root in 1974: a career that spanned 43 years. Engineering is a team effort with many talented people. I was just a silent team member. Doing my job year in and year out, I believe I could rise to heights and this would allow me to put my signature on personal achievements. At the end of all the projects I worked tirelessly on, it was the disciplines, Project Engineers and lead designers that walked away with accolades of greatness!

I would leave engineering for a period to pursue acting. After studying acting at The American Academy of Dramatic Arts in Pasadena in California and gaining the respect of my peers, I felt I was on my way to greatness! Only to find myself back in the mindset of Walter Mitty. I thought I was a great actor, but I never left the academy's rehearsal stage! I wrote and published two illustrated children books. I rediscovered my personal blunder again. Return to Walter Mittyville!!!

Les Brown's life quote, **"You don't have to be great to get started, but you have to get started to be great,"** changed my life! I didn't know I had started to do the things to be great. I finally realized I started down the road to be great and didn't know it. I know now I started to be great when I worked my way through college, when I sacrificed and went to California to study acting and when I studied at The Institute of Children's Literature and Columbia School of Broadcasting. The frustrations I've housed over the years are behind me now! I was sleep walking! Pride had clouded my mind! Mr. Brown set this captive free with his quote, "You don't have to be great to get started, but you have to get started to be great." Like a horse racing away from the starting gate, I dashed down the track. I didn't know I had started!

I'm Going To Make It
Amy Jane Chicoyne
Ontario, Canada

I'm Going To Make It

I grew up with a lot of post-traumatic stress disorders. My parents were addicts and separated. I was given away to my mother's ex-boyfriend's parents. I was molested, raped, suicidal, and always made bad choices. I became a young mother and lived in an abusive relationship for ten years. I then left that relationship and moved forward with another man who is now my husband.

One day, my husband lost his job and we landed on the welfare system here in Canada. The welfare system had an adult learning course that we could take to improve ourselves and get off of the welfare system. Our teacher had a series of videos for us to watch and that's when I saw Les Brown. It was like he was speaking to me and I felt him in my heart. My teacher asked me if I liked the videos and I said yes, of course. I then asked her who he was and she told me all about Les Brown and she said to me, 'I knew you would love Les Brown'. That night I went home, logged onto my computer and looked him up on YouTube. I started listening to his videos over and over actually for many years.

I started to listen to Les Brown in 2008 and the following year, I ran a community centre with two other women. We ran a teen program, and art program for the kids. We had events and had community professionals come to our Centre. After a while I went back to work, and we were laid off because they gave the company to India. So, I was out of work again. I was so depressed and one night I was listening to Les Brown's speech 'It's possible'. I don't know what happened but something just clicked in my mind. I saw an opportunity and I took action. I applied to college and I got in. There were so many obstacles I had to overcome just to get into school. I keep repeating these words from Les Brown:

- It's possible
- If you can look up you can get up
- You gotta be hungry
- It's not over until I win.

These words increased the hunger in me. Let me tell you I was hungry. I found a way to get into college even though the odds were stacked against me. I have used Les Brown's words to advise people when they are down: 'don't let someone's opinion of you become your reality'.

Listening to Les Brown's videos has given me confidence and belief in myself again. I graduated with honors and I am now an addiction and mental health counsellor. I still have bigger and better dreams. One of the most important dreams I have is to meet Les Brown so that I can say, 'Thank You'. Since I started listening to him, I live by his videos and today I am no longer that child who felt helpless and ashamed of herself and of life.

Dr Patrick Businge

Choosing My Future
Levan Adams
Michigan, USA

Choosing My Future

The time is 1995. I was entering my senior year of high school. However, I was still classified as a junior due to skipping school half of my 11th grade year. When I started the new school year in 1995, my mother would ask me to come and watch with her the Les Brown VHS tapes for 15 to 20 minutes before she would take me to school. Sometimes we would watch the same tapes over and over again but on different days. I now realize that watching those tapes helped me to determine my future.

Some of the things that changed was that I started to do better in school. I made it to the basketball team. I started going to an after-school program to receive credits. I also attended night school. In June 1996, I finally graduated on time after making those school credits up. In the Fall of 2016, I was admitted to Central State University in Ohio where I spent two years before living due to financial reasons.

If it wasn't for my mother's prayers and her being a big fan of Les Brown, who knows what would have happen to me and my future? Up to now, I listen to Les Brown. Some of my favorite messages from Les Brown are:

- 'You cannot expect to achieve new goals or move beyond your present circumstances unless you change'
- 'Other people's opinion of you do not have to become your reality'
- 'Forgive those who have hurt you'.

CHAPTER 8: ENCOUNTERS

It's Possible

I think that this extract from Les Brown's speech is all we need to set the scene for the stories in this chapter.

> So what I want you to do is think about something you want for you, that's real for you, that's important for you, that will give your life some special meaning and power. And I don't even want you to say I can do that. I don't want you to assume that. See, five years ago when I started out in this area, I would not have been able to make the mental leap that I would be up to where I am right now. I don't want you to begin to just psych yourself out. No, no, I want you to be able to say something to yourself that will enable you to maintain a level of integrity with yourself, that when you say this even when you face tremendous setbacks, it will be a benchmark to keep you in the game, to keep you moving forward and experimenting and readjusting your strategy and your plan of action continuously looking for ways to win.

> So what is that something? When you've got an idea you want to move on. You might not have the money, you might not have the education, you might not have the support or the resources you need. What is that something that can keep us going, that will enable us to act on our dream? What's one of those keys that will begin to help us to discover the secrets to our dream?

Here's what I want you to repeat after me please with power and conviction, say: **'It's Possible'**. It's all I want you to do when you look at your dream, just say to yourself every day: It's possible. Just say that every day to yourself: it's possible.

My advice as you read these stories, remember to say to yourself that 'It's Possible'.

Dr Patrick Businge

There is Power in Believing 'It's Possible'
Michelle Watson
England, UK

Author, Speaker, Book Creation Mentor and Life Coach
www.break-freeforever.com

There is Power in Believing 'It's Possible'

My name is Michelle Watson and I am a bestselling Author, Certified Life Coach, Speaker Trainer, Award Winning Speaker, Business book creation mentor & Publisher, Co-Pastor, Founder of Breakfree Forever Consultancy Ltd and Women Be. However, this is not how my story began. I was born in Enfield London England, but migrated to the Caribbean Jamaica with my grandparents at the age of three. I returned to the United Kingdom pregnant at the age of nineteen and felt like a fish in a mighty ocean. It was just that I was so used to being and dealing with issues on my own that even though I now had them, I managed to isolate myself somehow despite having a massive and loving family.

This led me into a relationship with a man I thought was the best thing to ever happen to me. We got married after which he changed drastically, and I suffered both verbal and domestic abuse from him This broke me and destroyed everything in me: my mentality, confidence, and self-esteem. It was during all of this that I then developed a tumour which I was told the possibilities were high that it would paralyze the left side of my face. All this happened whilst parenting a son from the marriage who had special needs. I managed to get out of the marriage, but he didn't leave my life as I was stalked, had my clothes stolen from the house, my car was vandalised daily, and I was scared to even fall asleep at nights.

There was one night I woke up and I found him standing over me! It really got bad, I became depressed, lost my job and was drowning in debt which led me to having suicidal tendencies. Many don't believe it today, but one day it came to the point when I attempted to take my life. I no longer felt that I was needed, and that the world would be a better place without me as I no longer believed that I had any value or abilities to offer. I eventually went back to my foundation - church. Though I grew up in church, I no longer had interest in it upon returning to the UK but here I was again back in God's presence. Things started to calm down, but I was still in a bad place as there was so much issues with my son and school. He used to get into terrible rages and I was so scared and ashamed to take him anywhere, the school had also informed me to not expect anything of him academically.

One day, a brother in my church who was aware of what was going on, wanting to encourage me, asked if I have ever heard of Les Brown. I said that I didn't. He sent me a YouTube link and I watched it. I started to gain hope. Funny though, I only started to have hope for my son but not for myself. One day that very same church brother called me and said Les Brown was coming to London and Success Resources was doing an event called *Pursuit to Happiness* with Les Brown, Chris Gardener, Gerry Roberts and others at the Excel Centre. At that time, I only had £140 in my account, but I went anyway. I can never forget speaker after speaker came but I just wanted to hear Les Brown.

As I waited, Gerry Robert, a book publisher came on and my cousin that came with me reminded me that I have always wanted to write a book and share my story. But how could I as I had no money or belief? After Gerry, it was Les Brown next on stage. He spoke to me without him even knowing. I sat in that seminar and cried – "someone's opinion of you is not who you are." I needed to hear him say those words. These words spoke to the life of my son and to me as I had allowed all the negatives that I was told from the abusive relationship, the doctors and school to hold both myself and my son back. I got up and went to the customer service and asked how much the book boot camp and they said it was £97. I paid it and left myself with the balance of £43.

That day changed my life. I started to sell items to raise money and my current husband Allain helped me a lot to gather items and sell even though he as well wasn't sure it would pay off but supported me none the less. I wrote my first book, Overcome and Raise above: How to turn the downside of challenges into the upside of renewing your life'. This book became a best seller. I started to get speaking events and things went up hill. However, there were still a few challenges here and there, but I was in a much better place mentally to see it through. I started to fight for my son (in prayer & with taking positive action) and got him as much help as I could find and afford.

I would listen to Les Brown as soon as I got up in the morning. Every single morning, Les Brown would make me laugh so much so that I made everyone in the house, my husband and 3 children, Santana, Rashaun & Alisha listen to him. Whenever I felt down or discouraged apart from the word of God and my church Les brown was the one, I would play his CD in the car or watch him on YouTube in the house and his laughter would make me laugh but his words would ignite something within me that made me believe again. I am now a multi award winning speaker and speaker trainer for Andy Harrington one of the men that spoke on the stage at the very event where I first saw Les Brown I have written my second book titled *Rise Above & Believe – How to Get Rid of Excuses and Create the Life You Desire.* I am now inspiring others and letting them know that 'Someone's opinion of them is not who they are' and that no matter what your circumstance is creating your desired life is still possible. As for my son he is now an exceptional student, who has obtained many certificates and was made to sit his exams at an early stage and passed with flying colours. That day sitting in that seminar I never dreamt I would be where I am today. If I did it so can you, thank you Les brown for being a mentor to me without you even knowing it – you changed my life

I am now the CEO of Breakfree Forever Consultancy Ltd. It specializes in working with ordinary individuals to become and live their extraordinary selves through the art of personal development, Business, Speaking and writing. The company's main entities are:

- *Breakfree Forever Publishing* which focuses on helping entrepreneurs to write & publish their business book and use it as a marketing tool for their business.

- *Vision 2 Success training* – This programme provides mentoring to individuals that have an idea and gives them the ability to turn their idea into a monetized business.

- *Speak From The Heart Academy* – Is for those who want to inspire, motivate, persuade, make an impact through their talk or even in interviews and sell YOU from the stage without the script.

- *Rise Above & Believe Academy* – Personal Development Coaching & accountability for those who are ready to create the life they have always desired.

'They could not kill me before I met Les Brown!'
Herman Thystere
Congo Brazaville and England, UK

'They could not kill me before I met Les Brown'

We are now going to travel to a special country that lies along the equator and is bathed by the blue waters of the Atlantic Ocean. This country was part of the French colony of Equatorial Africa and gained its political independence in 1960. It is called Congo Brazzaville. Its capital, Brazzaville, is located on the Congo River, immediately across from Kinshasa, the capital of the Democratic Republic of the Congo. This country has enjoyed political stability for more than two decades now and makes it a great tourist destination. Congo Brazzaville has produced great writers like Alain Mabankou, Tchicaya U Tam'si, Sony Lab'ou Tansi, Jean-Baptiste Tati Loutard, Henri Lopès, and Emmanuel Dongala. It is in this vast country and in its second largest city Pointe-Noire (Black Point) that we meet and discover the story of the emerging author Herman Thystere titled: 'They could not kill me before I met Les Brown'

My commitment to God

It was early in the morning one day of August 2003, and I wanted to fulfil my commitment to God. I woke up and looked at my wife who was profoundly asleep in the bed with our child. It was a one-bedroom rented house in one of the neighbourhoods of Pointe-Noire. It had rained all night. As usual, the tropical rain was so fierce, one could feel it by the type of raindrops banging on our tiny roof.

4 AM! This was the time I had to wake up and join my friend, Christian, who, from Monday to Friday, waited

outside of my compound, so that we could walk together the distance that separated us from our praying site. We had to lead prayer for one hour from 5AM to 6AM in our small group of prayer warriors. On this particular day, Christian could not make it as he had another engagement. So, I had to walk the dark streets on my own in that early hour of the morning, a walk that would normally take up to 30 minutes.

I got out of the bed without waking my wife and daughter up. I took my Bible and read a portion of the Scriptures that appealed to me and spoke about my divine protection. As my wife knew of this early morning programme, there was no need to disturb her sleep. I walked out of the house, knowing, I had God's protection during my journey to the prayer site. I found the streets were empty of people and it seemed I was the only one walking. The air was as fresh as the rain had just stopped falling. There were puddles of water everywhere.

Filled with trust

As I walked the badly maintained roads and the narrow avenues, my heart was filled with trust just like the Israelites as they ascended to Jerusalem for their pilgrimage. From my lips came Psalm 125, 'Those who trust in the LORD are as secure as Mount Zion; they will not be defeated but will endure forever. Just as the mountains surround Jerusalem, so the LORD surrounds his people, both now and forever'. I was also filled with joy as this Psalm had set the tune of my day. I had decided what my day was going to be. I was in control of the spirit of my day. To me, that day was made by providence, and I had a spiritual and prayerful contribution to make to mankind.

After I had walked for about 15 minutes without encountering anyone, I went passed a cemetery singing, with my Bible in my right hand. I reached the verge of a big puddle left by the stormy rain. As I wanted to jump it up to the other side, I noticed that there were two gentlemen coming towards me from the other side of the puddle. Moved by respect and consideration for my fellow human beings, I waited for them to jump first so I could follow thereafter. To my utter and dreadful surprise, the two men suddenly and violently grabbed me! They were far from being the gentlemen as I previously thought of. They were in fact thugs! They started uttering threats at me. I could not believe what was happening to me on my way to leading morning prayer.

'I am going to kill you'

I knew in me that I was done. There were no other people in the street. Whatever these two would decide to do to me was going to be devilishly successful! What were they after? One of them took out a gun from his pocket, and the other one a sharp and shining knife from its hiding. They manically asked me for money, and they were specific; they wanted 500 Central African CFA Franc, which is around £0.67! I said I did not have money on me. I showed my Bible to them. It got them so mad, that they threatened to kill me. The one with the knife was horrendously violent, shaking me. He asked me to kneel, which I did. In that position I said a loud prayer to God. But, he urged me to shut up and asked me to stand up again. And once again, I explained that I had no money, and the reason I was out in that early hour of the morning was to go and conduct a prayer meeting. They angrily thought I was lying to them. The apparent leader of the two said to me, "Because you are proving stubborn, I am going to *kill* you!" To this compatriot my life was worthless!

Sweat was running all over me. I thought of my wife and daughter I had left earlier on: what were they going to become without me? I thought about myself: what was I going to do? Scream? I dared not as they could kill me even before I finished the first scream! I had to trust God I prayed to for protection.

'Run for your life!'

As he resolved to implement his sordid and hideous decision by taking his knife and trying to stab me in my chest, his partner quickly and miraculously stopped him. The knife reached my chest, but I did not know it. He said to him that while palpating me, he found a Siemens mobile phone in a small bag I had tied up around my waist. Indeed, that small bag was where I carefully hid my identity documents and that phone. Providence used that small Siemens mobile phone to avert my assured death from these ruthless thugs! 'Don't kill him! Don't kill him! I have just found this phone after palpating him,' said the one with the gun. He then let go of me, and with a regretful near-miss burning desire for blood shed, said, "You are the luckiest man! Now, run for your life!"

I was so hypnotized by my sudden ordeal that I couldn't run. It seemed so surreal to me. Was it truly happening? I sensed tears rolling down my cheeks. And as I walked away from them, I felt a wet sensation on my chest. That's where the edge of the knife was abruptly stopped. It created a little perforation on my chest, provoking blood to gushing out. And while walking away from those human angels of death, I felt pity for them, not hatred! I prayed for them to reconsider their ways. They weren't born for that. There was too much they did not know about themselves… So, as I went my way, I promised or vowed to myself that wherever I would go into the world, I'll tell of this survival story.

Searching for my purpose

I survived, and I came to the realization of the preciousness of life. God gave me another chance. What was that for? Thousands of people got killed in that month of August 2003. Why not me? Why did I survive it? While I could not explain it in the natural way, I just remembered these words from Sholom Aleichem (1859-1916), "Life is a dream for the wise, a game for the fool, a comedy for the rich, a tragedy for the poor". My survival enhanced my consideration of life, my life. To me, life was going to be a dream to be lived in its fullest.

Lots of water flowed under the bridge and five years after this traumatic, near-miss death experience, I found myself in Liverpool, United Kingdom, as a refugee. It was hard, very hard. I knew nobody in this city, and my first night was spent in a police station. Indeed, I had to call for the police patrol to help me not to sleep rough in a city I had never lived in before. My first bed was police chairs!

The Voice

While waiting for my immigration situation to be officially sorted out, I lived on £35.00 a week given to me by the UK Immigration Services. I was not allowed to work. It was a very depressing and challenging moment. One day, after going to buy some food stuff, I came across 'The Voice,' a British national Afro-Caribbean weekly newspaper. This newspaper attracted my attention and I bought the issue of that week. Of all the news I could read from it, only one stood out; the article talking about a certain Leslie Calvin Brown, an African American Motivator, who was going to be in London in 2008 for a motivational speaking event. And the gate fee was £500.00!

What? Here I was surviving on £35.00 a week, and this man that I never heard of was going to speak, and people were going to pay a huge amount of money just to listen to him? Who is he anyway, I asked myself? I had to go to the local library and make some further researches about him from the internet. While on the internet, I was so impressed, overwhelmed, and stunned by this man's ability to motivate and arouse people. From YouTube, I found out that he had some video clips. I attentively and passionately listened to the messages like "It's Not Over until I Win; Getting Unstuck; Live Full and Die Empty; It's Possible; You Deserve; How to Become Successful; You Gotta be Hungry…"

'They could not kill me before I met Les Brown!'

I couldn't believe that a man could have such rhetorical skills. I felt like flying under his compelling encouragement to releasing the greatness locked within me. I thought what a man! This is a man I would not have met had the two thugs killed me that morning!

Les Brown's story of how he was born, his adoption by Mrs. Mamie Brown, his struggles in high school, being labelled EMR (Educable Mentally Retarded), the seeds of change brought or sowed into his life by Mr. Leroy Washington. His love for sublime and motivational driven quotes; his knowledge of books that he quoted from. The hardships of starting and running his own public speaking business… opened up the consciousness of possibilities in my own life in a foreign land. I heard him speak about Dr. Norman Vincent Peale, 'Shot for the moon, even if you miss you will land among the stars', Earl Nightingale, 'You become what you think about', Zig Ziglar, 'See you at the top', Dexter Yego, 'Don't Let Nobody Steal Your Dream', and many others I had never heard of.

Oh, I was literally transformed in my thinking. I found out that I could be someone that could reach out to and touch millions of lives around the world because I chose a path to success. His message appealed to me. "You have greatness within you!" Wow! It was too beautiful and powerful to be true in my case. I started dreaming of meeting Les Brown one day. But, still a small voice from deep within me whispered, 'Do you think you can do as well as Les Brown? Come out of it!' 'How can you even approach him? Are you worthy?'

'I was born for this!'

Against my life odds, I decided that I was going to be a motivational speaker, but my negative small voice still triumphed in shutting me up for many years. I would occasionally listen to Les Brown in my car and cry, knowing that I could do this. I was born for this. But somehow, I resisted this internal positive urge. But in the process, I overcame my fear, and listened to Les Brown, and I somehow succeeded in writing my first book in 2011, 'Now that You are Born Again, What Next?' Given that this book was not a success as I wished, I fell again a victim of the negative voice.

But one night, this year, as I was struggling to find sleep, I saw that my man, Les Brown, was doing a Facebook Live. While speaking, he said he was going to be in London on 20th January 2018. London again? I decided there and then to purchase my ticket for the Les Brown in London event. I said to myself I could not go to watch Les 10 years ago because I could not afford the ticket price. Now that I could, I would be the dumbest man in the world not to go. I wanted to be in his physical presence and to be impacted by his life. To me, this was the reason why the thugs that attempted to kill me could not succeed. I had to meet Les Brown, to receive my portion of motivational anointing and soar up in life to blessing mankind. Their threats were not as powerful as the willingness from Les Brown's heart to come help me.

Did they want to kill me? Of course! Was I traumatised by my life-threatening circumstance? Yes. But I chose to move on, believing that the world would hear of my survival story and why? In his book, *Live Your Dreams*, Les Brown wrote, "No life is without confrontations and failures. You will hear catcalls and encounter failure in your life. Be aware. Be ready. Absorb the blows, be wiser for them, and persevere because the possibilities are never exhausted." I encountered with the confrontation of precociously dying, but providence made sure that I did not die before I met Les Brown, Mrs. Mamie Brown's boy! There is a reason for that. That's why I absorbed that blow and did not let the emotional, psychological, and traumatic, effect of the attempted murder on my person, steal my joy of living and deny me of a glorious and impactful future.

Les Brown came for me

On the 20th January 2018, I was in London inside the Methodist Central Hall to fulfil my dream of seeing Les Brown physically. He came for me, in his ~~73th~~ 73rd year of existence, battling with cancer, checking himself out of the hospital where he was, travelled all the way from the US to London, just to talk to me. Why? Because Les subconsciously believed that we are two branches cut from the same tree. He had to come, pulled by the force of my dream!

I had given up of my dream of becoming a motivational speaker, and he came to help me pick it back up, dust it off and run with it. He did not come alone, he carried many others, so that I could be exposed to their skills and talents. The likes of Spencer Fearon, Raymond Aaron, Alfie Best, Douglas Vermeeren, and Ona Brown…I heard Les Brown, battling pain in his body, close the event by these words, "I can give because I can…" Then, with a youthful swag in his steps, he walked off the stage under the thunderous acclamation of a satisfied audience. I was over the moon, so proud of myself. I had my "so THERE!" attitude at myself by succeeding to achieve one of my dreams, seeing Les Brown! I received so much from him in order to give as well!

Les has never been in Congo Brazzaville where I was born and grew up but he has been there through me. I'll carry Les Brown wherever I go. Les has been given to me. Since I got to discover him, a lot has changed in my life. For example, I am taking flying lessons, learning to pilot a plane, with the aim of owning one, one day. I am once again writing my own book to be published by Raymond

Aaron this year (decision I made during the event in London), and working on starting my own motivational speaking business, becoming an entrepreneur!

I also met with Dr. Patrick Businge, member of the Les Brown Unlimited Team and Founder of Greatness University; bestselling author of '7 Steps to Greatness.' From this encounter at the Les Brown in London event, a collaborative and achievement driven relationship was born. Dr. Patrick Businge offered me the opportunity to tell my story on how Les Brown has touched my life in his forthcoming book, *Les Brown Changed Our Lives.*

I promised myself that wherever I'll go in the world, I'll tell of how two ruthless thugs were convinced by providence not to kill me because I carried greatness within me which had to be released. And meeting Les Brown from the pages of The Voice newspaper has given me an opportunity, fifteen years later, to tell my survival story to the world. All these years I had my story waiting for a larger platform to tell it. And Les Brown, through Dr Patrick Businge, has given me the opportunity to do just that. Does Les know about it? No! Who cares?

Les has taught me, Herman, without even knowing me in his "Live Your Dreams" lesson of motivation by saying, "You showed up on this planet with greatness within you. The possibilities are endless when you were born, and unless you allow life to batter you into submission, that does not change. You are in control until you abdicate control, and even then, you can seize it back." Yes, I showed up in this world with greatness, and I chose not to abdicate my control over this life by seizing this opportunity given unto me to be part of the adventure of the forthcoming book by Dr. Patrick Businge.

This is Herman Thystere, from Congo Brazzaville, telling you that no man, no condition is ruthless enough to prevent me from meeting with Les Brown. That meeting is so vital in getting you to the motivational runway of your destiny take off. Les Brown met Mr. Leroy Washington, and he changed his life. I met Les Brown from the pages of a newspaper and, unknowingly, he has changed my life.

A Random Encounter
Vinette Hoffman Jackson
England, UK

Empowerment Speaker, Communication &
Presentation Coach
www.vinettehoffmanjackson.com

An impromptu conversation

On the 15th of January 2018, I was invited to give a speech in Northampton. As is my custom, instead of sitting at the front of the room, I chose to sit at the back until I am called to the stage. I became engaged in a random conversation with a man I had just met named Raj. He started sharing his vision to become a speaker some day and wanted to know if I could offer some tips. I told him anytime he wanted to discuss it just give me a call and in true 21st century style, we added each other on Facebook. The conversation then shifted to who was my inspiration to become a motivational speaker. I was going to give a list but the first name out of my mouth was Les Brown. He quickly interrupted me to tell me he knew him. In my mind I thought 'sure'. I know him too, a thousand miles away through my phone screen. We all 'knew' him but I remained polite.

No chocolates

Raj told me Les was in town Saturday and I should come down to see him. Unfortunately I had another engagement so I declined the offer and thought nothing more about it. On Friday morning Raj sent me a message asking if I was sure I didn't want to come. I once again apologised but on a whim I added 'can you give Les a gift for me please? 'No chocolates, he's diabetic' he responded. I was not expecting any answer to be honest, maybe just a laugh or chuckle. Intrigued by his response I replied. 'No! I wanted to give him a copy of my book'. I waited anxiously for his response. 'Ok, but you need to be here by noon' came the reply. I was already at the door and putting my shoes on from the word okay. 'Send me your address' I typed. I was already in my car, my fingers poised above my Satnav waiting for the address. After getting the address I quickly punched it in and headed towards Raj to drop my book off.

Lowered expectations

On my way, the doubts started to creep in and I quickly lowered my expectations. Why would Les Brown even accept a book from someone like me? He probably had thousands of books sent to him daily anyway so mine would just join that pile. I had no hope, I arrived about half an hour later at my new-found friend's house and was invited in. We talked for a while then he suggested I make a quick video for Les about my book and why I was sending it to him. I declined at first but then I thought, well why not? I've got nothing to lose, so I quickly recorded a short message just to say hi and how much I admired his work. After I left I thought for sure that was it. I would never hear anything else from Les Brown. Maybe a polite mass email sent out just to say thanks. Maybe. I drove back home and crawled into bed watching television alone.

Shock and disbelief

What transpired in the next few minutes seemed surreal and was met by shock and disbelief by my family. I had always spoken my dreams out loud around my house and I had the habit of picking up my phone and loudly answering with phrases like 'Hello? Oh Oprah, I am so glad you called girl' or sometimes believe it or not I would answer and say 'Well hello Les Brown' then I would pause and then my conversation would continue 'What ? You want me to share the stage with you Les? Ok I'll do that just for you!' These virtual conversations would be greeted by loud laughter from family members and the occasional 'Shut up!' was not a misplaced comment whenever this happened.

Shut up, no way!

As I was there lying in bed, my phone rang. I looked at the number and did not recognise it so I didn't take the call. A few seconds later the phone rang and it was the same number so I decided to answer. 'Hello!' came the voice at the other end. Now for anyone who has ever heard Les Brown speak, you know he has the most charismatic and unmistakable voice in the world. I heard the voice but my brain could not believe it, so I sat up straight in bed and turned the TV off. 'Who is this?' I asked nervously. 'It's Les Brown, Vinette!' came the reply. 'Shut up, no way!' I shouted. 'Ok!' Les replied and I could hear the smile in his voice. 'No! No! I mean speak' I hastily added. I put my hand over the microphone and screamed 'It's Les Brown! It's Les Brown!' It was a case of the girl who cried wolf, no one actually believed. I rushed out into the passageway and put the phone on speaker.

No sales pitch

My mother and sons rushed out of their rooms with eyes big as saucers. They could hear that unmistakable voice. 'Vinette' Les continued. 'I have your book here. What an amazing title. And your stories are really thought provoking. They really made me think. I am going to send you a personal testimonial.' 'T-t-thank you.' I managed to mutter, then I waited on the line, and waited and waited for a few seconds, but it felt like an hour, but it never came. I was waiting for the sales pitch that all, well, most well-known people give you at the end of an amazing offer, but no sales pitch came and I sat there puzzled, if not a little bit stunned. For a moment I even thought I had been pranked. Then Raj came on the phone to let me know he was about to do the endorsement and once again I waited and waited and waited but the sales pitch still did not come. We said good bye and I turned to my mom with a quizzical look. Did I just speak to Les Brown just as I would with my next door neighbour? Did he just offer me an endorsement without any cost? Impossible.

When God says YES who can say NO?

Then I started smoking, then laughing uncontrollably. Even if the endorsement never came or I could not afford the cost I still expected, I had spoken to Les Brown and nobody in my home would ever forget it. It will be my go to story at every party until I die. Mom being a Christian started shouting about the power of God 'when my God say yes, who can say no?' She asked. I suspected my story would somehow become her story when she returned to Jamaica to share with her friends. 'My daughter spoke to Les Brown you know! And I was there to witness it all. Thank God almighty!' I could already hear her boasting. I smiled. A few minutes later my phone went ping! We stopped chatting and looked at the screen. It read video attachment. We looked at each other and opened the message.

It was Les just sitting there, speaking about my book. My book. No requests for money, nothing. He gave me a phenomenal and personal endorsement that would have cost thousands of dollars for not a single penny. It was only at this moment the tears started falling in gratitude. To repeat a famous phrase 'Les Brown, there is greatness in you!' But my sentence would not end there. There is also kindness, humility, authenticity and most all love. He is one of the few people who does exactly what it says on the label and I love him. So in return, let me give my endorsement of Les Brown, totally free of cost too.

Les Brown, 'You give from the heart'

To Les Brown: Les Brown, in a time when money means more to man, when it cost to even have someone hold your hand, when people do everything to gain the upper hand, you stand out. Though many may not even understand, for you give to people straight from your heart without thinking of what you get. Your kindness has lifted me when I was falling apart. You're an icon, a legend, a living stalwart to share my story I wouldn't know where to begin. Just know that you have changed something within me, my mom says thank you with the widest grin. She said for you, 'the right sperm did win.' I hope I can repay your kindness in some small way, I'll start by remembering you each time I kneel to pray. Thank you for what you did and had to say Les, I look forward to seeing you again someday!

CHAPTER 9: GREATNESS

The Road to Greatness

In his famous speech *It's Not Over Until You Win*, Les Brown makes this observation:

> Most people have done all that they're ever going to do. They raise a family, they earn a living and then they die. But people who are running toward their dreams life has a special kind of meaning. And here's what I will share with you, that in the process of working on your dreams you are going to incur a lot of disappointment, a lot of failure, a lot of pain, a lot of setbacks, a lot of defeat. But in the process of doing that you will discover some things about yourself that you don't know right now. What you will realize is that you have greatness within you. What you will realize is that you're more powerful than you can ever begin to imagine. What you will realize is that you're greater than your circumstances that you don't have to go through life being a victim.

In this, I understand that failure, pain, disappointment, struggle, are steps to greatness. Effectively, greatness is about following to where these steps are leading us in life. Nelson Mandela says, "Sometimes, it falls upon a generation to be great. You can be that great generation. Let your greatness blossom." In this chapter, you are going to discover people who have gone through these steps and are examples of this great generation. I leave you with this final thought, 'If you do what is easy, your life will be hard. If you do what is hard, your life will be easy' (Les Brown). Welcome to Greatness.

Discovering My Greatness
Maria-Lewis Ramadane
Virginia, USA

Discovering my Greatness

We now travel to Spotsylvania in Virginia, famously known as the home of several Civil War battles. Here we will meet Maria Ramadane: a Speaker, Teacher, Coach, and Proud Mother of raising "Men not Boys". Maria has a very special relationship with Les Brown. She is a founding member of the Les Brown Maximum Achievement Team. With the inspiration that she has got from Les Brown, she has gone on and become the CEO of TLS Consulting Group Inc: a business that helps others discover their dreams through personal and professional development. Let us now discover how Maria found her greatness after listening to these intriguing words of Les Brown in his keynote speech, 'It's Not Over Until You Win!'

> Most people have done all that they're ever going to do. They raise a family, they earn a living and then they die. But people who are running toward their dreams life has a special kind of meaning. And here's what I will share with you, that in the process of working on your dreams you are going to incur a lot of disappointment, a lot of failure, a lot of pain, a lot of setbacks, a lot of defeat. But in the process of doing that you will discover some things about yourself that you don't know right now. What you will realize is that you have greatness within you. What you will realize is that you're more powerful than you can ever begin to imagine. What you will realize is that you're greater than your circumstances that you don't have to go through life being a victim.

Les Brown Changed Our Lives

As Les Brown states, "You have Greatness within You!" Many recognize that early in life and that greatness is manifested in their walk and their talk. That baby girl knows her value and her worth from day one. As a forty-two-year-old divorced mother of two handsome and intelligent young African American men, I have not always believed that I was "Enough." But Les Brown said, "I don't know what you're up against, I don't know what you're facing. But here's what I do know: You've got something special, you have got greatness in you, and I know it's possible that you can live your dreams."

I was born and raised in the rural community of Spotsylvania County, Virginia, known as the home of several Civil War battles. I was blessed to be born into a family of strong and determined women and men. Our family was one of the first African American families in the area to be landowners. My father taught me to value our family land and to "hold on to it." Throughout my childhood I have wonderful memories. Living in the South, I did not escape the grips of racism. One day, an elementary aged girl loudly proclaimed that she "hated all niggers" except for me and my cousin, thus, implying that I was a "nigger." It was not until years later I fully comprehended the ingrained seed of racism implanted in the young minds of some of those around me. But again, Les Brown reminded me that, "The greatest revenge is massive success."

At the age of nine, I suffered from a debilitating illness, losing the ability to walk due to what was thought to be an unknown virus. I was told by a doctor that I was faking it and just did not want to go to school. I ultimately spent two weeks in the hospital and several months in a wheelchair. One of my first obstacles to overcome. I learned to walk, run, and play sports. Nine years after my mysterious illness, I earned a scholarship and played basketball at Elon College in Elon College, N.C. Yes, we can, when we put our mind to it! Mr. Brown would say, "If you set goals and go after them with all the determination you can muster, your gifts will take you places that will amaze you." I graduated with a Bachelor of Arts degree in Broadcast Journalism. I was on my way to be the next, Barbara Walters. At that time 20/20 and 60 Minutes were my favorite news magazine programs.

At the tender age of twenty-two, I had my first child, a busy baby boy. My husband, at the time, and I settled in an apartment. After a couple of years, I was fortunate to start a career in my chosen industry, broadcasting. I worked for the Public Broadcasting Service (PBS), for four years. I considered that a great entry into the field, I thought I would remain in for years to come. During that time my second prince was born, another baby boy with the deepest eyes that appeared to see directly into my soul.

When my children were young, like most suburban soccer moms, I over extended myself. We ran from activity to activity. Quickly strife and discourse entered our home, arguments turned to separation and before I knew it, my husband and I had an extremely toxic relationship. There is a great deal of stories within this story. But after 16 years of marriage, we legally departed ways; one more obstacle to overcome. "Forgive yourself for your faults and your mistakes and move on," Les Brown.

Back to my career, after four years at PBS, my passion changed. I went back to college, earned a Master's Degree in Education. I started teaching middle school students with special needs. I went on to earn a post graduate certificate in Administration and Supervision. I have taught Pre-K to post-secondary students and served as a school administrator. There are many stories to share! Our children truly are our future!

Remember, Les Brown told me that I had greatness within me. So, what is next on my journey to greatness? Along the journey I did discover my own strength! Strength to stand, when I could not walk, strength to stand in adversity, strength to stand against racism, strength to walk away from toxic relationships. I now stand on the shoulders of those that have gone before me. I stand in my authentic self. I stand to represent the countless beautiful phenomenal women of our past while bringing out the greatness in the young minds of our future!

In addition to serving as an administrator in public education, I am also a business owner. I incorporated Total Learning Solutions Consulting Group Inc in January 2017. I help others discover their dreams through personal and professional development. Les Brown taught me, "It takes someone with a vision of the possibilities to attain new levels of experience. Someone with the courage to live his (her) dreams." I am living my dreams thanks to the empowering words of Mr. Les Brown, those words have been the background chorus of my life.

Dr Patrick Businge

Change Your Mindset Change Your Life
Hannah Zemzam
England, UK

Founder of Zemzam Inspires Change

Change Your Mindset Change Your Life

We now travel to Luton: a small town a stone throw away from London. Luton is one of the most diverse places in the UK. It has a long history of welcoming people from overseas and more than 100 languages are spoken in this small town of less than 300,000 people. Every year, Lutonians have a carnival: a time when, from all walks of life, everyone comes together to celebrate the best of Luton. In this multicultural town, we meet one of the proudest Lutonians, Hannah Zemzam. In her welcoming words, she has this to say to you, 'Luton has opened many doors in my life and I hope that during your visit you too grasp the opportunities to hand like I have'.

Unexplainable feeling inside of me

Ever since I can remember, I have had an unexplainable feeling inside of me that has been hungry to strive, prosper and touch other people along the way. Life hasn't always been easy for me. I grew up on a council estate in Luton. My father left me when I was just 10 years old. I lived most of my life with my mother who suffered with bipolar and, from an early age, I witnessed the actions of her abusive boyfriend.

Used the fire inside me wrongly

The pain and confusion I encountered at a very young age resulted in me being a rebellious teenager both at home and school: a teenager who was always heading in the wrong direction. I was an angry young person who was lost. I always used the fire I had inside of me in the wrong places and at wrong times. It wasn't long before I was kicked out of school. At this point, I hit rock bottom. I was then diagnosed with chronic depression at tender age of 15 and I was driven to Spain by my uncle as my mum couldn't cope anymore. At this stage, I remember feeling like I didn't want to live anymore! What did I know? I was only 15 and my years had been filled with broken promises, broken parents, and a difficult life in a council estate in Luton Town.

God's footprints in my life

This was when I had my first encounter with God – they say he always shows up in people's time of need, and boy did he show up for me. I am reminded of the poem 'Footprints in the Sand' where Marianne Williamson writes,

> But I noticed that during the saddest and most troublesome times of my life, there was only one set of footprints. I don't understand why, when I needed You the most, You would leave me." He whispered, "My precious child, I love you and will never leave you never, ever, during your trials and testing. When you saw only one set of footprints, it was then that I carried you.

At this point in my life, God changed my thinking straight away. My mind was renewed – I didn't understand what had happened as I wasn't a strong believer before this. I made a decision to change my direction in life and used all of that fire inside of me in the right way, putting it into my education and right thinking. I came to understand and accept that I couldn't change the people around me and what they had done or were going to do, but I could change my destiny. I was not going to become a product of my environment.

One year later - I walked out of High School (the school I had been kicked out of) with a full set of GCSE's and joined their Sixth Form. That same year, I was chosen as a trusted pupil to show OFSTED inspectors around the school. I later went on to University and studied Business and Management at The University of Northampton where I achieved Second Class Upper in my Bachelor's degree. After University, I travelled to South East Asia for six months where I learned to appreciate the opportunities given to me in the UK. Upon my return from Asia, I started my career in marketing and now I am a Marketing and Events Specialist at the age of 25.

Others opinion is not my reality

It is at the university, with all its pressures and challenges that I got interested in motivational messages. I started searching for things that would help me grow. On my journey and searching, I was told about Les Brown. I was told, "Les Brown will change your life", so I thought – I must have a listen. After listening to Les for the first 5 minutes I knew I'd be following him from here on. Les Brown often says; "don't let someone else's opinion of you become your reality". This was a strong belief throughout my young life and I want to continue to share this message with other young people.

Unfortunately in life, we're often thrown into the fire quite young – when we don't actually know how to defend ourselves. I'd like to thank Les Brown as he has given me the positive mindset and thinking needed to inspire others.

I have started my own business in Motivation to inspire change in young people's lives.

After growing closer to God, I have come to understand the unexplainable feeling inside of me is the God within me. After following Les Brown for long, I have come to the realisation that the force driving me to fulfil my purpose in life is the greatness within me. I will continue to strive to reach my greatness in all circumstances. You too have something special. There is greatness within you. I therefore encourage to live your greatness no matter your circumstances.

Dr Patrick Businge

From Nobody to Somebody
Anonymous

Dr Patrick Businge

From Nobody to Somebody

I heard about Les Brown some years ago from someone who used to share his events on Facebook. I got used to reading his Facebook posts and watching his Facebook Lives. What stuck with me were these words from Les Brown, 'You've got something special, you've got greatness within you'. I would be feeling ill and after hearing these words, I started to believe them. I now believe that I am somebody. I now believe that I am living greatness in my speech. I am living greatness in my walk. I am living greatness in my life.

I never imagined it would be possible for me to afford to attend any of Les Brown's conferences. However when I saw the Les Brown in London Event on 20th January 2018 advertised at a discounted price, I knew that my time had come to be there. Just his words of encouragement, positivity, plus all the speakers at the event who have all overcome adversity, has changed me immensely.

A few days later after the event in London, I discovered that Les Brown was sick. Just seeing him on his sick bed in hospital doing a Facebook Live and still encouraging people, believing he will continue to overcome cancer, and laughing though he was in pain, has given me a different perspective on life. It has helped me to see how much of a life warrior he is. I have decided to keep pushing through life like him. For me, the change Les Brown has had in my life is not necessarily about earning more money. The change in my life is about a positive beneficial difference to my life and hopefully in that of others that I come into contact with. I now believe that I am somebody because of Les Brown.

CHAPTER 10: HEALTH

Breathing God's Free Air

One night in April 2018 after dinner, my wife told me this story that made me think about my own health. She

> A 78 year old man collapsed and was rushed to the hospital. He was given oxygen to sustain him for 24 hours. After some time he was getting better so that the doctor gave him his bill of £500, and when he saw the bill he started crying. The doctor told him not to cry because of the bill and that he could pay it in installments. But the main said, 'I am not crying because of the money, I can pay all in cash. I am crying because just for 24 hours of using oxygen I' m to pay £500. But I have been breathing God's free air for 78 years now. If I'm to pay, do you know how much I owe?

When I calculated, I found that this 78 year old man owed God approximately £14, 235,000 (fourteen million two hundred and thirty five thousand British pounds). In this chapter, you will read stories of people who have come to the realisation that their health is their wealth and how Les Brown has accompanied them to regain this wealth when it all seemed lost.

My Mentor Miracle
Dexter Patterson
Wisconsin, USA

Speaker and Social Media Specialist
www.dexterpatterson.com

I was sick of feeling worthless

I am honoured to share my testimony. Les Brown is an amazing person and mentor. For many years, I was lost and struggled to understand my WHY and what I was living for in this world. I lacked self-confidence and continually beat myself up every time I failed. I did not recognize the greatness within me, and it began taking a toll on my mental state in a big way. I was clinically depressed. So, I started going to therapy sessions and researching motivational speakers because I realized I needed some help. I was sick of feeling worthless on a daily basis.

My short-lived time with Zig Ziglar

At that time, I was working as a salesman. Zig Ziglar was one of the first motivational speakers I came across on YouTube. I listened to his voice and his message. I learnt his quotes and here are my top 10 that I could recite in the depth of my sleep:

- You don't have to be great at something to start, but you have to start to be great at something
- Your attitude, not your aptitude, will determine your altitude.
- If you can dream it, then you can achieve it.
- You will get all you want in life if you help enough other people get what they want.
- If you aim at nothing, you will hit it every time.
- You were born to win, but to be a winner, you must plan to win, prepare to win, and expect to win.
- Expect the best. Prepare for the worst. Capitalize on what comes.

- Don't become a wandering generality. Be a meaningful specific.
- There are not traffic jams on the extra mile.
- Make failure your teacher, not the undertaker.

Whenever I would listen and recite these quotes, I would feel motivated to go beyond my circumstances.

It's possible

In Africa, they have a saying that 'a child who does not travel thinks that his/ her mother is the best chef'. So, I thought Zig Ziglar was great until I clicked on a video clip featuring Les Brown. This video clip changed my life. I saw someone that looked like me. I saw someone that grew up like me. I had found someone that made me believe I was worthy and capable of success. This video was his famous speech 'It's Possible'. Speaking in a big crowd, he said,

> Oh, y'all look good! I want you to look at something right now. Think of some major goal you want or maybe it's one you're already working on and you have experienced a lot of setbacks, a lot of defeats. You've experienced a lot of disappointment. Maybe you've already given up and maybe you just need a little fun, little encouragement to get back in the game again.
>
> Here's what I want you to look at. There are winners and there are losers and there are people who have not discovered how to win. And all they need is some coaching. All they need is some help and assistance — just a little support.

All they need is some insight or different strategy or plan of action to make some adjustments that will open up the key to a whole new future for them, which will give them access to the unlimited power that they have within themselves. That's all that they need.

So what I want you to do is think about something you want for you, that's real for you, that's important for you that will give your life some special meaning and power. And I don't even want you to say I can do that. I don't want you to assume that. See, five years ago when I started out in this area, I would not have been able to make the mental leap that I would be up to where I am right now. I don't want you to begin to just psych yourself out. No, no, I want you to be able to say something to yourself that will enable you to maintain a level of integrity with yourself, that when you say this even when you face tremendous setbacks, it will be a benchmark to keep you in the game, to keep you moving forward and experimenting and readjusting your strategy and your plan of action continuously looking for ways to win.

So what is that something? When you've got an idea you want to move on. You might not have the money, you might not have the education, you might not have the support or the resources you need. What is that something that can keep us going, that will enable us to act on our dream? What's one of those keys that will begin to help us to discover the secrets to our dream?

Here's what I want you to repeat after me please with power and conviction, say: 'It's Possible'. It's all I want you to do when you look at your dream, just say to yourself every day: It's possible. Just say that every day to yourself: it's possible.

This message changed my life. I heard his voice not just in my ears but in my heart. Les made me think anything was possible. For weeks I watched this video clip over and over again. I also looked for whatever I could about Les Brown's material on YouTube. I listened, l learned, and I did my best to apply his tips in my daily life. I stopped living in fear and started dreaming again. Though I had fallen because life had knocked me down, I was able to look up and get up. I believed it was possible every hour of my being. Before you knew it, the person who did not think he was worthy started winning and boy did that feel good. Every day I began looking in the mirror and telling myself, "It is possible. I'm going to make it." Before I knew it, I was more motivated, and I was eager to take action to change my life.

First to graduate

I enrolled in a college transfer program at a local technical college, and two years later, I became the first person in my family to not only attend but also graduate from college. I graduated with honours and had offers to attend some of the best four-year universities in the country. I went on to get my bachelor's degree from the University of Wisconsin and my master's degree from the University of Purdue all within six years. It was arguably the most challenging six years of my life but also the most rewarding. Me, Dexter, finally realized that I was a winner and in full control of my destiny.

I have since started to share my testimony via my #TefTalk video series that has reached thousands of people all over the world on Facebook. I encourage my audience to embrace the power of mentors, and I always recommend that they check out Les Brown's material. I want everyone I know to believe they are going to make it. I want them to realize they are worthy of success. I want them to know that they cannot be the best version of themselves until they start believing that they have greatness in them.

My mentor miracle

I want to thank Mr. Brown for helping me become a more patient, driven, focused, and a grateful man. I no longer beat myself up for common mistakes or failures. Instead, I have taken responsibility for my happiness. Les says, "When you feel good about yourself you act differently." This is happening to me now. I will never give up on ME until I win. It is possible for you too. Thanks, Les Brown!

'Your Health is Your Wealth'
Paul Kenny
Tasmania, Australia

**Educator, Music Producer, Speaker and
Entrepreneur
www.paulkenny.com**

'Your Health is Your Health'

We now journey to Tasmania in Australia. Doing his daily morning walk by the seaside, we meet Paul Kenny: a renowned musician and composer. Paul is now ready to tell his journey of transformation.

Before I met Les Brown, I was getting bigger and bigger. My life was not great. Trying to keep up with my life and 3 children was hard. My wife would take the children out to the park and I would just stay at home. I would be left on the couch as I could not walk to the park because of my weight. I had also had several knee operations that had been a disaster. I got to a point where I was in so much pain. I also suffered from chronic pain syndrome. I had been stuck on the couch for over 7 years. I wasn't the nice person to see or meet. This was my life before meeting Les Brown.

In October 2016, I started thinking of setting myself goals for 2017. I thought about goals related to my mindset, health, fitness and life in general. After thinking about my goals, I then asked myself, why wait till 2017? I said, I can start right now. Why stay stuck on the couch for longer? 2017 was to become a year of change for me but it was only the start on my journey.

I decided to have a total change. The first thing I did was to sort out my nutrition. I changed my diet and this was the first step to my transformation. If you are not healthy on the inside then how can you function on the outside? I then started working on my mindset. I started listening to motivational recordings and videos from a lot of people. As I did this, I seemed to always go back to Les Brown. Just using him as an inspiration from where he started to where he is today, it made a huge improvement in my life. His words of inspiration have lifted me from where I was to where I am and to where I am going. My mindset has changed, everything has changed for me. What an amazing 2017 it was and what amazing years to look forward to.

Today, I am doing motivational videos and writing a book about my journey. People have been contacting me and thanking me for changing their lives. This has come about by listening to Les Brown. People seem to be trapped in life. I found a way by listening to Les Brown and my passion is to now help them find their way in life. I help people change their lives and feel awesome so that they can then achieve a lot in life. I help them to get a can-do attitude so that they achieve their goals.

This works only with a change of mindset and attitude that I now have and pass on to so many people. My goal at the end of this is to do motivational speaking. I have spoken at smaller events and I now assist schools, universities and businesses to change their mindset. They can do anything if they change their mindset. Everyone is on the journey building a better tomorrow.

If I look back where I was 12 months ago, it is amazing. I can see it in my face. I can see it in my eyes. I can feel it in my body. Thank you Les Brown for being a massive part of what I am doing. I have lost about 28 kilos and have a total new outlook on life because of you. My family also thanks you for your help. Hoping and inspiring others through the words of Les Brown, 'You have greatness within you'. A lot of people are lost, they are stuck, and all they need is someone to show them the door to their greatness.

Dr Patrick Businge

CHAPTER 11: KIDPRENEURS

Be Like Little Children

Approximately a third of the world population has been touched by the message of Jesus Christ. In Matthew 18, his disciples came to him and asked, 'Who, then, is the greatest in the kingdom of heaven?' In response, Jesus called a little child and said, 'Truly I tell you, unless you change and become like little children, you will never enter the kingdom of heaven'. From this response, I think that if we want to step into our greatness, we have to become like little children. This reminds of a story told by Les Brown:

> Two young boys were skating on ice when all of a sudden, one of them fell through and got trapped under. His friend started to punch the ice in hopes of breaking it but could not get through. In desperation, the friend climbed a tree and broke off a huge branch, came back down the tree and started smashing the ice, eventually breaking it and saving his friend. As emergency services came after the boy was safe, they sat in amazement and wondered how the little boy was able to break off the branch, smash the ice and save his friend. As they were sharing their amazement, an old man walked up and said, "the boy was able to do it because there was no one here that told him he couldn't.

Little children are open-minded, creative, and above all willing to risk to get what they want. If you want to be great, be like a little child. Here are stories from two girls who are stepping into their greatness like these little boys.

From Sorry to Story
Inspiring Vanessa
England, UK

Author and Kidpreneur

My Name is Vanessa. I'm 11 years old and I'm a Multi-award winning motivational speaker, YouTuber, Kidpreneur, Artist and Author. My story started off when I was born in August 2006. I was a very joyful girl and happy baby. As from 4 years old till now I still love art and drawing, because it's my passion. But in 2008 everything changed. My dad left me and my mum. I still think about him even now. It was a very hard time for me and my mum. We were in a sad and sorry state of mind. However, deep down, we both knew that we had to stay happy and that we had each other- me and my mum.

Have you ever lived with a single parent? If you do, you may know how it feels! It is really hard to overcome these types of things but as people say "share your story" and "someone could be in the same situation as you!" According to me, the reason people don't overcome these things is because they focus on the person about why they have done it. They focus on someone else's story and not THEIRS! My mum listens a lot to Les Brown and I often listen with her. One sentence I have heard many times from Les Brown and it keeps coming to me is, 'It's possible'.

What I have focused on is my story, not my feeling sorry for my dad leaving us. It is because of this that I have shared the stage with the likes of Eric Ho, Jairek Robbins, Caleb Maddix, Eric Thomas, Douglas Vermeeran and many more… My dream is to meet Ellen DeGeneres. As I have heard from Les Brown, I know it's possible. My journey has been incredible and I can't wait for the future. I hope you have been inspired by my story and remember, you are the hero of your own story.

You Help Me Become Confident
Stella Businge
England, UK

Author and Kidpreneur
www.stellabusinge.com

You Help Me Become Confident

Dear Les Brown, my name is Stella Businge. I am 8 years old and I live in England. I first heard about you from my mummy and dad. My mum listens to you at home and when she is taking me to school. My dad puts on your radio when he is taking me to gymnastics.

I heard you say that you were born on the floor. How were you born on the floor in an abandoned building? I've heard you and mummy always laugh. I think you are funny. When I meet you, I will ask you about how many books have you written? Which book is your favourite? I like reading and writing books. My book is called 'Ella and the Pink Creature'. I will tell you more about the pink creature when I see you.

I know that you are a motivational speaker and entrepreneur. You help me to be confident when I go to book fairs and I have to speak to people when they ask me questions. You also help me in gymnastics to win when I go for competitions because I believe your words 'It's possible'. Thank you and see you soon. Say hello to your children.

Stella Businge

CHAPTER 12: LEGACY

The Ghosts of Your Dreams

Have you ever been or driven a car with a flat tyre? When all the four tyres are flat, the car is slower and the tyres makes a lot of noise. I find this example of a car with flat tyres to be the best analogy to explain part of our human condition. There are times we lead our lives like cars with flat tyres. We live as if there is no pressure inside. We go through life with neither hope nor excitement as if we have nothing to live for. During these moments, this is the advice that Les Brown gives us:

> So, I say that your life is worth finding, what it is that you are supposed to do. Imagine if you being on your death bed and standing around your bed the ghosts of the dreams, the ideas, the abilities, the talents, given to you by life but you, for whatever reason, you never pursued those dreams, you never acted on those ideas, and you never used those gifts. You never used those talents, and there they are staring at you as you are lying on your bed, with large angry eyes, saying we came to you only you could have given us life, and now we must die with you forever. And the question is: if you died today, what dreams, what talents, what abilities, what gifts, what ideas would die with you? Les Brown

Take time to reflect on this question. What is the purpose of your life? Why are you in this world? What is your personal mission in this universe? How will future generations know that your life was worth living? Let us discover how some people have decided to make marks not on their bodies but on this great universe.

Living my Best Life Yet
Nikki Garcia
New Mexico, USA

249

Living my Best Life Yet
Nikki Garcia
New Mexico, USA

Living My Best Life Yet

Travelling to Sante Fe in New Mexico is like travelling to wonderland. It is a wonderful place famous for its Art Galleries, New Mexican Food, and Sunsets. They don't call it the Land of Enchantment for nothing. There are also beautiful mountains and forest sceneries just a few kilometres from the town. New Mexico is at a higher altitude so for those who aren't used to it, you definitely need to stay hydrated especially during the summer times. Here we meet Nikki Garcia, who is craving to make the rest of her life the best of her life.

I am the one

Hello! It's a pleasure meeting you. Les Brown has changed my life in so many ways. Just a few examples are when I would hear him talk and talk about being "the one", my eyes would fill with tears and I'd feel the goosebumps on my arm and I just remember feeling I am "the one" too!

Leave a legacy

It is after listening to him and his story that is when I got to work. I wanted a life where I can survive and live comfortably but more importantly give back to others. I started my own business about 6 months ago called "Ever Beauty Skincare". I make handcrafted soaps, body balms, and bath bombs. And as a way for me to help others I donate a 2oz bar from every soap loaf that is made for my business. As of today, I have donated over 60 bars to the homeless shelter. Les Brown, as well as other motivators, have helped me realize it's not about me - it's about those who are coming behind me. As common courtesy, I have got to leave this place better than I found it.

Hold your head up

My famous quote from Les Brown is 'You have greatness within you'. Whenever I am feeling challenged with my business I have to remember this quote or listen to one of his speeches. Another good quote is when he left the new house he bought for his mom and she tells him 'Boy, you better hold your head up! Hold your head up!' That's a really good one, especially when you are feeling down about your work or just life period. And last but not least, I have to say: 'every setback is a setup for a comeback'.

Dr Patrick Businge

A letter to from Coronado Island
Carolina Lanfair
California, USA

A letter to from Coronado Island
Carolina Lanfair
California, USA

A Letter From Coronado Island

Lawd, Lawd, I'm soooooooooooo tied! Not tired! Tiiieeeeed! I worked late evening hours tonight. I would have done a video for you, Mr. Brown, but, it's very late right now.

Hello, Mr. Brown. How are you doing, post- post-surgery? How are Calvin and John Lesley doing? Okay, so this is Carolina Lanfair. I can't wait to meet you and learn so much from you in Deerfield, Florida! Registration, airfare, hotel, and meal package – all booked! I'm not in a financial position to attend your seminar, but I'm taking a GIGANTIC step of faith and doing this! You said if you really want to come to Deerfield, Florida, you will find a way. God blessed me to find a way!

My career is California Licensed Court Reporter and Captioner. I caption for the deaf- and hard-of-hearing community in various on-site venues (colleges, elementary schools, universities, prisons, meetings, conferences) as well as remote-captioning. I also report court proceedings and depositions. Captioning is very humbling, gratifying, and rewarding but extremely challenging. It constantly tests psychological and physical psychological. I love using my skill that opens the door wide for me to boldly walk in servant hood. I love meeting and working with people. Additionally, I'm a professional proof-reader and editor. The hazards of court reporting: no talking! So, when I get the chance to talk, I'm the Energizer Bunny! And I can't read anything without proofreading. Initially, unconsciously. Now, automatic-pilot!

My immediate dream is to be THE BEST CAPTIONER I CAN BE and segue into becoming a broadcast-captioner – caption live TV programming. Do you realize how fast people talk on TV – especially news programs? They speak at the speed of light! Then there's foreign news and foreign names! The Olympics, sports games – extensive dictionary preparation entries required!

I am so glad I'm dreaming in color now! It feels so unnatural, but I continue to dream! I was never taught to visualize. Visualizing is painful for me! And sustaining the vision is tough for me too! But I visualize myself writing a book to help those who have stinkin-thinkin' and who don't know how to dream and visualize! And I visualize writing an accompaniment movie! MY GREATEST DREAM IS ENTREPRENEURSHIP WITH STEADY STREAMS OF INCOME AS MY LEGACY! ALL IT TAKES IS ONE IDEA! I know I can do it! I will do it!

I have a Bachelor's of Science degree in Business Management/Administration with emphasis on leadership. I graduated summa cum laude. I'm the only one in my family to complete a college degree. Generational curse broken!

Man, I came to the GET MOTIVATED event in San Diego just to see Mr. Brown! I took off the plantation (forfeited a few hundred dollars for the day) and also convinced my two friends to take off the plantation to come see Les Brown. Neither friend had ever heard of you. Amber Castillo and Anne Tolch.

Brother, the ONLY REASON we stayed was to see you, Mr. Brown! OMG, you didn't come on until 5:15PM! I had to do a lot of begging to keep my two friends in tow to see you! We were all exhausted, but worth the long wait! Unfortunately, Amber ended up leaving because she had to go pick up her son from school. Anne and I stuck it out -- the ONLY REASON -- to see you, Mr. Brown! The ONLY REASON the whole audience stayed was to see you, Mr. Brown, live! That was back on Tuesday, February

16, 2016. Remember that? The venue changed at the last minute to accommodate all registrants coming to hear you speak!

I came to know Les Brown from a DVD that was in a goodies package from a seminar I attended, its headquarters in Provo, Utah. I went through the bag and threw everything out. I was a second away from throwing out the DVD, but for some reason, I decided to check out the DVD. It was a DVD of Les Brown speaking. I was always into self-improvement- and self-development materials, but Les Brown took it farther and deeper! Funny as all get-out! And when I heard your crazy laugh, Mr. Brown, I WAS HOOKED! I played the grooves off that DVD!

All of your stories touch me, Mr. Brown. However, particularly, your start in life, being born in an abandoned building, your twin brother and you and Mrs. Mamie Brown adopting seven children! I also love your defining moment with Leroy Washington. Then there's your persistence when breaking into DJ'ing and transitioning from politics to motivational speaking! How you went in every day for a break! "Drink, Rock, drink!" "I called my mama and my girlfriend Cassandra and told them to turn on the radio, I'm about to come on the air!" Most touching is when you left the Senate to take care of your mother – how you stood your ground with your siblings not to put your mama in a nursing home. You said mama took care of all seven children and yet seven people can't take care of one person.

I lost everything and ended up homeless, living in my car. I had nobody to turn to for help. I had no ride-or-die friends. Nobody cared whether I was breathing, dead or alive, including me. I was homeless for 3.5 years, living in my car – the darkest moment in my whole life. I was suicidal. I have never been homeless. I was a college-educated homeless person. I finally got still and surrendered to God. I listened to your videos, Mr. Brown, and also to Dr. Tony Evans' message, YOUR GREATEST FAITH LESSONS ARE LEARNED IN THE DARK -- through my tears of despair, hopelessness, agony. That kept my mind from turning to mush.

My FAVORITE quotes by you are: "You have greatness in you!" "YOU'VE GOTTA BE HUNGRY!" "You've got to develop a sense of urgency!" "Do not go where the path may lead, but go where there is no path and leave a trail!" "WHEN YOU FALL, IF YOU CAN LOOK UP, you can get up!" "Get rid of the emotional vampires in your life." "Stop wasting valuable time!" "Valuing each moment we're blessed with!" "Live with urgency!"

BLB (Before Les Brown), no one said words like yours to me! Your motivational speaking convicts me to not live a mediocre life, to not settle – to live full and not take anything to the grave.

There are times when I decide that I give up because I'm spent and don't believe that I can live my best life. That it's just too late for me because I missed my life. And something compels me to fight! Every time I listen to you, Mr. Brown, your passion, your messages won't let me give up. Your exhortation changes my countenance, my thinking, my mood. I asked God to clean house and get rid of all emotional vampires, and He did! Be careful what you ask for! It's lonely, but I'm taking this time to master my gifts and go introspective to find out who I am – always mindful to surround myself with those who are smarter than I am! People who uplift and want the best for me. People who believe in me when I don't believe in myself, people who can see my gifts that I don't see in myself.

Mr. Brown, you are the "defining moment" for millions! I consider you my very own personal "defining moment".

You see, nobody was excited that I was born. That injures my heart so much, and it messed me up. That damaged me. I have sabotaged my life. Neither of my parents showed me love, never said they loved me, and I never felt love from or was loved by them. As a result, that left me broken, lost, always unsure of myself, doubting myself, with no sense of belonging. I have never felt I belong anywhere. Then came you, telling me that I have greatness in me. I have NEVER heard those words before. No one has ever told me that I have greatness in me. I grew up with dream-killing parents who didn't teach me, guide me, and speak life into my mind. My dark and unloving childhood traumatized me. I realize that most likely no one spoke life into my parents either. I'm sorry that both chose to continue to pass down garbage and not take a stand to get rid of the generational curse of existing and not having dreams for a better life.

Mr. Brown, you wake up my spirit! You say, PRESS ON when you fall and if you can look up, get up!

And admit it. I made an appointment to be where I am today. I had no purpose or plan. I didn't know anything about dreaming big and in color. I was taught that circumstances determine outcome.

My take-home message is: Don't be casual about life, or you'll become a casualty. Life will move on you. Live full and die empty! I love your saying here. And then face your fears. I'm not living my best life. And I admit I don't know what my best life looks like. Again, I made an appointment to be where my life is now. I'm also ashamed to admit that I don't know what my gifts are. For some reason, I feel strongly that I have multiple gifts. I believe I was creative as a child but believe that I have to always be realistic.

But I am so incredibly thankful and grateful to you, Mr. Brown, for being my "defining moment", for feeding my brain with what it should have been fed in my childhood. You know, it was ALWAYS my dream to be the first millionaire in my family. I remember I told my mother this when I was about 14. Man, by the time she got done telling me how stupid and unrealistic and crazy I was, I never shared anything else with my mother. Even worse, I believed my mother and stopped dreaming. The thing is, I STILL WANT TO BE THE FIRST PERSON IN MY FAMILY TO MAKE $1 MILLION. But even more germane than $1 million is MY WHY? My skin-in-the-game! My why is to give back. To remove the generational curse of stinkin'-thinkin'. I want to leave a legacy to my future generations that I will never meet that IT IS POSSIBLE!

Mr. Brown, I want to be a speaker to encourage others, to tell my story because I want to make a difference in the world. I want to make God proud of me. I want to touch lives like you do! I have to be totally transparent. I don't know what God gifted me with that I do better than anyone else, what my passions are. I don't know why I have no passion. But I'm so grateful to you, Mr. Brown, that you got my brain wanting to dig deep to find out my gifts and see where they take me. I don't want to take anything to the grave with me. I want to live my best life!

Thank you, Mr. Brown, for changing my life! Thank you, Mr. Brown, for arming me with wisdom, for shaking up my thoughts and interpreting mental activity that has sabotaged and never served me. I want to thank you for your heart of exhortation! You love what you do! You are sooooooooooo inspiring! And it is just so natural for you to motivate and inspire! There are others, but NOBODY CAN DO IT LIKE YOU DO! And I give kudos to MIKE WILLIAMS for seeing this Les Brown, renowned motivational speaker that you couldn't see! THANK YOU, MIKE WILLIAMS! Mr. Brown, you epitomize living your best life! I want in! And yes, I have a LES BROWN PUBLIC SPEAKER IN ME! I don't have your infectious laugh, but I have stories! I have passion to serve! Thank you for ALWAYS telling us, NEVER GIVE UP! For having that mindset that, there's room at the top for everyone! I've never met you, Mr. Brown, but you have impacted and affected my mind and health in positive ways. Thank you for getting me to believe in myself no matter my circumstances.

Thank you for caring about people! Thank you for telling us to live our best life! Thank you for telling us that the university is waiting on us to share what we have! It's so hard because I don't want to face that I don't know the second most important piece of information in my life! The first important is the day I was born. The second most important piece of information is the date I find out why I was born.

Thank you, Mr. Brown, for making me OCD, obsessed, nonstop-preoccupied with searching for and finding out WHY I WAS BORN! WHAT WAS I BORN TO DO? WHAT IS IT THAT I DO BETTER THAN ANYONE ELSE! WHAT IS MY PASSION? WHAT IS MY WHY? Daunting homework, but I accept the challenge! And even though we have never met, Mr. Brown, I feel loved by you and that you really do care about my life and that you really want me to live my best life! Even though I have never met you Mr. Brown, I genuinely believe that you want the best life for me! Mr. Brown you are my defining moment because prior to you,

NO ONE has ever told me that I have greatness in me! This was and is truly a labor of love for me to do this write-up!

I want all of that for myself too, Mr. Brown! My old-habit thoughts put up resistance, but it's a DONE DEAL! I BELIEVE AND KNOW I HAVE GREATNESS IN ME! I fight back and am very cognizant of my self-talk! Shut up! Right?!!!

Carolina Lanfair

Dr Patrick Businge

CHAPTER 13: MINDSET

Change Your Mindset Change Your Life

After decades of research on achievement and success, the World-renowned Stanford University psychologist Carol Dweck discovered a ground-breaking idea about the power of mindset. In her book 'Mindset', Carol Dweck explains why it's not just our abilities and talent that bring us success but whether we approach them with a fixed or growth mindset. With a growth mindset, we can achieve far beyond our horizons in any area.

This chapter is a clear testimony on the extent to which the enabling words of Les Brown have allowed people to approach their abilities and talents with a growth mindset. Les Brown has done to them what Mr Leroy Washington did for him as he narrates in his speech:

> But I met a high school teacher who one day changed my life. I was waiting on another student and when he came in, he said to me, 'Young man, go to the board and write what I'm about to tell you.' And I said, 'I can't do that, sir.' He said, 'Why not?' I said, 'I'm not one of your students.' He said, 'It doesn't matter. Follow my directions now.' I said, 'I can't do that, sir'. He said, 'Why not?' I said, 'Because I am educable mentally retarded.' And he came from behind his desk and he looked at me, he said, 'Don't ever say that again. Someone's opinion of you does not have to become your reality.'

As you read these stories, read them with a growth mindset that will allow you to create the best version of you.

A Soul's Paradigm Shift
Elda Gjoka
Albania

Trainer & Motivational Speaker
Founder & CEO of Genuine Effect
www.eldagjoka.com

A Soul's Paradigm Shift

We now travel to Albania: a country located in the Balkan Peninsula, in the South Easter Europe. It borders with Greece, Macedonia, Kosovo and Montenegro and it touches both Adriatic and Ionian Sea. Albania is a country of adventure and has been officially dubbed as the 'New Mediterranean Love'. It is here we meet Elda who shares her story on how Les Brown effected a paradigm shift in her life.

My world crumbled

As a woman entrepreneur, a team leader, speaker, a role model as an ex-athlete, and 11 times National Champion in Table Tennis for many years, as well as an ambitious person who strives for success through integrity, I found myself at a point where all what I had dear to me, or I have been fighting for, and sacrificing for, was like blown away. All my plans were crushed and I lost orientation. I started to feel hit, lost and in pain mostly because I understood that I couldn't stop the pain, emotional suffering and disappointment of people who were dear to me.

Devastated spiritually, financially, and heartbroken when discovering that you may wake up one day after 37 years on earth and you realize that your world has crumbled and you didn't see it coming. This is where you are lost as your most important purpose in life, was no longer as you had always envisioned. This really crushes your emotions and also your belief in right and wrong.

Les Brown mentored me while I was crying inside and when I was lost in the darkness. They say, when the night is darkest the stars come out. These dark times, revealed to me the truly great people who are my friends for life now, they are proof that loyalty makes you family, not blood. I am privileged to have had so much emotional support from my old friends and the new ones, to make it possible to came out with a clearer vision on what surrounded us, but the special gift was also these bad times made me discover a new friend in life: Les Brown.

My inner mentor

During this time when my world crumbled and I was suffering deep emotional pain, one of my Facebook friends shared a "Dream Motivation" motivational video. This friend occasionally shared these videos but I had not developed any interest in watching them at all. As I was going through my pain, one evening I clicked on one of the videos. The voice of Les Brown and the message in his opening words hit exactly where my pain was. He said…

> That some of you already know. It's not easy. It's hard changing your life. That in the process of working on your dreams you are going to incur a lot of disappointment, a lot of failure, a lot of pain. There are moments when you are going to doubt yourself. You will say, God why, why is this happening to me? It's okay to have disappointments in life. But when life knocks you down, make sure you lay on your back, because if you can look up you can get back up.

At this point, I suddenly found my inner mentor that was going to accompany me in my "why?-s". Ever since, I heard, reheard, and went on looking for more of his motivational speeches. I learned about his life, the challenges he overcame, the proud moment when he bought the first house and handed the keys to his mom, also with the challenges of the debt and pain to have to give the house back soon over a business deal done under naivety as well. Les Brown healed my pain and became my inner mentor up to now. His wisdom enabled me to heal my thoughts whenever I felt in emotional pain.

Trusted person

Les Brown is the trusted person whom I refer to during my inner thoughts and conversations. I talk to him and he talks to me in my thoughts and dreams. He reminds me to not take failure personally but instead to get back up each time and learn the lesson. He says, other people's opinion of you does not have to become your reality. "Just because fate doesn't deal you the right cards, it doesn't mean you should give up. It just means you have to play the cards you get to their maximum potential."

> Now let me tell you something, ladies and gentlemen. What will reasons do, Les? Nietzsche said if you know the 'why' for doing you can endure almost any 'how'. What do you mean by that? If you know why you're doing something when the hard times come and they're going to come, when the disappointments and rejections come and they're going to come by the truckloads, your reasons will be your rod and staff to comfort to pick you up. Once again I got

a saying on one of my tapes: if life knocks you down, try and land on your back, because if you can look up you can get up. Let your reasons get you back up.

Les Brown tells a story, and gives a message that empowers and talks to your core beliefs. It awakens in you the attitude of confidence and takes you forward, despite the hurdles and disappointments you face. Now almost 3 years later, I am continuing my journey, and as motivational speaker and trainer, I often refer to his message and to his quotes whenever I want to share and emphasize a point on how powerful a person is and has to become aware to be.

Spiritually walk again

Les Brown made me walk again when life brought me to my knees. With his many videos, he enriched my perspective and made me go deeper in understanding myself and the world around me. He made me perceive that if I am in a chaotic environment, I must not allow chaos to lead me. I started believing that difficult times had not come to stay. I now aspire to meet him here in Albania. I want to make more people meet Les Brown in person in Albania and in the region. He is my inspiration for life and I would like everyone in Albania to know him and to have the chance to meet him. If you meet him, he would effect a paradigm shift in your soul and in mind by his wisdom. He will touch your heart and mind just like how he touched my heart and mind. I am now more than ever committed to never give up despite my circumstances.

At a time when I was drowning into negative thoughts of a cause that was already lost, Les Brown, changed my life. He effected an inside revolution in me. He made me realise again that life is wonderful. He has supported me to keep going forward no matter what life was throwing at me. I am always inspired by his speech 'It's Possible'. In that speech, there is a story that gives me motivation to continue. It goes:

> Well, I was working, I kept saying it's possible, they got other speakers on this program. I can be on that program too. I kept selling myself, I got all fired up. And I was calling in every day, every day. And the lady finally said, 'Mr. Brown, I tell you what! We want you to come in and talk to our sales executive. You've got the kind of fire and guts that they want that will motivate them. And let me tell you something else. We want you to bring your motivational tapes. You're going to need at least $50,000 worth of tapes. Is that right? Yes because they want to keep that drive alive.

> I said, 'All right. I'll call a guy to duplicate my tape'. I said, 'Don, how you doing? This is Les. Let me tell you, I've got a major speaking engagement. Man, it's the speakers' dream. I need over $50,000 worth of product'. He said, 'Les, you don't have that kind of credit'. I said. 'I know but Don, I can sell that. Just right after the speaking engagement, I'll give your money in four days'. He said, 'Are you sure, Les?' I said, 'Yes, but I got a major speaking engagement and they told me to do it.' He said, 'Man, that's a big

odd. Let me talk with the lady with you'. I said, 'Hold on just a minute, man'.

I called the lady back. 'Hello, Evelyn, how you doing? This is Les Brown. I got Don on the phone. What did you say? Do I have the speaking engagement?' 'Yes, you do.' 'And what else do you suggest?' 'Les, our people, they buy a lot of tapes, your tapes are very popular among them. I'm saying bring at least $50,000 worth of tapes, Les. You'll sell everything you've got and more.' 'I said, 'did you hear that Don?' He said, 'Yes.' I said, 'Now, if anybody else has to make a decision, are you the final person?' She said, 'I'm the final person. I will send you the contract. I want you'. I said, 'did you hear that, Don?' I said, 'Oh ye of little faith!'

Well, he duplicated tapes. One week passed by, I'm checking her mail every day. No contract. I said, 'Come on Murphy, don't start on that. Come on, man. Give me a break, come on'. I'd talk to myself. I don't want to call him right now. Two weeks passed by, Murphy said, 'Don't you think you ought to call?' I said, OK. I called her and say, 'Hello, this is Les Brown calling'. 'How you doing, Les?' I said fine. I said, 'Evelyn hasn't sent my contract out yet. Any additional information you need?' 'So Les, you haven't heard?' I said no. 'Evelyn died. How soon she died!' I said, 'Did she say anything about me?'

When I got home I was so wiped out. And Murphy was in the house waiting for me.

Murphy said, 'Is it possible you want to listen to some of your tapes?' Well, ladies and gentlemen here is what I had to do. I had to begin to focus on what was the solution, that this was not the only place that I'll be able to sell those products. And as I began to challenge myself and got in help and support and some other input, I eventually did, it took longer. But it was challenging but I did it. Repeat after me please. No matter how bad it is, or how bad it gets, I'm going to make it. I'm going to make it.

I repeat these words to myself everyday: "No matter how bad it is, or how bad it gets, I'm going to make it. I'm going to make it. It is not over until I win!" Truly, Les Brown has made me walk again and I am forever grateful. He has made me walk from the other side of the storm. I have survived and I am no longer the same person I was before entering the storm. Les Brown has embraced life in the most vivid ways. He is an example and an inspiration for me that my life is a gift and I should embrace it with all it brings me.

My therapy out of an emotional trauma

When I received Patrick Businge's request to share my story with you, I could not believe it! For me, to have the possibility to share my story with Les Brown, and potentially let him know how he has affected and changed my life, brings me great satisfaction. It is a blessing to say, 'Thank you Les Brown for making me spiritually walk again. You have been an important part in my therapy through all the emotional trauma I have been going through'.

My life was on track until I got hit by an emotional trauma. Les Brown you rescued me. At the time of writing this story, I am still in an in-between state of considering where I am now and where I want to be in the future. You have affected my life by your voice and by your message. You have inspired me to touch people's souls and minds. You have told me that, "If there is no enemy within, the enemy outside can do us no harm." Though I am still getting over what hit me like an unexpected thunder from a clear blue sky, I am a now motivational speaker and I look very much forward to welcoming you to Tirana in Albania.

'When life throws you lemons make lemonade'
Kevin Miguel Langford
North Carolina, USA

Facing life challenges is inescapable. Overcoming life challenges is only possible through positive energy and the will to overcome them. As the youngest of five brothers and from a single-family household, I had a lot of adversaries throughout life and to this very day. For example, school teachers gave me negative feedback when I was pursuing my military school matriculation. I had to drop out and then pursued "regular college-athlete"... The reoccurring dilemmas of making life decisions, not sure which direction to take, is my story even to this very day.

Being the "dreamer" and the creative-artist type, I looked for inspirational and uplifting messages from different people and places. Les Brown has been and still remains as one of my treasured sources for positive energy. Since I was in college over 35 years ago up to now, Les Brown's motivational messages via social media have been for me. It is because of Les Brown that I have not given up on myself when so many people have given up on me. While Les Brown was posting his personal and current health issues and that of his sons, as well as reflecting on the challenges that he faced, I had let go. At that time, I was reflecting on my life after having been fired from a job that I held for approximately 7 years.

As I write my story, I am 2 weeks jobless but I have a "no worries" and positive attitude. I have learnt this attitude from Les Brown: the attitude he was demonstrating prior to his surgery. One of his messages is when life throws you a "curve ball" or a "straight ball" get back up and move on and make "lemonade out of lemons". And so it is, my brief story without the details. Believe me, I could even write a book. For now, I am getting back up, starting a new chapter, I will pick up where I left off...

From a Dummy to a Mastermind Mentality
Anonymous

From a Dummy to a Mastermind Mentality

I am intrigued to share my story with you. I am the oldest sibling of five. My mom and dad had us when they were young: at 19 to be exact. I always knew that life had to have a "secret" to success and I was willing to die looking for it and put it into practice.

I met Les Brown when I was 20 years old. At this point in my life, I was looking for answers and direction for my life. It was a leader in our company that recommended me to hear Les Brown. I decided to listen to him and I was immediately connected with him on the fact that I also want the best for my family. I was willing to change my mindset to achieve my goals. More than anything, it is his story that inspires me as a Network Marketer. This is one of the parts that motivates me in his video 'It's possible':

> It takes courage to act. Part of being hungry, when you've been defeated, it takes courage to start over again. I used to do door-to-door sales, and I was working with another friend of mine. And door-to-door sales, I mean it's punishing, it's cruel and unusual punishment. And I was a little boy, knocking on the door, *"Hello, would you like to buy a nice working television set?"* No, bam! They slam the door in your face. And the friend of mine that was working with me, they slam the door on his face and I look back and he was gone to the car. He said, *'I can't do this'.* And he sat down in the car and he said, *'You go ahead. I'll be here when you get back'.*

Now he had a mother and father to take care of him. My mother was ill. I'm adopted. I was hungry. I had to go on. I learned something about myself, that when you step into your feet, somebody said it was Winston Churchill, he said that *courage is going from failure to failure without losing enthusiasm*. When you step into your fears and continue to push yourself to go on, something happens for you. It will enable you to transcend yourself.

I went to the next door, *'Would you like to buy a nice working television?'* No, bam! Went to the next door, no, bam! After a while, I no longer took it personal. And I began to play a game. I say, well, I know there's a yes out here somewhere. And I'm going to keep on till I find it. And I'm not going home until I do. And I continue to knock on doors. And then somebody eventually would say yes and I said, *are you sure?* And I would go in there and I would get the sale.

When you have something you want to do, if you don't develop the courage to do that which has been given you to do and you spend a lot of time going around trying to convince other people of trying to get their approval, what will happen is that you will lose your nerve. And other people will convince you that what you are doing doesn't have any value and you give up on your dream. It's an interesting thing about life, I've also found, that if you don't have the courage to act, sometimes and particularly if you have something special to do, life will move on you.

In this story, I am able to see what is not there yet. I am able to develop the courage to act and break through the limitation of my life. I am able to develop a mastermind mentality. This has become my secret to success. Each time I listen to this story, I understand that most things are attainable and the only reason they are is because of the master mind mentality that one develops through investing time and great effort to create it. I now know if I want to be responsible for my life and live my dreams I must have a master mind mentality. Now after meeting Les Brown through his videos on YouTube, my life will never be the same. Thank God for people with great minds like him that I now have the key to step into my desired reality.

I am 22 at the moment and I choose to do network marketing to achieve my goals. Every day I hear Les Brown's voice: "YOU HAVE GREATNESS WITHIN YOU!" That's my story and I will surely teach this Master Mind Mentality to my future descendants.

CHAPTER 14: MOTIVATION

There is a Time For Everything

I would like to open this Chapter with this reflection from Les Brown taken from his famous keynote speech 'You Gotta be Hungry'.

> When would a baby walk? It will walk when it walks. That's when it will walk. Les, when will you be known nationally as the motivator? I will be known when I am known. That's when I'll be known. Don't get caught up in — well, I've tried it four or five times and things didn't work out. If there's something that you want and you're hungry for it, you've got to do whatever is necessary until and when you give the best you can and that's not enough, you must do what is required. And don't give up on yourself. Don't throw the towel in so quickly. Many people give up on the one yard line. What if they have the determination just to keep on knocking, there is a funny thing about life. If you are home one day and someone is knocking on the door and you say I don't want to be bothered today. And if that person just keeps on knocking, can you believe that the fool is still knocking? Pretty soon you say what is it? What do you want? And that's how you got to be about your dream.

Effectively, the hunger within us sustains our motivation. Here are stories of people who had deep hunger that has allowed them, like the babies, to go before they are ready. In effect, they share how they have transitioned from their comfort zones to chasing their dreams, and from being broken to breakthrough.

From Comfort Zone to Chasing my Dreams
Julian Businge
England, UK

Author, Entrepreneur and Property Coach
www.peacepropertyeducation.co.uk

From Comfort Zone to Chasing my Dreams

We now travel to Luton: a small town in the outskirts of London in the UK. Luton is one of the most diverse places. It has a long history of welcoming people from overseas and more than 100 languages are spoken in this town of less than 300,000 people. In this multicultural town, we are going to meet Julian Businge. She co-founded various businesses, including Peace Apartments that offers high class apartments to guests and Peace Property Education which helps people who want to invest in property. Here is her story.

Every morning, before I would leave home, I would randomly watch motivational videos on YouTube. Sometimes I would continue listening to them in the car while driving my children to school or going to business meetings. The thing that I never would have expected about this experience was not the fact that the motivational videos seemed to give me more energy and drive each day. Listening to them was re-programming my mindset and this would change *the entire focus of my life* and destiny. There were lots of motivational quotes from Les Brown that struck me like a bullet. This is something that I'll never forget.

Les Brown spoke into my heart and this created hunger in me to look out for all his videos on YouTube. This hunger led me to start following him on social media. My favourite quote is "never let someone's opinion of you become your reality." that was the moment of realization and turn around for my life. Never again to live in fear and seek someone else's approval of my dream.

As I paid attention to each of the words in his speeches, I started looking around at my life closely and at the things I took for granted. I began to see value in my life. I have the potential to turn my life around for good. I discovered that the unfulfilling habits I had formed were for comfort rather than for chasing my dreams. I now believe that it's possible for my dreams to come true. I am on my journey to greatness, I am implementing the knowledge I have received from him to change my life.

I have found these keys very helpful in improving and planning for my dreams to manifest. I do the following: I write my goals down; I use affirmations; I have Les Brown as my mentor; and I read personal development books. You might find these helpful on your way to your dreams.

From Broken to Breakthrough
Jorge Alejandro Valdez
Texas, USA

From Broken to Breakthrough

We now move to San Antonio in Texas. The inner city neighborhood is very notorious for drugs, alcohol, violence, and many other things. According to the person we are going to meet, there are lots of broken homes here and the income levels are some of the lowest. He says, 'this place gets a lot of bad reputation in the news, but for me it is my home where I have grown up. Just like in anything else I would say that there are still good people in my neighborhood'. This person is none other than Jorge Alejandro. Let us now discover his story.

Indeed, Mr. Les Brown has changed my life from where I was only a couple of years ago. I discovered him through his YouTube videos and from then on the rest is history. His story and courage throughout was something that I could also relate to since I was also raised by a single mother. Just the trials and tribulations in his personal story from a simple DJ to a congressman and motivational speaker inspired me to excel. I like it when Les Brown says,

> When would a baby walk? It will walk when it walks. That's when it will walk. Les, when will you be known nationally as the motivator? I will be known when I am known. That's when I'll be known. Don't get caught up in — well, I've tried it four or five times and things didn't work out. If there's something that you want and you're hungry for it, you've got to do whatever is necessary until and when you give the best you can and that's not enough, you must do what is required. And don't give up on yourself. Don't throw the towel in so quickly. Many people give

up on the one yard line. What if they have the determination just to keep on knocking, there is a funny thing about life. If you are home one day and someone is knocking on the door and you say I don't want to be bothered today. And if that person just keeps on knocking, can you believe that the fool is still knocking? Pretty soon you say what is it? What do you want? And that's how you got to be about your dream.

Looking back on my life, I went from living in a broken home with a single mother working multiple jobs with 4 children to completing my college education in finance and working for a top tier federal agency in a matter of 10 years. Today, I am close to achieving complete financial independence by having my home paid off in my 30s and this is just the beginning. Health has been a recent concern for me lately. I'm battling through all sorts of weight gain and such. A few weeks ago, I discovered a live video of Mr. Les Brown in a hospital bed with the will to motivate once more. He said, 'Fear not because you are more powerful than you are aware'.

I am currently week two into my routine of disciplined diet and exercise after an episode last week where my right hand went numb and wouldn't respond right away. It was a scary 15 minutes because my heart began to race and I felt a sweat of nervousness coming on. I found out that I was overweight and had high cholesterol. So after that day, I used what I learned from Les on his health concerns and applied it to my situation. No longer will I let my body become second fiddle to anything else. Through Les Brown, I have become more aware that my health is my wealth. So, I have decided to completely revamp my diet and not just exercise like crazy and then eat it all away.

I am not completely out of the woods on this one yet, but I know that through Les Brown's encouragement, I will make it through this as well. That's why his message has changed my life. Soon, I will become an entrepreneur and investor in the field of finance. This is my dream. I know that there is still so much to do. I hope my story will inspire someone one day.

Go Before You Are Ready
Reginald L Russell
Arizona, USA

www.reginaldlrussell.com

Go Before You Are Ready

My story with Les Brown started when I was given an audio CD with his clips on it. As I listened to them, the thing that resonated with me during my period of reluctance and apprehension was when he said, "Go before you are ready". This really stuck with me and motivated me to move and take action. It allowed me to understand more clearly that I did not have to be necessarily qualified to take action. It let me realize that I did not have to wait for somebody to create a space for me, that I capacitated the ability to act and control my ability to provide energy to my goal. I did not have to wait for someone to empower me as the empowerment came from within me and in my willingness to make things happen. Ever since listening to Les Brown, I have been going before I am ready realizing that preparation often takes place during the process. I'm not saying that one should not take initiative in preparing themselves, but don't allow the need for a perfect preparation to stifle your start.

By using the "go before you are ready method", I have started a publishing company, written a book, started a clothing line, and created a non-profit community organization working with kids and sports in the community. My understanding that qualification comes from God and not from human beings has really empowered me to feel strong, courageous and bold in the face of adversity. So if you feel apprehensive about your passions and ambitions, "go before you are ready". You can thank me later, see you at the top!

Running Away From Pain to Les Brown
Jonathan Nicolas
Florida, USA

Actor, Motivational Comedian and
Member of Les Brown Unlimited Team
www.jonnicolas-mca.com

Running Away from Pain to Les Brown

I live in The Sunshine State otherwise known as Florida, I say that because it is always sure to be shining each and every day. It doesn't matter if the sun is out or not, there are always things to do that make you feel great! You don't need to go far to find a beach and let me tell you, here in this State it has some of the best beaches in the world. Whether you are in the Southwest part of Florida in Sarasota at Siesta Key Beach, with your feet buried in the cool white sand and the little fish that swim around you, or if you decide to go much further to the "Deep South" of the famous Miami Beach with the banging of the Cuban Congo drums and the charismatic people, you will always enjoy yourself. Florida is also globally known as "Walt Disney World" because of the famous Disney's Magic Kingdom which I'm sure the kids would enjoy. Never have I lived in a place that has so many open roads and exotic creatures to see. The Sunshine state has a certain type of solitude that is hard to match. If you're looking for a place to get away or a place to call home I would have to recommend "The Sunshine State", from the amazing types of food and the number of resort-like locations, you can never go wrong. It's where I found my peace and I know it's where you will find yours.

Unusual childhood

My story isn't your typical one where I get to tell you about how I had supportive parents and they raised me right and told me I can be whatever I wanted to be when I grew up. I didn't get to play catch with daddy outside while mom was in the kitchen cooking our favorite meal. I didn't get to lay on my mother's lap while she sang to me and told me stories about my father and how great he was. Unfortunately, I won't be able to make you smile this early in my story because that just wasn't my reality and that isn't what happened to me. To ones born with a head start they get to say they had mom and dad to look up to, to guide them and tell them great stories that made them smile and be happy to wake up every day, excited to see what the next day would bring. I'm not going to lead you a stray and fill your head up with untrue events. Oh no! I wouldn't do that to you. You deserve so much more than that: you deserve the truth.

Born in the back of the car

The truth of the matter is I was born with odds stacked up against me. I was born on a warm night in the middle of summer in a 1980 Chevrolet Monte Carlo. Yes, I was born in a car. I told you this wasn't going to be your typical story. The reason I was born in a Monte Carlo was because my grandfather who was driving the car at the time, bless his heart, with my mother and grandmother in the car thought it would be a good idea to take us to a Psychiatric Ward, assuming they were like a hospital. Sadly, they were informed that it wasn't that type of hospital, so my grandmother did what she had to do and delivered me right there in the back seat.

Most people don't believe me when I tell them I was born in a car. It wasn't that hard for me to believe because I always had something I was going through, so needless to say I wasn't surprised. I'm just relieved that my grandmother saved me from being named Monte Carlo, since my mother wasn't that creative. Whenever I could start remembering my younger years, it wasn't the best of memories.

Abused by my mother

My mother was always upset or at least it seemed with me. I could never figure out why. I just knew every time she was upset, it was me she was taking it out on. She would abuse me mentally and physically. The fact that there wasn't a dad present to offset the attacks didn't help. I had a hard time dealing with getting beaten often and no one came to my rescue. My only rescue was when I went to sleep. I remember dreaming of playing basketball like the great "Michael Jordan" and acting in movies like the legend "Denzel Washington". Only to wake up and realize it was just a dream and I had to go back to the harsh reality that was my life. I dealt with a lot of anger issues in my younger years. I didn't put it together at that time that my anger stemmed from years of abuse by the hands of the woman who was supposed to love me.

I was special

Somehow, no matter what I knew I was special because I always made people laugh around me. I guess this was from all that television I watched with all the funny great comedians like Eddie Murphy, Martin Lawrence and the late great Richard Pryor. However, I still struggled with the pain of the continuous abuse. I remember one day the physical abuse had stopped because my mother didn't feel like dealing with me anymore and she sent me away. I was free!! Or at least I thought I was free.

Many years later passed and I'm in Brooklyn, New York. Now, I'm in my deep teens still not having a clue of what I'm doing with my life. I was struggling to make it out of high school while becoming a father at a young age of nineteen, homeless, and trying to graduate from college. I would always try to dig deep within myself and bring some type of joy to me, but it seemed like joy wanted nothing to do with me. For many years, I would go on struggling with pain, hiding it from most people, and masking it with my humor and funny outlook on life.

Things didn't work out with my son's mother due to the abusive relationship I was used to with my mother. I just couldn't figure it out. Soon after separating with her, I went and got married to a woman who brought me the right type of distraction that I needed. This woman also gave me a beautiful little angel that showed me what love was. This was the second time in my life I felt true joy, the other is when I first held my son in my arms... I am now a father of two.

Running from pain

Brooklyn's never changing harsh winters and daily violence forced me to take my family and move to Florida. Here, I am in The Sunshine State. The sun is shining and nature is all around me thinking that everything was going to change. Sadly, it didn't. The pain has followed me here. I thought I could get away from it when I left Brooklyn. My wife of seven years and I developed more problems in my marriage and I struggled to discover why. I learned a few years later it was because of the pain that I had deep inside and I didn't know how to address it. I took another attempt to escape the pain and made the decision to get divorced.

From my mother to Brooklyn, from Brooklyn to Orlando, now this time I ran to Miami, and now I'm a grown man and a father of three children. I am still struggling with the questions of life: Who I am? What am I doing with my life? What do I want to do about my career? I had a job I was unhappy in. I was in a relationship that didn't serve me. I still have the pain inside and barely could face the man I was. I had moved away from my children because of the divorce. I was at the end of the line. Darkness had consumed me and I couldn't see the light or a way out. I had no idea that what was coming next was going to be a life changer for me.

Les Brown breathed life into me

I called a very good friend of mine and I told him about how I was feeling, what I had been going through and how I felt like I couldn't breathe. I vividly remember what he said to me: 'I know that can't be easy, have you ever heard of Les Brown?' My response was, 'I have never heard of him and who is he?' My friend then sent me a link that I would quickly discover would change my life forever. I put my head phones in and clicked on the link that took me to this video where I began to hear a powerful voice saying 'You have greatness within you'. This man went on to say 'many people are just existing and not truly living'. He shared his own story on how he was born and given away for adoption, how he was labelled educable mentally retarded and he was put back from the 5th grade to the 4th grade. How he was homeless and slept in his office because he couldn't afford a place to live. This man was breathing life to me through my headphones.

Things that he was saying reminded me of when I was younger and I would hear about God, and how he creates us to be great, how we are filled with his love, and how we need not to conform to this world. Les Brown said he wanted me to listen to his voice at night and in the morning. He said what you listen to in the first twenty minutes of the day controls the spirit of your day. So, I began to do that day in and day out. I also began to read the Bible. I started to read as much as I could and listen to as much as I could of this man because with each video I watched and each audio I listened to, I began to come alive and find my way out of the darkness. One day I was listening to Les Brown and he said a poem that spoke volumes to me. He said, 'many a flower has bloomed unceasingly and wasted sweetness upon the cold desert air' and he translates that into so many talented people the world would never come to know because they would fall through the cracks by never believing in themselves and manifesting their God given gifts to reality.

I decided to get baptized

At his point, I vowed to myself that I would never let this happen to me. I was born with a purpose and I have greatness within me. Mr. Les Brown had changed my life. He inspired me to stop feeling sorry for myself and to forgive myself. I decided to get baptized and start an entire new life with a new positive mindset. This mindset would one day put me closer to this man, as I thought that one day I would meet him because we shared many things in common and spoke the same language.

In August 2017, he came across my Instagram saying, "you have a story to tell and I want to help you tell it". He offered me to join his institute where he would teach me how to use the power of my voice to tell my story and how I could inspire thousands upon thousands as he did me. So, I did. For the first time in my life, I invested in myself and joined his movement. After months of listening to him day in and day out, the day finally came in October of 2017 that I met the man that changed my life. I finally did it! I finally figured out how to rid myself of the years of pain that had been tormenting me. Les Brown had inspired me to achieve greatness by looking from within.

I am a motivational speaker and life coach

Now I have the title of a Motivational Speaker and Life Coach. I am working diligently to inspire many people out there who think they are not good enough to live this life and live it to the fullest. He came into my life at a time where I desperately needed to hear his words. It is because of him that each and every day I seek to inspire everyone around me and live the life I have always dreamed. Les Brown said to me, "It's possible" and I say to you, "I know it's possible". As you read my story, know that you are not alone. You have amazing gifts inside you waiting to be born into this world. I love you and always remember you are special and you have greatness within you.

CHAPTER 15: PERSEVERANCE

I will persevere until I succeed

Allow me to share with you a summary of what I wrote about fear in my bestselling book '7 Steps to Greatness'. Fear is the number one killer of dreams. Fear steals our peace. Fear stops us from getting on in life. Fear hinders us from taking action. When fear takes over, we sit in the back seat and do not know where we are going to end up. Sometimes we make fear bigger than us and it takes over our lives. There will be times when you will fear and therefore not persevere. You will listen to your negative inner voice and conversation and these will hold you back. Not everyone will support you. Not everyone will be happy with your dream. Not everyone will encourage you to continue. Even some of your closest friends will become your great discouragers. Your life will feel like an ongoing war characterised by unpredictable explosions, landmines, insecurities, and fears. It is during these moments that you will need to stand up within yourself against fear and persevere with your dreams.

Before you read this Chapter on how people have persevered amidst the violent storms of life, I would like to share with you this reflection I received from Les Brown on 18th January 2018. So, my advice to you is not to choose to be a permanent victim of fear in your life. Read these stories and stand to life and its challenges. Like them, you have got what it takes to find a way to win and get a message from misery. I look forward to you becoming an example of a person who says to life, 'I will persevere until I succeed'.

Find a Way to Win
Toni Thompson
California, USA

Visionary
Transformational Speaker
Agent of Change

A letter from Victorville

February 7, 2018

Dear Mr. Les Brown,

My name is Toni Viola. Over 32 years ago, you made an impact on my life. I was 18 years old, just graduated from high school and like most teens, scared out of my mind of the thing referred to as "adulthood". Nonetheless, I had to do it anyway. Filled with uncertainty about what I was going to do I had taken a job working at ***In N Out Burger.*** That wasn't exactly what I had in mind throughout high school. You see, I desired to be a child psychologist and optometrist sprinkled with awesome communication skills. Unfortunately, life choices took me down a different path of self-discovery.

I grew up in a home where my parents worked to make ends meet. We didn't talk much about my goals but I remember creating a Vision Board and mailing it to myself, giving a copy also to my mom to keep. Somewhere within the first year post high school I came across your cassette tapes at a yard sale… "You have greatness within you" would become the mantra sewn in my spirit and heart that saw me through some difficult times through early adulthood, becoming a single mom at 19, selling encyclopaedias in a desert community in Las Vegas to support myself and child. No baby daddy to turn to, in fact, he became conveniently AWOL…! It was a very challenging time in this young woman's life. You see from the time I was 5 years old, I envisioned becoming someone great, a millionaire, a movie star, or great speaker. By the age of 30 I was on my 3rd child, on and off welfare, feeling like I had failed, those dreams were dying... Then here comes that voice again... "You have greatness within you".

Mr. Les, tears are forming right now even as I write this letter... wow... I would pray to God and ask him: What is my purpose? What is my gift? What do I have to give back to humanity? Church was a way of life and taught me the rules of religion, but a relationship with God didn't happen until I was around 35 years old. Mr. Les, my dad had passed away; he was a diabetic, narcissistic, and functioning alcoholic prior to his demise. Grief stricken and worried about my mom, I moved back home....prayed some more and asked God to tell me who I am... what does he see in me...again. Here's that voice again, "You have greatness within you"... ! Okay, I hear that but life was showing me nothing but struggle after struggle...!

To add to my already complex journey, I met a PK (Preacher's Kid). He was tall, dark, well dressed, a handsome deacon in training. Alright God, this must be answered prayer... Dad was dead... I was feeling lonely and afraid of raising my sons by myself. This man worked and made decent money, had musical gifts and was really a smooth operator. I was taken by his charm. However, manipulation and verbal abuse would take place right after we said 'I do'. Mr. Les Brown, that entanglement turned out to be a distraction and a disaster which lasted 17 years.

Before I bore you let me speed up to tell you how much those words "you have greatness within you" surfaced again. I turned 50 in 2017, I suffered a bad car accident, and my husband and my mom were both aneurysm survivors living with me. Do you know that I learned what the true meaning of greatness is coupled with resilience? I am so thankful to share this with you. I began to download and listen to all your motivational messages, your stories about being educable mentally retarded, your first job as a disc jockey, your first speaking engagement, the first time you got cheated out of buying your precious mom her first home, how you slept at the office and managed employees, and so many other inspiring stories… I am so grateful because you spoke into my spirit and over my life the same blessing I found in God's holy word which says I am fearfully and wonderfully made.

Mr. Les, I am an inspirational, transformational speaker under construction today. I launched an online women support group called Mysistafriend Network. It has grown global with over 1,500 members. I have recently been asked to facilitate a Vision Board workshop to the youth in my community. I am becoming who God sees… I may not be where I desire to be yet…. But I know now that greatness is definitely within me… Peace and blessings to Mamie's Baby Boy.

Love,
Toni Viola Thompson

Homeless Millionaire
Steve Mcmenamin
Victoria, Australia

Life changed for me and I pretty well ended up being a homeless millionaire. I used to sleep in my office. During this time, Les Brown seemed to appear out of nowhere. He would show up on a podcast and YouTube when I needed him. His stories of sleeping in the office and working hard to buy his mother a home helped me not to give up. They stopped me from being embarrassed about my situation which no one knew about. I would sneak to the gym, as I had no power, water, and got fit. I would shower there and then get into my suit. After the office, I moved into a huge house under construction while it was being built. I slept there illegally. I wanted to give up but whenever I would listen to Les Brown, I knew quitting would not help. He would say to me:

> You do what it is you're supposed to, you're supposed to build something, you're supposed to create something, I don't know how to do it. Learn. Do whatever is required. Just go out there. It's possible you can get what you want. It's necessary. If you want it, you got to go into action, you've got to be willing to experiment. You've got to be willing to fail and to succeed. You've got to be willing to form and develop new relationships. It's you, it's on you, you've got to make that happen. Nobody's going to bring it to you on a silver platter and say: 'Here's your dream manifested'. No, it's hard. Yes, it's hard. It's difficult, yes right and it's worth it.

With this, I saw and heard how his vision got him through life. His laughs made me smile. I am happy that I shared my story. I know this is a small story compared to other people that Les Brown has touched.

From Misery to Message
Veronika Sam
England, UK

International Health and Wellness Mentor

From Misery to Message

Have you ever been concerned about your way of living? Have you ever imagined that there must be more to life than hard work and paying bills? Have you ever thought that you need more spare time with your loved ones? This is what I was thinking back in 2008 after my marriage ended. I was worried about what I was going to do with my life! Listening to Les Brown and learning from him has helped me grow as a person till this day.

I first came to London from Czech Republic in 2000 with the intention to study English for only 6 months. Surprisingly, I have been in London for 18 years. I first met my husband in 2001 and got married but in 2008 it all changed. My husband left me and my 2 year old daughter with loads of debt and with no support. He went back to his home country in Africa and we never saw him again. In order to pay the bills and cover my debt payments, I worked over 50 hours as a child carer. I wanted a job like this so that I could have my daughter with me while I worked. The problem is that in the last two years, I have been made redundant 3 times. It feels like an exhausting profession with little job security. Now I work part time and term time only so that I am able to fit everything around.

If someone told me two years ago that I would be running two businesses (my daughter's and mine), helping charities, and traveling the world, I will say no that's not me. To arrive at this stage, I had to change. This has only been possible thanks to personal development that has become our number one priority for myself and my daughter. It has changed our mindset and we can see the change in our lives. We are meeting incredible people and helping many others. We have been on TV and interviewed by local newspapers. We are living our dream.

My mission now is to help other people, especially single mothers, become independent, become better role models, and learn to become positive in hard times. You might be asking why me? It is because I can relate to this. I have been in many situations where I thought there is no way out. I almost lost my house. I have been in a lot of debt, but step by step my life is taking a turn. I can now see the light at the end of the tunnel! Mr Les Brown has been lifting the mood in our house, we have been learning so much especially when he was fighting his illness after visiting London in January 2018. My daughter Vanessa aka "Inspiring Vanessa" has sent her book as a gift to him. My favourite message from him to you is that 'keep the faith' and 'It's not over until you win'.

CHAPTER 16: POWER

Power is Our Deepest Fear

Early 2018, I was talking to a head teacher of a school in England, UK. He told me that one of the deepest fears children in his school had was the fear of being stabbed. To deal with this fear, some of the boys in his school came wearing three pairs of trousers. This was the way they managed their deepest fear. However, reading this timeless message written by Marianne Williamson in her book 'A Return to Love', I get a different perspective on our deepest fear. She writes:

> Our deepest fear is not that we are inadequate. Our deepest fear is that we are powerful beyond measure. It is our light, not our darkness that most frightens us. We ask ourselves, Who am I to be brilliant, gorgeous, talented, fabulous? Actually, who are you not to be? You are a child of God. Your playing small does not serve the world. There is nothing enlightened about shrinking so that other people won't feel insecure around you. We are all meant to shine, as children do. We were born to make manifest the glory of God that is within us. It's not just in some of us; it's in everyone. And as we let our own light shine, we unconsciously give other people permission to do the same. As we are liberated from our own fear, our presence automatically liberates others.

The boys in this school in England had not yet realized that they were powerful beyond their current circumstances. They did not know that there was greater power in them than their fear of knives. Though they were in a faith school, they did not realise what the author of 1 John meant 'who is in you is greater than who is in the world' (1John 4:4). As you read this Chapter on Power, I would like you to reflect on this question: What is my deepest fear? It is my hope that the stories in this chapter will be a testimony for you to turn to your deepest fear and get the courage to turn your tragedy into triumph and your test into a testimony. I leave you with the words of Nelson Mandela, 'There is no passion to be found playing small in settling for a life that is less than the one you are capable of living'.

From Poverty to Power
Rogers Mbaziira
Uganda

Business Coach and Founder of Mbaziira Foods

Dr Patrick Businge

From Poverty to Power

We start by travelling to Uganda in East Africa where we meet the 27 year old Rogers Mbaziira. Seeing its natural beauty, one of the earliest explorers Henry Morton Stanley referred to Uganda as 'The Pearl of Africa' in 1871. One year after making his first trip to Uganda in 1907, Sir Winston Churchill wrote his book 'My African Journey'. Read about how he felt about Uganda, 'for magnificence, for variety of form and colour, for profusion of brilliant life — bird, insect, reptile, beast — for vast scale — Uganda is truly the Pearl of Africa'. Rogers lives in The Pearl of Africa where he has tapped into its natural resources to make a transition from poverty to power'. He has two businesses: Mbaziira Foods that deals in fresh food products, and a personal development company that trains, mentors and coaches salespeople and entrepreneurs. Here is Roger's story.

I started listening to Les Brown messages a few years ago. While passing in the streets of Kampala, I saw a CD that had the title 'You have greatness in you'. It caught my attention and I bought it because I needed something that could help me cool down as I was going through some terrible situations. My bosses had delayed paying my salary and I was facing a lot of challenges in paying my bills. I also needed to plan my future since I had a poor background where I lacked everything in life. So, I discovered Les Brown when I was behind on my bills and in my plans. I listened to this video several times whenever I was down. Here is what I often heard from Les Brown:

> And here's what I will share with you, that in the process of working on your dreams you are

going to incur a lot of disappointment, a lot of failure, a lot of pain, a lot of setbacks, a lot of defeat. But in the process of doing that you will discover some things about yourself that you don't know right now. What you will realize is that you have greatness within you. What you will realize is that you're more powerful than you can ever begin to imagine. What you will realize is that you're greater than your circumstances, which you don't have to go through life being a victim.

At this point, I realized that I could actually do more than I was doing. Immediately, I stopped leaving everything to chance. Since that time, I have developed confidence and self-esteem. Since that time, I have increased my income. Since that time, I have started businesses: I am mentoring and speaking to people who now pay me for my services. In addition, I have learnt a good formula for success and am determined to live the rest of my life as the best of my life.

I am hopeful that I will achieve this each year because of Les Brown. I watch his motivational messages and I follow him on social media every day. Here are some of the quotes from Les Brown that fuel my life on a daily basis:

- 'Life is a fight for territory if you don't fight for what you want, what you don't want will take over'
- 'Most people fail in life not because they aim too high and miss, but because they aim too low and hit'
- 'You gotta be hungry'

- 'You have something special. There is greatness within you'.

I am grateful that I landed on Les Brown's CD in the streets of Kampala. He has changed my life and not so many people are able to change people's lives like him. Just as I met his CD in the streets of Kampala, I now wish to meet him one day in Kampala. My dream is to bring him to Uganda so that he can change people lives in this Pearl of Africa.

Turning My Tragedy Into Triumph
Tyler Jamal Smith
Florida, USA

Motivational Speaker and Mentor

Turning My Tragedy Into Triumph

I have been serving in the United States Army for the past 7 years. Serving with a multitude of highly prestigious units. Of those to include, 10th Mountain Division, 82nd Airborne Division and finishing off with 7th Special Forces Group. As an Airborne Paratrooper and elite professional, there's a lot of demands that are expected of one. However, during my tenure with the military, I have always faced a lot of adversity. Rather it was racial discrimination, double standards or unfair treatment. It started to take its toll on me during the last 2 1/2 years of my career serving with 7th. As with any major organization, there's always toxicity as you can always expect a few rotten apples on every big apple tree.

I dealt with PTSD, depression, anxiety and panic attacks on a daily. It got to a point where I felt as if I were walking on egg shells every day. There was nothing I could do right, and I was being heavily punished for the most tedious things. This led to extreme depression, which affected every area of my life. I brought my troubles into my home and it began chipping away at my marriage. I felt like a complete failure; both as a soldier and as a family man. As I neared my separation date from the military, I found myself with a lot of time on my hands. At this point, my marriage was in shambles. I was living separate from my wife and kids. I was being separated from the Army involuntarily and it became a very dark time in my life. However, all the pain and adversity actually pushed me closer to the things I was genuinely passionate about, which was motivational speaking.

I began sifting through YouTube videos of speakers and I listened to them every day. But it was when I heard Les Brown's voice that it did something to me internally. I was no longer hearing him with my ears, but also with my heart. "You don't have to be great to get started, but you have to get started to be great", "Sometimes life will move on you when it's time for you to move onto your destiny". By listening to him and deeply considering his philosophies, it gave me the courage to act on my dreams. To turn tragedy into triumph. To understand that there's "Greatness within me!" and that "It's possible!" I viewed my current storms in life as experiences designed to propel me into my destiny. Thanks to Les, my perspective completely changed and so did my life.

I decided to let go of the things that were destroying my life and let God have his way in my life. I focused my efforts on becoming better in every way. As a father, husband and son of God. Listening to Les helped me develop the courage to face my depression and anxiety, which subsequently led to me overcoming my mental health battles. I went from a place where I was being flooded with anti-depressants medicine, even actually being admitted into a mental health hospital as an outpatient; to not even seeing the need to take the medicine because I knew that I was capable of over-turning my situation by changing the way I viewed. I understood that everything I was going through was necessary for my growth and transition into greatness. I reached out to Les Brown, and joined his institute and the rest is history.

I have now left the military and I am walking into my destiny full speed. I've had multiple speaking engagements and I offer encouragement to others on the daily. I have also personally met Les Brown during his live event and now we have a personal relationship. Who would've thought that would be my reality less than a year ago while I was going through the storm? I am a firm believer that the best is yet to come and I'm so thankful to God for bringing me through and giving me a mentor like Les Brown. I thank God for his life and legacy and I plan on continuing the greatness throughout the world.

He changed my life by changing my philosophy
Philly Figo Matsepa
South Africa

We travel to South Africa: the home of Nelson Mandela who, according to Philly, is the man who spent 27 years of his life in jail for fighting for us today to be free, and still that didn't stop him from fighting until he was named the first South African black president. Indeed, Nelson Mandela's life proves Les Brown's words, 'there is greatness within everyone'. Let us now discover the greatness in Philly Matsepa, a 28 year old South African living in Johannesburg.

'I was raised as a good Christian'

I'm from the family of 9 children. I am the 8th born with 5 brothers and 3 sisters. As I grew up and throughout my school years, life was not easy. My Mother passed away when I was only 4 years old. I was very young, I cannot even recall any of my time with her. I was raised by my father who was a decent man who wanted his children to be raised with love, respect, truth, and prayers. He was a very strict man but he always wanted the best for us. Even when he couldn't afford much, he would make sure that there is food on the table for us to eat at night before we went to bed. He made sure that we all had clothes to wear. He did all this with just one single income. He worked hard to keep us happy and to have love and peace.

My mother taught my brothers and sisters to always pray and go to church on the Sabbath day. My father was happy and proud knowing that when he was not with us, he knew we were in good behavior because we spent most of the time at the church praying and being thankful to God. As time went on, my brothers and sisters went to town and I was left alone with my younger brother. I was only 17 years of age by that time. We looked after each other. Financially, life was hard at that time as I had to cut people's hair to get money for food. It was hard. I really looked up to my father, who was strong and a real father figure.

'I lost focus'

I will never forget the day my younger brother and I were playing pool. I received a phone call, and someone said, 'Philly your father is dead'. I was quiet for some time as the person was trying to comfort me over the phone. I then asked, 'Are you serious?' He replied, 'Yes'. I asked him again, 'Are you sure?' He replied, 'Yes. I'm sorry young man! Go home now, people are coming'. I said, 'Ok, it is alright'. I hang up phone. Now I had to break the news to my younger brother. It was not easy. It was hard but I did it anyway and we comforted each other and went back home.

The death of my father turned my life around. My brother and I were the youngest at that time and we were left with no one to be our role model or to talk to. I then started to be negative and lost all my focus. I would talk about how hard life was as I was financially broke and I didn't have any source of income. I became a person of negativity. And lost the fight of being the person I always wanted to be. I stopped going to church the way my parents taught me because my focus was on my toxic attitude. The only good thing I did was pass my matric (final year of high school). My brothers and I agreed to go on in our higher learning, but I didn't do that. I don't have any college qualifications. I did what was easy. Which is to stay at home, do nothing and develop a toxic attitude. Everything I had planned went down the drain.

See, my dream was to be a police officer. I wanted to get that job after my Matric. I was never successful with my dream and that was painful. Life began to be harder for me. I was hopeless and I didn't have any back up plans. I was in this situation till the age of 27 to the extent that I couldn't afford to buy myself a roll-on, toothpaste, body lotion, and other small essential things. By then, my brothers and sisters were already working and they took over the responsibility to look after us, the younger ones. People would start to complain, and put pressure on you. You're too old, you need to get a job. By the time these complaints started, I was staying alone at home busy with my toxic attitude.

'It was hard growing up'

It was hard seeing my brothers and sisters making a difference in their lives and I was here stuck depending on them. I started a small business as a barber but the money I got I used to build toxic relationships. I did all I could to get out of that situation but I was never successful. With much pressure on me, I got a job at the casino to clean toilets. I then told myself that's it.... Philly this is it.... There was nothing making me happy there but free Wi-Fi.

One evening, I was playing a compilation of motivational clips. As I was listening, a man with a signature voice said, 'In what have you done with your life so far is it giving you what you want? When you look towards the Future, is life giving you what you want?' Inside my heart the answer was, 'No it's not'. This man continued, 'If you look at your life and you are not getting what you want, you owe it to yourself to do something differently about it. See 85% of Americans are doing something 8 hours a day that they don't like'. This statement touched my heart, knowing I'm one of the 85%. He then said, 'most people will resist change as if change is worse than what they are facing everyday'. As I looked at what I was doing, I said to myself I need to change from cleaning toilets. This is not for me. He continued, 'whatever you need to change that situation, you've got that in you. You've got genius in you. You've got goodness in you. You got creativeness in you and you have greatness within you and if you take a chance to work on that, you will find that the world is on your side'. Wow, this made a lot of sense to me.

'I loved his voice'

I loved his voice. I loved his way of talking and how he put his words together. I loved how he told stories. I loved him. I kept on searching for his voice on videos until I knew his name: Les Brown. I then downloaded all his videos I found on YouTube. I started listening to him every day: morning, midday, at noon and night. I would listen to Les Brown for a long time and never got bored listening to him over and over again. Before I heard Les Brown's voice, I didn't know that I had greatness within me. The possibility of living a happy life was never in my mind. Les Brown told me that 'It's possible'. Les Brown told me, 'I must be willing to do things today others won't do in order to have the things tomorrow others won't have'. I asked myself, what are these things?

They were: make discipline my vitamin, for the undisciplined life is an insane life. Make it ok to fail because anything worth doing, is worth doing badly if I don't know how to do it right. After hearing these messages, I looked at my life and the things that kept me from living my dreams. I worked on my behaviour and started doing things differently. It was not easy for me to do this.

'I was dying'

Les Brown said something I won't forget in my life. This has helped me make good decisions and I believe it will always help me make many more in the future. He said, 'check your relationships if you are living together or dying together'. As I looked at myself and reflecting on these words, I realized that I was dying. I was not aware until Les Brown put this awareness into my mind. With this, I had the power to end those toxic relationships without any fear of getting hurt. He also said, 'in order to be someone you have never been, you have to do something you have never done before'. This gave me the power to feel good about the decisions I was about to make. I was positive and I did it. Even though it was painful, I did it anyhow. I did all that was possible to get out of toxic relationships and disciplined myself to be single and work on myself. I decided to develop some good behavior, treat people with love and respect, and be humble the way my parents taught me. I decided to go back to church.

'Leave dead people alone'

One of the challenges I had was that there were some people I loved and cared about and their behavior was holding them back and stopping them from achieving their goals. I used to be upset when I saw these people. This would break my heart whenever I was around to them. Until Les Brown said on one of his Monday Motivational Calls, 'some people, no one can change them or educate them but life…No matter what you do or say you are wasting your time. They will learn from life. It is a full time job changing yourself. Leave dead people alone'. This changed my mind on how I used to look at these people.

Now I'm happy and feeling good knowing I'm not responsible for any man or woman's mistake. I'm so thankful for the vision and mindset Les Brown has given to me.

'His story changed my pain'

I don't remember anything about my mother and that used to upset me so bad. That situation was pain to me, seriously. Then the man with the signature voice, Les Brown, told a story of how he was born, adopted and raised in Miami, Florida. His story changed my pain and he made me feel better. Now I have accepted the situation and I'm thankful for my mother because she gave birth to me before she passed away. Knowing that giving birth to me was the greatest gift I could ever get from my mother. To show how thankful I am, I have respect for all the mothers in the world and I love them all. That's how grateful I am to be pain free from losing my mother at an early age of my life. All thanks to Les Brown.

My dream was to be a police officer after I finished my Matric. I was hoping to get a job at SAPS (South African Police Service). I was applying but my application has never been answered. I was hopeless, it was hard for me to accept. Then I began to be negative. I told myself it will never happen to me because I have been applying but nothing happened. In my mind it was done that this will never happen to me, this is not going to work for me. I was hopeless. Les Brown said we must check what kind of thoughts we entertain because thoughts are so powerful. He quoted someone who said that our life is a gift from God and how we live it is a gift to God. After hearing this, the question for me was: what kind of gift am I giving? At this point, I realized that most of the things I did were wrong. I questioned if this was because I had left church? It was at church where I was taught to live the life God always wanted me to live.

'I kept my commitment to my commitment'

One of his best speeches at the Manpower Conference, Les Brown said the Bible is the most motivational book ever written. At the time I was doing so many wrong things the Bible didn't allow me to do. I prayed but my behavior was bad. I said to myself, if I continue this way, I won't allow God to be alive in me. This is one of the things that was holding me back from living my dreams or unlocking doors to my dreams. I was living an insane life. I was living an undisciplined Life. I had to change, stop all the wrong things I used to do and make a commitment to myself never to do those things again. I was afraid of the pain I was going to feel when ending or letting go of what I was used to.

It was Les Brown's words that kept me strong. I had to feel the pain and do it anyhow because it is worth it. I had to keep my commitment to my commitment. It was not easy, it was hard but I was well prepared because Les Brown told me that 'It's possible…Easy is not an option…If it's hard, do it hard'. Les taught me whenever I'm going through some hard times I have to have faith. I have to believe in myself. I have to believe it's possible and have some plan of action to keep me going.

My plan of action was to listen to Les Brown's video clips every day. This gave me faith. I believed I could and I had to change. Changing was not easy because at some point I would be sad, but it was part of change. Change was painful for me. As I changed, I began to see my life getting better. I developed a positive attitude. I started to smile with people and good things were happening to me.

'You gotta be hungry!'

I used Les Brown's story of how he became a disk jockey to work on my mind, attitude and behaviour. This is the conversation that ensued: Les Brown: Philly, what do you want to do in life?' I replied, 'Sir I want to marry, have a home, have a family and help people live their dreams'. Les Brown: 'How are you planning to do that?'. I said, 'Sir I want to be a police officer and have my own businesses. Les Brown: 'You gotta be hungry…People that are hungry are willing to do the things today others won't do in order to have the things tomorrow others won't have. You have to work on yourself, Philly. Develop your mind. You don't get in life what you want, you get in life what you are. Always strive to get on to the top because it is the bottom that is overcrowded. You got to be hungry!'. I said, 'Yes sir I'm hungry!' Les Brown replied, 'change your behaviour, have positive thoughts, and work on your mind and attitude because how you behave is important… Develop your communication skills because how you express yourself once you open your mouth you tell the world what you are… See yourself as a police officer, start working to get knowledge. Create relationships and train yourself because it's better to be prepared for an opportunity and not have one than to have an opportunity and never be prepared'.

At this point, I started working on myself by changing my behaviour and attitude. As I did this, Les Brown said,

'Philly, talk to people…ask for help not because you are weak but because you want to remain strong'. So I started talking to people on how to become a police officer. I behaved like a police officer. I was ready. My inner voice continued to tell me, 'remember you don't have any college qualification… This is a crowded place but if you are hungry enough the world will make a place for you'. With my deep hunger, I went and applied for the job of becoming a police officer.

In South Africa, the post for the South African Police Service (SAPS) comes out only once a year. For the past 7 years I had been applying, my application had never been successful. This is what made me become negative and scared that if this doesn't come through, I will be sad. As Mr. Les Brown had told me in my mind, I shouldn't take anything personal and that some people are so negative that they have to say no 7 times before they can say yes. I developed the courage to apply for the 7th time.

'Yes I can'

I'm happy to say that it is done, I've got the job and I'm now going to be a police officer. We are going to training. My life has changed since I started listening to Les Brown. Mr. Les Brown said that most people don't live their dreams not because they aim too high and miss but because they aim too low and hit. Before Mr. Les Brown changed my philosophy, I used to say I'm not good enough to have my own business. The story I would tell myself was that without college qualifications, whatever I do would not make a difference in my life especially after getting the job to clean toilets. I couldn't see anything different. When Les Brown said, 'It's possible…You have greatness within you…You can do more than you can ever imagine', my reply was, 'Yes I can'.

In my mind I wanted to have a business of my own but I didn't know how I was going to do that. Les Brown changed all that by saying when you want to do something in life don't worry about how you are going to do it. 'How' is none of your business. That is for God to decide. This opened my mind because my heart was already in. Les Brown said that the most important investment you can make in this day is to invest in yourself. I then knew that it is important to invest in myself by setting time aside to listen to his tapes, watch his speech videos 3 to 4 times a day for as long as I can.

'If you do what is easy, your life will be hard…'

I always wanted things to be easy for me. However, Les Brown told me that if I do what is easy, my life will be hard but if I do what is hard, my life will be easy. That is why I ended up cleaning toilets because I did what was easy. I was afraid to try because I knew it was hard, so I was driven by fear of failure. Mr. Les Brown changed all of that when he said you have to be a risk taker because if you can't risk, you cannot grow. If you can't grow, you cannot become your best. If you cannot become your best, you cannot be happy. If you cannot be happy, what else is there!

To me, what was there was fear. I was really afraid to fail. However, Les Brown told me that I will fail my way to success. I understand this better now as it has happened to me many times in my life. Les Brown told me that I am going to make a lot of mistakes in life. This has happened to me too. His teachings have changed my philosophy.

'Les Brown has changed my life by changing my philosophy'

I believe the richest gift you can give to someone is the power to change their philosophy. That is what Mr. Les Brown has done for me. He changed my belief system about how I see myself. This has given me the power to change my life. Les Brown has changed my life by changing my philosophy.

Thank you, Les Brown, for making me go out of my comfort zone and educate myself. People live empty and die full because of what I was going through: possibility blindness. To change that, they need to listen to you with an open mind and relaxed belief that it is possible. This is what I did and it changed my philosophy. I am so thankful for what you have put in my mind. Without any college qualifications, I am an entrepreneur today. It feels good to overcome my fears and do what I never thought I could do. I have a new friend because of you. Dr. Patrick Businge, whom I never knew before and now he is one of the people I am willing to learn a lot from. Thank you, Dr. Patrick Businge, for giving me the opportunity to share my story in your book. Sharing our stories is one of the best things God wants us to do while we are alive. I am so happy and grateful.

CHAPTER 17: RELIGION

Faith

While religion is the number one cause of conflict in the world, it is also the number one cause of peace. At the heart of any religion is faith: from the Latin word 'fidere' which means to trust. This leads me to St Paul definition that: 'Faith is being sure of what we hope for and certain of what we do not see'. This means we are sure of what we do not see as a result of our faith.

Life is full of examples of people who have lived by faith in extraordinary ways: Mother Teresa, Nelson Mandela, Martin Luther King, Dietrich Bonhoeffer, and many others. Life is also full of people who have lived by faith in ordinary ways: our parents, siblings, neighbours, etc. In my case, faith is one of the treasures I got from my parents when they walked to their dreams with great determination and unwavering hope. This taught me that I can achieve my dreams if I lived from a place of faith and hope.

As you read this chapter, you will discover people with faith. It is their faith that led them to move from prison to the pulpit, from loss to wealth and from self to God. If yo believe as I believe, their faith might take you to another hemisphere with a different time zone where your dreams are possible.

From Prison to the Pulpit
Charles and Nadia Anthony
Texas, USA

From Prison to the Pulpit

Let us travel to Texas: the second largest state in the United States of America and where dust rises from the shoes of horses. Texas is known as the Lone Star State where its motto is friendship. Like any other place Texas has its own downside but for the most part Texans love people. It is a great place to scale opportunity and to live your dreams alongside Texans. Here we meet Anthony Bond who is ready to share his story 'From Prison to the Pulpit' using quotes that have had the most impact in his life.

"Don't let someone else's opinion of you become your reality"

Les Brown, I did all in my human power to embrace this quote which eventually became my reality. When you grow up in poverty and around individuals whose goals are not a reality to them, you have a tendency to live the same way. All I heard was negative criticism because my father and every other male figure that had influence on me couldn't overcome recidivism and seemed to keep landing in the pits of doom (prison). So, this became the reality that I knew and the reality I carried forward. However, I am doing my best to help the next generation avoid it.

"You don't get in life what you want you get in life what you are"

Les Brown, I had to become a warrior and change the seat of my mind. I first allowed the word of God to transform me. I didn't have to look for purpose around me because I discovered it was within. In turn, I waited for it to manifest.

Discovering that I am first a man of God, a husband to my lovely wife Nadia and a father to our seven kids and one to come. Once I embraced these responsibilities, the manifestation of my hidden abilities became a driving force of my life style.

"If life knocks you down, fall on your back because if you can look up you can get up"

Les Brown, I have learned to have no more excuses, knowing that an ongoing process is progress if it is productive. No matter past nor present nor what the future holds I will continue to seek all that is purposed for me and be blessed on purpose. And as someone once said I will allow God to use me up until he calls me home. Once again, thank you Les Brown for your courage to allow yourself to be used for greatness and to pour not only into my life but into the life of others.

"That's my story and I'm sticking to it."

Les Brown, I have been listening to your YouTube videos for approximately 5 years. These videos has inspired me to be the best that I can be in all I do. I have set out to accomplish the greatness that has been buried inside of me all of my 34 years on this earth. I went from prison to the pulpit and within that transition, Les Brown, you have been one of the anchors to my ship. My wife and I have both followed you together and in our worst moments we have allowed ourselves to be fed by your soul piercing words. We are so thankful that God has allowed us to cross your path which has contributed greatly to our growth as a married couple, as parents, as children of our own, and as individuals. We continue to follow you on Facebook because we love to stay fueled by your inspiration. Lastly, we are gracefully encouraged by being chosen by Dr. Patrick Businge to share part of our story. There is more that we have overcome because of you and it is not written here. That's my story and I'm sticking to it.

'Lost faith in me, found faith in God'
Umana Anieka
Nigeria

'Lost faith in me, found faith in God'
Umana Anieka
Nigeria

Welcome to the populous country in Africa

Let us now travel to Nigeria: a beautiful country located in West Africa. It has the largest black population in the world, with nearly 200,000,000 people. Nigeria has an agriculture-based economy and is the fifth largest oil producing nation in the world. Its people are hardworking, industrious and welcoming. It is in this vibrant country that we meet Umana Aniekan, known among his peers as Africa's Nehemiah. He is hungry to share his story on how he lost faith in himself and found faith in God.

I lost faith in myself but found it in God

Getting dismissed from school can be traumatic especially if you are from a typical competitive and strict Nigerian home. I was a high achiever as a child, quiet but doggedly inquisitive. My parents always complained of my nosiness and urge to know everything. My father who was a disciplinarian never spared the rod at any point. My mother the softer one spared the rod a few times but didn't spare the prophecies and promises from heaven's gates. She always believed I was born for greater things than the world has ever seen. When I was younger, I believed in my mother wholeheartedly but as time passed and I grew up, I went through trials and tribulations to the extent that I lost faith in myself.

Fear killed my dreams

The most prominent of these experiences was my dismissal after 3 years of university education. Yes, I got into university at an early age of 16 years and in 2014, I was advised to withdraw, at the age of 19. This was the darkest day in my life. It was as depressing as it was traumatic. I wondered how I'd get back up. I pondered day in day out where I'd start from and how the world would think about me. This reminds me of the famous quote from Les Brown that, "When life knocks you down, try to land on your back. Because if you can look up, you can get up. Let your reason get you back up." Blessed be God, I got into another university. After getting up, I started dreaming again. However, I still lacked direction and what's the point of life without direction and purpose? And then it happened.

Setbacks require comebacks

In life there are moments that you will never forget. You not only define the moments but they define you. The 10th of April 2016 was one of these moments. Why? It is the day I first listened to Les Brown. I was attending a seminar and while we were waiting, the organisers decided to keep us occupied by playing Les Brown's speech *It Is Not Over Until I Win*. Like most people, I didn't care much for motivational videos and messages but then Les started speaking and underneath my headphones, I could hear him. I stopped my music and listened. For the first time in my life, I heard someone in my heart. My ears were doing the hearing but I knew my heart was doing the listening.

Born for a purpose

Midway into the tape, they stopped to start the seminar. I wrote Les Brown's name in my idea book, got home and downloaded the full video despite having limited data. That night, I listened to the tape over 3 times and every time, I felt this energy that I could do anything that I was born for a purpose that I could live my dreams. Les spoke to me in a way that made me feel special. He said things that introduced me to a new level of confidence and the next day, I went on YouTube, and downloaded as many motivational clips as I could find. Fast forward to 2017, I still listen to Les Brown alongside Myles Munroe, T. D. Jakes and others at least three times a day.

Les Brown changed my life

Les changed my life. I see things differently now, I discovered my purpose in God and that is what has kept me going despite all the trials I have gone through. I am building an e-commerce company (eMALL.ng), I have better relationships, I help people every day, and I am continuously and consciously stepping out of my comfort zone. Sometimes, when I feel down, I just play back some of Les Brown's tapes. Nothing just happens, I know Les Brown was sent for me and I can only pray that other people who were lost like me can give him a try. He has helped me achieve my dreams. I hope he will help you achieve your dreams. One of my goals is to meet Les Brown and if possible, speak alongside him. Aniekan Umana, Nigeria.

From Loss to Wealth
Felix Kawawa
Nigeria

347

Pastor and Author of 'Think Why God'

From Loss to Wealth

We are going to stay in Nigeria and meet Felix Kawawa in the Nigerian city of Lagos. He is ready and hungry to share his story with us. Felix writes this story not just from the heart but types it into his famous phone, the Galaxy Grand Neo Plus GT190601. This story has taken Felix 6 attempts to get it into its present state. Due to the lack of electricity in his house for several weeks, he types it from his phone. There are moments Felix is about to send it to me, he presses the wrong key or the phone battery runs flat and he loses everything. He has to start again. Les Brown, says, 'When your dreams are too big, the odds do not matter'. Felix is a testament of this and he now shares with you his transition from loss to wealth because of Les Brown.

I lost everything

I lost everything that I have and who I am. After spending some time in Singapore, I came back to the waiting cold and emptiness hands in Nigeria. It was a sad experience, and I can't wish it upon my worst enemies. To say that I was living comfortably, was to be likened to the proverbial prodigal son. Being wasteful, degenerated and unwanted by family and friends. Hopeful, I needed to start afresh, but I wasn't motivated at all. From the one million and five hundred Nigerian Naira that my friend gave me, I started a restaurant and bar business. At this point in time, it was looking like my life was beginning to get together again. Finally, I could see the smile on my face as I looked myself in the mirror every morning as I woke up. I was making profit and my business was going great.

All of a sudden, I lost it to the ill wind which blew one fateful night. My restaurant and bar happened to fall, and collapsed. Life caught me on the blind side at the moment I least expected it. I needed to build everything again. I had just got married to my beautiful wife, Gift, who was my only delight and pleasure. Together we started to build the restaurant business again. Then suddenly came the storm; my benevolent friend who assisted me with the money, falls out with me on principle. Overnight, he told all my consumers and friends to desist from patronizing me. They heard him, even though he wasn't living in Nigeria at this time. Again, my restaurant and bar business was losing money and patronage. It was at this moment that I decided to go back to the Lord having left the church, many years ago. This was a difficult decision for me but with faith, I decided to give my life back to God. Even though I had become a drunkard, I still haven't lost my sharpness and agility with the scriptures.

Returning to God

One evening, a certain Bishop Johnson came into my restaurant to cool off his heels as his car was under repair. Then a conversation ensued between us and one thing lead to another. After talking to him for over two hours, Bishop Johnson invited me to his church which I hesitantly obliged him. This kick-started my journey to God. It gave me a chance to start what I knew best as I had grown up as Christian. Can you imagine that at fourteen I have spoken at one of the biggest Christian gatherings in my city (Benin City Scripture Union)? At the time, 1983 precisely, I was a little wonder and one of the best sought after young preachers of my time!

Les Brown multivitamins

When Bishop Johnson opened a branch of his church in Lagos, he asked me to go and take charge of it. I hurriedly looked for someone to buy my restaurant and bar. All the people whose interest I could ascertain did not come up with the capital value of the restaurant. Reluctantly, I accepted the last person who came for the property, which I sold on a giveaway price. My Lagos journey wasn't smooth either but it was worth it. I have since conquered my fears and doubts as a result of the motivational messages from Les Brown. Just like Victor Hugo once said, "An invasion of armies can be resisted, but not an idea whose time has come". Like an idea, I had come a long way from where I was before I came into contact with what I call 'Les Brown's multivitamins'. Les Brown has become my daily vitamin.

The first time I listened to a Les Brown motivational video, I was blown away in awesome wonder. He spoke to my heart and his words stained my soul forever. There are really too many of his quotes that I have committed to my memory. One of his mantra which I recite daily is:

> If you want a thing bad enough, go out and fight for it. Work day and night for it, to give up your time, your peace and your sleep for it. If all that you dream and scheme is about it, life seems useless and worthless without it. And if you gladly sweat for it, fret for it, plan for it, and lose all your terror of the opposition for it. If you simply go after that thing that you want, with all of your capacity, strength and sagacity, faith, hope and confidence and stern pertinacity. If neither cold, poverty, famine, nor

gout, sickness, or pains of body and brain can keep you away from the thing that you want. If dogged and grim, you beseech and beset it, with the help of God, you will get it.

It is all coming back

Within two years of listening to Les Brown's webinars and YouTube videos, everything I thought l lost came back to me. Ever since, I have learned to put a handle on my life and I have everything under control. Listening to Les Brown via YouTube has once again proven that distance is not a barrier to advancement. The sun and moon may be 93 million and 240 thousand miles away, respectively, but that does not reduce its effectiveness. The moon only has to copy the sun to give her light. It is only when there is no hope of escape, will an army fight to the finish. Still steering my ship of success on purpose, towards the ideas and principles of my mentor Les Brown. In his speech *The Power to Change* he says: 'See, if you don't decide to act on your dream, if you don't decide to make a decision to live your life, if you don't decide to step into your fears, if you don't decide to say yes to your life, it will never work for you'. I had to be consistent and persevere in order to make things happen for me at all costs. Once I quietly made up my mind that there is nothing that I cannot endure, my fears left me. Today, I tell stories based on my life and that of an animal's instincts to explain the innate ability that resides in me. I gave up my restaurant and bar just to find my purpose in life.

Les Brown has changed my life

Les Brown has changed my life. I have not met him yet but he touched my life from afar. He made me a useful instrument and now I am redeeming my lost time. I am a motivational speaker like him, a relationship counselor, graphics designer, author and publisher. I have been able to write my phenomenal book THINK WHY GOD, which Miss Carolyn Maloney helped me to put in Les Brown's hands. I am now a pastor, and founder of JACOB'S WELL HERITAGE CENTER AND JACOB'S WELL HERITAGE INSTITUTE in LAGOS NIGERIA. I speak in various conferences around my locality. I am writing my third book titled GET INTO CHARACTER. My question to you is: What will you sacrifice in order for you to reach your goals and dreams? I look forward to getting your answer to this question.

CHAPTER 18: RISKING

'If you touch it, I will sue you'

The first time I saw Les Brown was during the Les Brown Institute Certification in July 2017 in Florida. During this certification, I met a lot of people whose lives had been touched by Les Brown. I vividly remember when he entered the room and how people cried, gave shouts of excitement, and sung with jubilation seeing him for the first time. As I witnessed this emotionally charged experience unfold, I could hear my inner voice telling me, 'Patrick, you must write a book about what you are witnessing'. During break time, I spoke to his two sons, Patrick and Calvin Brown about my idea of writing a book on how their father had changed people's lives. Though I thought I was going to get resistance from them, they both welcomed the idea. At this point in time, I did not have the time to start writing as I was completing my book, '7 Steps to Greatness'.

In January 2018, I sent an email to Les Brown and started collecting stories of people whose lives had been changed by him. When one of the women who was not even a relative of Les Brown got my Facebook invitation to share her story in my book, her reply was, 'You have stolen my idea. I have had it for many years. If you touch it, I will sue you'.

Where did I get the courage to continue after this unexpected response? You can easily guess: it is from Les Brown. He says, 'You wanna become a risk-taker. You wanna raise the bar on yourself. Most people won't do that. See most people engage in low-life living, low-risk living...If you're not willing to risk, you cannot grow. And if you cannot grow, you cannot become your best. And if you cannot become your best, you can't be happy. And if you can't be happy, then what else is there?'

As I wanted to do what I loved and be happy, I became a risk taker. Had I continued living a low-risk life, you would not be reading this book. As you read this chapter, you will discover how to make a transition from living a life as victim to being victorious. You will learn to follow your heart and take risks so that you discover your treasure. If you believe as I believe, I feel it is time for you to leap and grow your wings on the way down. This is because of what I learnt from the greatest professional boxer Muhammad Ali that 'He who is not courageous enough to take risks will accomplish nothing in life'.

Les Brown Changed Our Lives

From Victim to Victorious
Rachael Krasny
Florida, USA

Singer, Healer and
Founder of Read Head Credit Repair

From Victim to Victorious

Three years ago I broke my foot training for a six minute mile marathon; I had no bones in my foot. I was diagnosed with a nerve disorder and degenerative arthritis. I was told that running wasn't a good option for me anymore and that I have "an 80 year old ankle," as my doctor would say. My injury was so severe that I couldn't walk for two years. Thankfully, I received Stem Cell Growth (PRP) which saved my mobility.

At that point in my life, I felt so deflated. I felt like I had lost everything. I had been an athlete my entire life, first in competitive gymnastics; then in running, I felt as if I lost a part of me. I was extremely depressed; and it wasn't helping that I was feeling sorry for myself. There has been many times that I have felt alienated and alone; my disorder is so rare and invisible to the eye that some people assume that it doesn't exist. I also tend to hide the pain and keep it to myself because many don't understand.

As I went through this life as a victim, I encountered someone who changed my life. It was a night when I could not sleep and I was surfing the internet. Suddenly, I came across a YouTube Clip titled 'You have greatness within you'. This clip was to change my life. I started listening and all I could hear was an irresistible voice of the Great Les Brown. From this night onwards, I turned to Mr. Les Brown for relief, for wisdom, and for support.

The videos and speeches that had the greatest impact on me were, "There is Greatness Within You", "Challenge Your Limits", and "It's Not Over Until You Win". Here is one of those messages I always identify myself with from Les Brown:

> And here's what I will share with you, that in the process of working on your dreams you are going to incur a lot of disappointment, a lot of failure, a lot of pain, a lot of setbacks, a lot of defeat. But in the process of doing that you will discover some things about yourself that you don't know right now. What you will realize is that you have greatness within you. What you will realize is that you're more powerful than you can ever begin to imagine. What you will realize is that you're greater than your circumstances that you don't have to go through life being a victim.

Listening to Les Brown helped me change my mindset. One of my favorite quotes from Les Brown is, 'You wanna become a risk-taker. You wanna raise the bar on yourself. Most people won't do that. See most people engage in low-life living, low-risk living...If you're not willing to risk, you cannot grow. And if you cannot grow, you cannot become your best. And if you cannot become your best, you can't be happy. And if you can't be happy, then what else is there?' As a result, Les Brown has given me the power to take calculated risks and become successful. He has given me the confidence that I was lacking. He has inspired me to start taking action and believe in my dreams; which is to be a Motivational Speaker, Singer, and Healer.

Today, I am the Founder of an empowering community on Facebook called, #MotivatedPositive. We are a community of loving and supportive brothers and sisters that thrive on adding value in each other's lives daily. We are about unity, acceleration, and collaboration. We are obsessed with personal growth and development and we are committed to benefiting each other's lives.

Seeing Mr. Les Brown at the 4% Conference in Orlando was truly impactful; his strength and his perseverance towered over me. I was thankful to see that he was healthier than when I saw him at Grant Cardone's 10x Growth Con. Hearing his story inspired me to take risks and be the entrepreneur that I am today. It is because of Mr. Les Brown that I did not give up.

Even though I knew that gymnastics and running were out of the question I was able to turn to Pole Fitness because of my flexibility. My flexible attitude taught me gratitude; which Mr. Brown spoke very highly of. I have also adapted Mr. Brown's belief in financial freedom; I teach, I train, and I focus on educating our youth about how they can become debt free. I help people daily repair their credit and boost their credit score. My background in corporate sales and knowledge in branding, content, marketing, business development, and social media training has allowed me to be the freelance entrepreneur that I am; this year is about expansion. Les Brown taught me to use what I learned and to focus on creating solutions. He stated that effort and being prepared go a long way; that our reputation is defined by our values. Thank you, Les Brown, for changing me from victim to victorious.

Follow Your Heart
Rich Fontaine
Florida, USA

www.powerofselfent.com

Follow Your Heart

We are now going to meet Rich Fontaine in Florida. Rich is a Certified Speaker with the Les Brown Unlimited Team and an AAMCB nominated Best Selling Author who has dedicated his life to helping others find their purpose. He is the son of two lovely parents from the small island of Haiti who did not have much in the ways of finances but had abundance in love. They instilled in him to always work hard and walk an ethical and moral path. Though his family always raised him with character, Rich still fell down the wrong path, getting into trouble and engaging in fist fights at school. He left college to find a better way but instead found himself flunked out with no aims or goals. Through great study and research of all the greatest and most successful people in the world, and after reading hundreds of books, Rich found the answers to success and a proper mindset. Using his loved quotes from Les Brown, he now shares how his life has changed.

'Someone's opinion of you does not have to become your reality'

When I was a child, I remember I always felt adventurous and excited about life. It is not until I reached the age of about 10 that I started to feel different from everybody else, as in this feeling of not fitting in. The puzzle piece that just didn't sit right with all the other pieces. Being chubby did not help, as it made me an easy target for bullying. Little girls would tease me about how unattractive I was. Boys would throw papers at my head while in the bus. Though it was many years ago, I could still hear the remarks from the girl making all the kids laugh at me and the punch from the boy who thought I looked at him wrong. Even though it is in the past, these memories will always linger because what happens in our past does affect our future. At least that is what I thought.

I went through college with the same mentality, believing I was second rate because of all the affirmations that were told to me by my young peers. Unconsciously, I would sabotage myself at every turn. I failed out of college twice and I was having run ins with the law. I felt completely lost, until one day, someone said to me in an audio that made hairs on my back stand tall and straight. He said, 'Someone's opinion of you does not have to become your reality'. I turned up the volume and listened to this man's voice whose story was similar to mine.

He was teased as a child, I was teased. He dealt with poverty, so did I. He had problems with self-esteem and I had problems with self-esteem. He was a dreamer and I, too, was a dreamer. Who was this man? I began to go through the audio description and finally read the name of the man who would change my life. Les Brown. 'This is me LB triple P. Les Brown your platter playing papa.' His charisma and laughter caught my attention immediately. I began doing more research and listening to more speeches, I was instantly hooked. He became my mentor even before we met in person. I listened to his speeches every morning for one year and it kept me hungry for success. I became relentless with my goals and pushed through the adversities and suddenly I became bigger. Not physically, but spiritually, emotionally and mentally. I caught my stride, which got me to study more mentors and in turn taught me all the things I know and wrote in my best-selling book: *Destiny on Purpose.*

I graduated and began to contract as a project engineer and now I own my own Real Estate Investment Company *The Vortex PM.*

'If you ever have a choice between your heart and your mind, follow your heart'

I would have never taken the leap of faith was it not because of Mr. Les Brown: the Wiseman, the guru, the sage, the speaker, the teacher and especially the Motivator. Fear would have been running too deep in me but because of Mr. Les Brown's voice always in my mind encouraging me, I knew I could never fail. He is the master speaker and I worship his ability to light a stage on fire. I learned so much from his speaking style, but I learned even more from his heart. The day he sung my wife happy birthday over the phone, I knew I was in the right Institute, I knew I was with the right people and I had the right mentor. With his mentorship, I have spoken on stage with him and become CEO of the Power of Self Entertainment Group that provides access to other inspiring speakers to large events and venues.

The Road to Les Brown Institute
Tommy Pichardo
Florida, USA

Founder of Tommy Pichardo Enterprises LLC
Transformational Trainer, Coach, & Speaker

The Road to Les Brown Unlimited

On April 6-8th 2018, I attended my fourth Les Brown Live Certification Training Event. This marked 15 months of being enrolled in Les Brown Institute, where I was involved in the various trainings offered by the Institute to help me be a professional speaker, trainer, and coach. I also spent 9 months working as an ambassador with the Institute. My role involved talking to people who were interested in training with Les Brown Unlimited as speakers, trainers, and coaches. It was an exhilarating experience for me, as every day I was in an extremely positive environment working alongside the C.E.O, President, Vice President, and Chief Learning Officer and other ambassadors of the Institute.

While I was working there, the great Les Brown would drop in from time to time. I remember the first time he came in when I was there, my heart started racing, I didn't know what to do or how to act. I was star struck and actually it was that way for the first several times I would see him come in. Eventually I did calm down and was able to be and act normal when he would be there with us. I remember one time at the end of a day at the office, leaving to go home, Les Brown and I walking out of the office, down the stairs and into the parking lot conversing like we were long time buddies. Anyone that knows Les, knows he loves people and genuinely cares for people. It was truly an unbelievable experience for me that I will cherish for the rest of my life. You might be asking, how did I end up joining Les Brown Institute? What motivated me? Here is the rest of my story.

Les Brown Changed Our Lives

In 1989, a friend of mine invited me to go with him to go see this up and coming speaker. So, we went and after this man spoke, I remember thinking to myself, 'My God I want to do what he is doing'. It was so powerful as I had looked around the room there were people with tears in their eyes, and the rest of us, myself included had that look on our faces like - OH MY GOD!!! - It was that powerful. That was the first time I was told, "You have greatness within you!" and "It's not over until you win".

I left the event not realizing at the time that, that was the beginning of "my preparation". That same year, I went through my first divorce, and consequently had two more divorces after that. Also, I went through all kinds of adversity and failures not only in my life and relationships but also I had business failures. During and after all these failures, I was personally and financially bankrupt and even ended up homeless. I resorted to drug addictions and at one time I tried to commit suicide.

Fast forward to November 8th 2016, I went to see that speaker again. This time, he mentioned from the stage that right after this event he was having a "meet and greet" event at his office right here in Fort Lauderdale, Florida. So, I showed up and there he introduced the launching of Les Brown Institute which is now called Les Brown Unlimited. You can imagine what I'm thinking: OH MY GOD!!! (again). This was the opportunity of a lifetime for me. You can't even imagine how I felt. My words in this book cannot not described it. The only thing I remember was these words from a popular rapper that resonated loudly with me, "If you had one shot... one opportunity to seize everything you ever wanted, in one moment… would you capture it or would you let it slip?

I was in the very same predicament that many of you are in and want to pursue an aspiration, goal or dream. I was thinking to myself, 'how am I going to do this? I don't have the money. I don't have the resources. I have no formal training in public speaking. I Am too old to start doing this (after all I was 57 years old by this time)! However, inside me I felt that I wanted to do it and I wanted to do it badly, and as Les often says that when you want to do something "How is none of your business". So, I came up with some ideas on how to get the money for the tuition: sell my little trailer home and sleep in my pick-up truck.

When I mentioned to my daughter that I was going to sell my little trailer home to get the money to join the Les Brown Institute and that I would be fine sleeping in my pick-up truck, my daughter said to me, "No! Wait! Dad you can't sell your home!" At this point, I could see in her eyes and tone of voice the urgency of her not wanting me sell my home. Afterwards, I came to my senses and realized that she was right. She suggested that I sell something else. I decided that I would sell my "prized" camera, which I had paid almost $1500.

Now by this time it was the holidays. Thanksgiving was coming up, people were doing holiday shopping and I put my camera up for sale thinking I could get maybe $1000 for it. As it turned out, the best offer I got was only $200. Needless to say I couldn't let it go for that and I didn't have anything else of value to sell. I started a crowdfunding page and appealed to my friends and family for some financial support and much to my disbelief, no one contributed anything, not even a single dime!

The end of November 2016 was just a couple of days away and by this time I was in "panic mode". All I could hear in my head was, "Or would you let it slip?...do da dum...do da dum…" On November 30th 2016, I called the ambassador that was working with me to enroll me. I asked what was the minimum down payment I could put to hold my spot in the enrolment process. She said that if I can do a $500 deposit, then she could do a payment schedule. So this was it...the only opportunity to act on the opportunity of a lifetime. The very next day, December 1st, first thing in the morning, I headed to the pawn shop and pawned my gold chain, knowing that I could get $500. I got the $500.

After this, I called my kids and grandchildren to tell them that I was postponing Christmas for them and I would exchange gifts on January 25th, 2017 because I needed extra time so I could come up with the money to retrieve my gold chain, which would cost $580 to buy back from the pawn shop 30 days later. After this, I called my ambassador at Les Brown Institute and let her know that I had got the money. I got enrolled in Les Brown Unlimited on December 1st, 2016 and became a Founding Member of Les Brown Institute. My life has not been the same since then. I have been able to leave a mark on the people I encounter and I have had the privilege of encouraging and inspiring others to go after their goals and dreams. I have paid off all the tuition and I have continued doing all the training. As I write this story, I am a Gold Certified Les Brown Transformational Trainer, Coach, and Speaker. As I write this story, I have recovered my gold chain and if you see me around, pay attention to what I am wearing on my neck. You can live your dreams! GO FORTH! God Bless you. God bless your dreams, too. It's not over until you win.

CHAPTER 19: SPEAKING

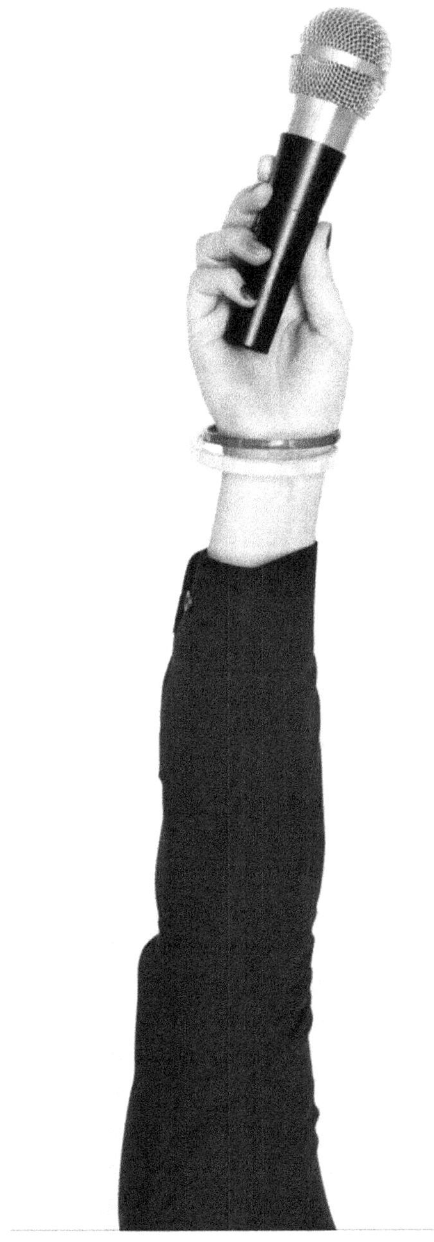

Do you want to unleash your story?

The great American poet, singer, and civil rights activist Maya Angelou said, 'There is nothing more painful than an "Untold Story" buried in your soul'. Trapped within the confines of your story are healing and transformational powers waiting to be unleashed. I believe there is a great story within you. Your story has the power to shift minds, mend broken hearts and transform the world.

In this chapter, you will read five stories from people who have been transformed by the way Les Brown tells his story. As you read Dr Ruben West's story and Jacek Salek's story, you will discover Les Brown's three key principles of storytelling. First, when you are telling a story, aim to distract the audience from the story in their head, dispute the story that the audience has convinced themselves of, and inspire them to a new life. Second, do not let what you want to say get in the way of what the audience wants to hear. Third and most important, never make a point without a story, and never tell a story without a point. As you read David Hall's story, you will discover how Les Brown's voice gave him the power to change his perception and led him to sharing the story given to him through life's experiences in Iraq, Afghanistan and the USA. As you read Ires Alliston's story and Wilken Dorcilien's story, you will learn how they rose above their circumstances, discovered their powerful voice and went on to become international speakers.

If, after reading these stories, you feel that it is time for you to unleash the story buried within your soul, get in touch. I believe that the world is waiting to hear your story.

Les Brown Changed Our Lives

The Helium to my Balloon
Dr. Ruben West
Illinois, USA

International Speaker, Author, Certified
Professional Success Coach, and Founder of
Black Belt Speakers
www.RubenWest360.com

The Helium To My Balloon

I remember watching the news and they were talking about a few raging forest fires that were out of control in the California area. They talked about how widespread the forest fires were. They talked about how rapidly they were growing and picking up speed. Interesting enough a few days later while watching the news again, I heard that these raging fires were started by an individual who was camping. It's hard to believe that a small flame from a campfire could result in such an unprecedented blaze. With that being said, the unexpected turns and growth that have taken place in my life have come about much the same way as the forest fires that I just mentioned. They came about from an encounter with Les Brown.

My name is Ruben West and while I think my current story is quite amazing I think it is still being written. Let me quickly bring you up to speed on what I have going on and why, just a few short years ago it would have been unheard of. I just returned from speaking in Dubai for the second time and being awarded a certificate from the governor of Bahrain after speaking at an event there as well. At the event in Bahrain, I had three speakers that I have personally worked with and trained participating. They spoke at the same event and each received standing ovations for their content, their delivery and their impact.

I've gotten a chance to speak in Oman, London England, Johannesburg South Africa and at present, I am booked in Calgary Canada, Amsterdam Holland and Madrid Spain. Being from the United States, I have numerous events booked around the country. I authored my own book and authored a book anthology series with six titles so far and no end in sight. I have appeared on TV numerous times and taken 30+ authors and speakers on network television. I have hosted nine live training or motivational events in various cities around the U.S. over the past 4 years. The students that I have trained have hosted events around the country as well. You may ask yourself, what does all this mean? It means that with the right connection, anything is possible.

I was originally born in Topeka, Kansas to modest yet committed parents, Robert and Rosetta West. Together they instilled in me drive and determination as well as a sound work ethic. While they told me that I could be anything I wanted to be, for some reason my dreams didn't match my possibility. I don't think this is unusual. Many times, we have people in our family or close friends that encourage us and push us to do more. But sometimes it feels as if they are obligated to say those things as opposed to saying them because they see something special or extraordinary in us. Other times I think when people are in close contact with us, it makes them "too near to hear." Therefore, it is easy to overlook what they are saying.

I remember a fifth-grade educator telling me that I would never amount to anything because I was a quitter. She came to this conclusion because she wanted me to switch from being left-handed to right-handed. As she put it, "there is no room in this world for left-handers." Well, as you can imagine switching at this stage of my life was impossible for me. Furthermore, being right-handed wasn't who I was. Isn't it funny that so many people want us to switch from being who we were made to be to something they would prefer us to be? Furthermore, the switch that they desire is not for our own benefit but for their sake. It wasn't my fault that I was left-handed. It was her fault for being an educator and not knowing how to deal with or teach a left-handed student. Unfortunately, I didn't have the ability to discern that the problem was her and not me. When she said I would never amount to anything it planted a seed in the back of my mind. I thought to myself, she must know. She meets so many students and has seen so many throughout the years go on to do great things that she must know the ones who have what it takes.

In spite of what she said, I still tried to get the most out of my life. I was not a quitter nor a slouch. I was willing to work hard and I was committed to doing great work when I was working towards something that I believed in. I remember watching Oprah Winfrey on her network television show. In this particular episode, she had the co-authors of the book called *The Secret*. They were talking about the endless possibilities for our lives and how we could change the trajectory of our lives by focus, the power of attraction and the use of vision boards. I was so engaged and intrigued that at the end of the show I created a vision board. I had pictures of me speaking to different audiences on the vision board. I had pictures of other speakers that I knew on there as well. I put this board up on my wall and committed to looking at it every day in an effort to give my life a new possibility.

Unfortunately, my enthusiasm was short-lived. The pictures on the board could not compete with the negative information that was constantly running in my subconscious mind. After about two weeks I pulled the board off the wall and threw it behind the couch. My thought was, who would want to listen to me? I am not smart and I have nothing to say.

Many years later while visiting Topeka, Kansas and sharing an idea that I had with my uncle Charles Byrd, he told me that I should look up Les Brown. Believe it or not, I was 44 years old at the time and had not heard of Les Brown. I took his suggestion and on the way back to Bloomington, Illinois I searched on YouTube for Les Brown. I saw a video of him speaking in the Georgia Dome. I got two immediate thoughts. The first one was, "this guy is amazing." He had the crowd captivated and hanging on his every word. The second thought was "why would this guy ever speak to me? He is way out of my league." In that moment, I put the phone down and let the idea go.

Six months or so later I was preparing to assist one of the surgeons that I worked with regularly on a new procedure that was taking place the very next day. He had advised me to do some research on the procedure and see if there is anything that we should be concerned with as we prepared to do the surgery the following morning. I was standing in my kitchen writing a few notes for the procedure. I walked away and then returned to read what I've written. I remember saying out loud "I'm smart!" My wife said, "what did you say?" I said "I'm smart!" She said, "I know you're smart, you married me but what are you talking about?" I laughed and said, "I just read what I have written and it gave me an insight to my true intelligence."

That moment was a shift for me. For so long I had wanted to speak but I did not believe anyone would listen to me because I was not smart and had nothing smart to say. However, with this new revelation I believed people would want to listen to me. I call that instant my break through moment. And it just so happened that six months prior I saw a video of the person that I needed to connect with. I made up my mind that I was going to call Les Brown. I looked on the Internet and found the phone number for his company. I called and asked to speak to him. The person on the phone informed me that he was not there but that they can take any order that I wanted to place. I let them know that my true intention was to speak with Les Brown. "We cannot give out his phone number." She replied. But if you send him an email he will read it and respond.

After she gave me the email address I hung up the phone and immediately sent him an email. I let him know who I was and where I was from. I let him know that I realized that I was supposed to connect with him. I also told him that if he reached out to me he would not be disappointed.

Interesting enough, the very next day when I finished assisting the doctor on the surgery we had prepared for I walked over to the counter and looked at my phone and realized that I had a message that said; "Call me" from Les Brown. That was the beginning of a whole new life.

I called him and he said "I've been looking for you." I don't know if this was something he said to everyone or just me but his words were like helium to my balloon. He informed me of a training he was having in New York and invited me to participate. I eagerly accepted and made travel arrangements. I was struck by how personable he was. He was very down to earth yet at the same time larger-than-life. In the time that I talked to him over the phone and went to the training in New York, I watched every video that I could find of him on YouTube. The truth is, my whole life I had a burning desire to speak but never thought anyone would listen. My mother is an associate pastor, I have four uncles that are bishops and my grandfather was a pastor. Speaking ran in our family but as much as I wanted to do it, something was missing. It was the confidence.

Les Brown had me go up and speak for three minutes at the training. After I sat down he walked up behind me and said softly in my ear, "we're going to share the stage together." That was more helium for my balloon. I don't think that I could have sat up any taller in that chair. My mind was racing with possibilities.

What I've come to realize is while two individuals can speak the same language they still may not be on the same frequency. There are many people who told me that they believed in me, that I can do or be whatever I wanted. But it was something about his voice! Something about his frequency. He didn't speak to my head, he spoke to my heart. It literally changed what I believed was possible for my life. I couldn't have been more hooked if I was a fish on a pole. I was all in. I attended additional trainings and continued to watch and listen to videos and CDs of him speaking at various places around the country. I remember telling him one day you will be able to call me and I will fill in for you at a speaking event. I know this was a bold statement but I truly believed it.

I remember him saying that he wanted to train one hundred thousand voices of hope. I thought to myself, I'm going to make sure he reaches his goal. I'm going to help him reach it! Just like the levels in a multilevel marketing company, I believe God placed me in Les Brown's downline in an effort to help carry on the work. I planned to amplify his efforts and magnify the message.

"Ruben, some people will not be able to hear me. They will only respond to your voice." I remember Les telling me these words as I listened in amazement. He went on to say "as much as you have chosen speaking, speaking has chosen you. You were born to do this work!" How did it affect me, you ask? Helium, helium, helium!

Here are two undeniable ways that Les Brown has changed my life. He is the high Joker and gasoline.

If you've ever played spades you know that spades override every other suit in the deck. With that being said, what's better than having just any spade? You can have the King of spades, the ace of spades, the Joker, or the high Joker. The best thing about having the high Joker is it overrides every other card that can be played. As I look back over my life, so many people have said things to me. Some of them positive and some of them negative. The educator that told me that I would never amount to anything caught me at the right time for her negative message to take hold. I was young and naïve. I believed she knew what she was talking about. At that time in the spade game of life she was the ace of spades and her voice overrode so many people who were trying to speak positivity over me. However, when Les Brown said "you were born to do this work", that was the trump card. It came at the right time from the right person. Game over!

The other undeniable way that Les Brown has changed my life is that he recognized that I was a young flame. I had a burning desire to do something greater. I had a burning desire to do something more. I had a burning desire to make a greater impact on the lives of others. He became the gasoline to that burning desire. Now I rage on, just like the California wildfires.

Has Les Brown and myself shared the stage together? Yes, we have, even internationally. Are there people who seemingly only hear my voice and react and respond to the words that I say? It appears so.

But here's one more thing I have to share with you. I was at the mall with my wife and my phone rang. I looked at it and it said Les Brown and his picture displayed on my screen.

"Hey Les. How are you doing"?

"Fine. Ruben, I have a question for you."

"Yes sir?"

"Listen, I have a presentation I'm supposed to do tomorrow in Detroit but I can't make it. I was wondering if you would be able to fill in for me?"

"Les, I've been waiting several years for this call. "YES I CAN!"

More helium for my balloon. More fuel for my fire. I wanted to take my life to the next level. I needed a secret ingredient. It wasn't more time, more money, more education or more material things. As a matter fact, the key wasn't getting more, the key was getting Les.

Thank you, Les Brown, for answering the call on your life.

Ruben West, Les Brown Legacy Team
www.RubenWest360.com

A New Me
Jacek Salek
Netherlands

Author, Business Coach and Entrepreneur

A New Me

I now invite you to travel with me to the Netherlands. Before we meet Jacek, here are some facts. The Netherlands is also called Holland. Its capital city Amsterdam is built on poles. It is inhabited by the Dutch people who are considered to be the tallest in the world. Here we meet Jacek who grew up in communist Poland.

While in Poland, Jacek participated in the democratic opposition against the communist government. He actively supported the Solidarity Movement during its legal and illegal operations to the extent that he was arrested twice by the communistic regime. After finishing medical university and receiving a grant to work on his PhD, he decided to change his career and become an entrepreneur. When in 1989 he lost all his money, he decided to emigrate to Holland in 1991. Today, Jacek is co-owner of a number of companies and travels nationally and internationally. Out of his beautiful office overlooking the North Sea, he shares with you the day that changed his life.

Tell the story

Life has given me special opportunities. It has given me special moments to be present on great events and to meet great people. One of these special opportunities happened on 30th April 2015 in Poznan, Poland when I met Les Brown during a very powerful event called 'Life without limits'. With over 25,000 people present in the stadium, it was the biggest personal development event ever in Poland. As it was a powerful day that changed my life, I decided to share my story with you.

Les Brown Changed Our Lives

When I met Les Brown, he said something that touched me. He told me, 'We all have a story and we all have a voice. If we have a voice, we can help other people'. I now believe that we all have a story. We all have a voice. It is sad to see so many stories going unheard and this is a big mistake that people are making. My life was touched by these words from Les Brown. I then asked Les Brown, 'How can I become a storyteller?' Remember, before meeting Les Brown, I never knew I could be a speaker or tell my story. With his mentorship, I have become a speaker. During this journey, I have joined Toastmasters. I can now tell my story, speak to people and motivate them more than before. Les Brown has inspired me to share what was within me.

One the key principles that I learnt from Les Brown and now use in my speaking is 'Do not allow what you want to say stand in the way of what people need to hear!' You could imagine that a person like Les Brown, a legendary speaker, does not need much in the form of preparation. I was surprised when one of the first questions he asked me and other people in Poland was: What does this crowd need to hear? What should be the main message they need to receive? I come from Poland, I should know what the people need to hear: a message of hope, faith, and responsibility for their own destiny. Then the message of unwavering persistence, unlimited opportunities, and victory. I knew all of this, but how could I tell this to Les Brown within one sentence?

At this moment, I learnt three things about speaking. This was epitomized in his quote, 'Never make a point without a story, and never tell a story without a point'. First, communication is an art! It is not about the speaker but about the public needs and expectations that makes a speech a success or failure. Second, it is not the information that counts, it is the experience one can create on stage that makes the impact. A good speech is like old Jazz. You get the general line and then you use your skills, energy and interpretation trying to make it into something special, something unforgettable. Third and last, your message must come from your heart, not from your brain!

Create the experience

After the speech I saw different people coming to Les Brown telling him what was important in his speech for them. What I noticed is that he was very warm and very open to everybody. He was listening and from time to time gave his feedback or comments. Always uplifting, always positive. At one moment a young man from the organization came with his younger sister. She wanted to thank Les Brown for telling his "twin brother story" as she felt that she was living in the shadow of her big brother. Les Brown did not only listen to her and give her a very uplifting message but he also asked if his parents were nearby. He invited them to the control room where the event was being broadcast. When the parents arrived he made them shine by telling them how fantastic their kids were and how well they had done by raising such fantastic kids. It was incredible for me to witness this. At this point, I learnt from Les Brown that as a speaker, my message on the stage needed to be consistent with who I was! It is therefore very important to create a special experience for people not only on the stage, but also in your daily life.

Become a messenger

Meeting Les Brown on the 30th April 2015 in Poland was an incredible day that I will not forget. Not only have I learned a lot, but it gave me tons to think about. He spoke to my soul when he said, 'I think of myself as a catalyst of action and a messenger of hope, turning people onto themselves and turning people onto their dreams'.

When he said this, I was with people who really cared about what was happening around the world. I was with people who were dreaming of raising half a million USD per day to fight poverty. I was surrounded with people who wanted more from life and wanted to become better. I was with people who were searching for purpose and hungry to live their dreams. This quotation made me wonder what my own purpose in life was. I question myself: What was I born for? What kind of greatness is within me? From this day forth, I decided to figure it out but for now I would like to thank to Les Brown for entering my life and transforming it into a new me.

A New Me

After meeting Les Brown and hearing his message of hope, encouragement, taking responsibility for my own life and that of others, I have gone on to write and publish a book titled *A New Me: The Art of Personal Reinvention and Continuous Improvement*. Les Brown has written a Foreword to this book. In this book, I tell the story on how I have re-invented myself partly because of meeting Les Brown.

Here is my final message to you. You need to believe that it's possible to live your dreams not your fears. Like me, you need to always be looking for possibilities in life. You need to realise that life is not always downhill. If you fall look up and get up. You have to fight through life. Les Brown says it best, 'Life is a fight for territory and once you stop fighting for what you want, what you don't want will automatically take over'. Everyone needs to know this and prepare for the fight. There is something greater in you than what you may be going through. Let what you are going through not hypnotise you. Every day, call into being the greatest in you. You have this choice. You have this challenge. Let the greatness within you continue to transform you into a new you.

'There is more to life than this'
David Hall
California, USA

I would take any drug I would get my hands on

I was born in California where I lived until I was 5 years old. My parents got a divorce and for five years I was bouncing back and forth across the country while they decided who was going to keep me. At the beginning of 6th Grade, I eventually moved back to California and stayed with my dad and my new step-mom. Shortly after moving back to California, I began to realize that my dad and my step-mom were alcoholics. They were drinking every day. I started school and before long I got involved with the wrong people and started doing drugs and drinking alcohol at the tender age of 15. I would take any drug I could get my hands on and nearly overdosed on multiple occasions.

I ended up homeless

As I was at risk of dropping out of high school, I ended up in a military academy for my senior year of high school. I graduated 6 months earlier than everyone else. At this point, I thought I was going to be on a good road to changing my life forever. However, once I moved back home, I started getting involved in drugs again and I was kicked out of my house by my dad and step-mom. I ended up homeless. I would stay with my friends but as time passed, I burned all my bridges. I had no job. I had no money. And I had no hope. After a few months, I ended up in a hotel room where I was staying with a cocaine dealer. One night, there was a knock at the door. As soon as he opened the door, I watched him get kidnapped right in front of me. I remember these two guys snatching him and putting him into a car. One of them told me that they were going to kill me if I left the room. I was so scared as I watched this man getting kidnapped right in front of my eyes. After a period of time, I said I can't stay here. Scared, I walked down the long corridor and I got out to the road. I saw the car with these guys sitting there. Immediately I ran for about 4 miles to a local hospital where my grandmother was recovering from a stroke. I slept on the floor of the hospital that night. I was homeless, a drug addict and rejected by everyone I knew. It was at this point that I realized I needed to make a decision with my life.

The roadside bomb

I joined the Marine Corps in the summer of 2006 and it was one of the best decisions I have ever made. It got me off the streets and I stayed there for 4 years. I worked mainly in Iraq and Afghanistan. At times there were literally bombs falling from everywhere in the sky. I remember in October 2009, the vehicle I was driving was hit by a roadside bomb. I was absolutely stunned, my senses were all shot, though I could hear the person next to me gasping for air. I had no clue what was going on! I couldn't see my body! I survived this but my vehicle was destroyed.

I then came back to the USA a few months later, and I went from the Marine Corps, which was a very structured environment, to living an unstructured civilian life. This transition was hard for me. I started dealing with Post Traumatic Stress Disorder (PTSD), stress, anxiety, depression, insomnia and many other illnesses. I can't tell you how many times I have been in mental institutions, being put on drugs and counselling as I was having serious problems adapting to life outside of the Marine Corps. I worried about everything. I had no idea what my life purpose was. I had no idea what to do. The first 4 years I was going to a city college, I was working a job, and I was spending all my money on alcohol and drugs every day. It was so depressing. I felt purposeless and useless. I was so self-conscious and always wondering if people really cared about me or if I was even worthy of love.

I immediately felt at peace

After moving up here to California, I spent 4 years on and off school. I would take one semester on and another off. I was having a hard time in life and with school. Suicide crossed my mind so many times. One day, I was studying in a coffee shop, and I was randomly approached by a man who asked me about what I was studying. He carried himself in a certain way. Something about him made me think it would be a good idea to ask him if I could sit down with him and have a cup of coffee, so I did. This was a man I could learn from and I aspired to be like. He was working with people at risk. After the talk, I wrote him a little letter and told him how much I appreciated his time. The next day, he invited me to his house. I texted one of my friends and said this is the address I am at. If you don't hear from me again, this is where I am. I walked into this peaceful, serene, quiet home. I immediately felt at peace. We spent the evening talking about what he was doing with his life. My initial reaction was that this guy is wealthy and he was going to be my business coach. Little did I know that he was going to dig into my soul and bring out a side of me that I never knew. He introduced me to different books and different ideas. He started planting new kinds of seeds into my mind. As time went on, I began to see myself differently. He got me on the path of self-development. For a few years, as I was working with him, he would share his wisdom with me. He started me on a journey of self-discovery and at one point, I got involved with a multi-level marketing company. I didn't do very well in the company, but as I was involved in this business I began to listen to motivational speakers.

Without your health, what else is there?

At the age of 27, I was diagnosed with testicular cancer. It came out of nowhere. A week after I was diagnosed, they removed one of my testicles. I never expected it. My doctor telling me I had cancer was the most scary, surreal experience I had ever had. It's crazy how when you are healthy, you have lots of worries and concerns in the world, but when your doctor tells you that you have cancer, nothing matters except your health. In one second, you realize that the only thing you have is your health and without your health, what else is there?

I continued going to school and I am currently in an undergraduate school. I have been plugging away at the courses and I only have a year left until I graduate with a Bachelor's degree in psychology. During this time, I started seeking God and living a godly life. I struggled with it because of the bad habits I had developed and I continued to use drugs. From the outside, it seemed things were going well, but internally I was lonely, depressed, and anxious. I couldn't sleep. Sometimes I would spend three or four nights without sleeping. My doctor tried all kinds of medication. I started regularly going to the gym. I thought I was on the right path…

Nobody thought I was going to survive

Last year, in February 2017, I was driving down the freeway and it was raining heavily. My car hydroplaned and I lost control of the vehicle, spinning around until I drifted across all three lanes and totaled my car into the guard rail. My car came to a stop still half-way in the right-hand lane. I checked myself and I realized that another truck had crashed off the side of the road as well. After a short period of time, there was a whole scene. Multiple cars had pulled over to help out. At one point I was standing near the guard rail and as I looked to the right, I saw a vehicle coming towards me that had lost control as well. Suddenly, I was hit by an SUV going nearly 60 miles an hour. My body was sent flying through the air, over the guard rail, down the embankment, and into some bushes. It took a while for the rescue team to find me. I remember laying on the ground and praying, knowing I was crossing over, but eventually I started to wiggle my fingers and toes and I realized that I was not paralyzed, even though I thought I would be. My shoulder was shattered, my leg was broken, and my whole body was in a tremendous amount of pain. I was put on a stretcher and taken to the hospital. Nobody thought I was going to survive. I didn't understand what had happened to me. I was in shock. I was on pain killers for about two months and that was about a year ago. This last year has been difficult for me. I have been dealing with stress, anxiety, insomnia, drug use, and everything else that comes with it. I felt trapped. In one night, all that I was working on was taken away from me.

There has to be more to life than this

Over the course of the last few weeks, I have been praying a lot. I have been asking God to tell me why I have been spared. Why me? A kid who has been addicted to drugs since the age of 16. A kid who grew up with alcoholic parents. A person who was blown up in Afghanistan. A person who was run over by an SUV in America? All these things could have killed me. I got to this point where I had to ask: how is this possible? Over the last weeks, I have come to the realization that God has a purpose for my life. There is a reason I am here. What I have begun to discover about myself is that I have a story and testimony that is powerful. Even though I have dealt with lots of things, I have never given up this idea that there has got to be more to life than this.

Opening my heart and my mind to my own possibilities

I have started every single day listening to Les Brown, Zig Ziglar, Earl Nightingale, and Jim Rohn. I began drilling these tapes into my mind and reading different books that have begun to open my heart and my mind to my own possibilities. One day, as I was driving and listening to a Les Brown audio recording, I began to cry heavily. He spoke the words that my heart needed to hear. His words and his voice gave me the power to change my perception and belief about myself, and change my mindset about what was possible for me. I truly began to realize that I am here to share my life and my story that I have been given through my experience and the people God has given me. I have committed myself to becoming a speaker and help people understand that if someone like me can bounce back from what I have experienced, there is no reason why they can't be successful.

I refuse to accept that there is no higher purpose for my life. I believe my purpose is to help inspire others and improve their quality of life. I have to give thanks to John Ramos who has helped me for years. I have to give thanks to Les Brown who has become a huge inspiration in my life. This man has changed everything I see about myself and my future. I have partnered with his company to develop myself as a speaker. I am incredibly excited for my future and I am fully committed to living my God-given purpose. What I know is that I am here for a purpose and I don't believe that any of us are here with no purpose. My purpose is to help people find their purpose in life. There is more to life than we experience. Les brown says we all have something special within us. I totally believe this. I am grateful to God and to people that have been there for me that could have easily let me give up. I am seeing a better future for myself.

Discovering My Powerful Voice
Ires Alliston
Georgia, USA

**Branding Expert and Founder of the
Alliston Group
www.AllistonGroup.com**

Discovering My Powerful Voice

We now travel to Kennesaw: a city northwest of Atlanta in Georgia. Here we meet Ires Alliston: Founder and CEO of the Alliston Group. For the past few years, as a Branding and Leadership Expert, Ires has had the pleasure of working with top leaders, coaches, trainers, athletes, and entrepreneurs educating them on how to create more success with their professional brands, develop their unique signature programs and monetize their intellectual property. Here is her story on how Les Brown impacted her life.

Growing up in a third world country as a young girl, I've always known that my voice mattered even though I was ridiculed and made fun of by my classmates because I wasn't a tall girl, my voice was weak or soft and I was an introvert. Needless to say, there were moments in my life that I was misunderstood and not accepted by others. However, I've often thought about bettering myself and finding ways to create an impact in me and in others.

Although I am now a mother, a small business owner, an entrepreneur and I have found my "calling" if you will, to serve, and help others to reach their maximum potential, Les Brown has also changed how I felt about my voice even more. I discovered my "powerful voice" even more as an international speaker, certified trainer and certified coach when I became a Les Brown student and began to dive deeper into my study on how to tell my story in a more effective, impactful way. Whatever self-limiting beliefs I had placed upon myself as well as what others thought of me, I discovered that my voice is a powerful tool to use to motivate and inspire others to do more!

There's this well-known quote by Les that even to this day, I carry close to my heart and that is, "You have something special. You have greatness within you!" To me, this phrase is such a critical element. It reaches deep into one's emotional and mental level. We must not allow ourselves to be distracted with what we are here on earth to do. One of our fundamental duties is to share our expertise, knowledge, experiences, stories and bless others with what we're designed to do.

In life and on our way to success, our road is often travelled alone by ourselves. Yet, we must stay focused and determined to succeed. If we want to create that greater impact – to help others, to leave a legacy for our family and make a positive difference in others, these are worth striving for.

I am honored to be one of the founding members and blessed to have the opportunity to be a part of the Les Brown conference in Florida as one of the speakers. Thank you, thank you, thank you! To those reading my story, be great! Continue to shine even more and be that light to someone who is waiting to hear from you especially the ones you have not even met, yet.

Love, Ires

From Motherland to Promised Land
Wilken Dorcilien
Florida, USA

Evangelist, Coach and Motivational Speaker
www.wilkendorcilien.com

From the Motherland to the Promised Land

I was born in a very small village in a very small country Haiti, in a traditional family, where my father worked and my mother took care of the kids. Compared to our neighbors who were very poor, my family had a very good life. This all changed one Sunday afternoon, when a good friend of my father approached me and asked for my mother. His face was very pale.

My mother came out to speak to him. He was trying to hide what he had to say so I would not hear him, but I heard him say something that changed the course of my life," Mariw malad ampil, li lopital": your husband is very sick, he is at the hospital. In our culture, that means, your husband died. Needless to say, we were very, very sad. At the funeral, I looked at my mother's face and my siblings, and knew they were crying not just because our father died but also because now we didn't know how in the world we would cope with life.

While my father was alive, we had enough money, we had enough to eat and we had a lot of friends. That all changed after the funeral. I remember a few months after our tragedy, I saw coming towards me a very good friend of the family - he used to eat with us, almost every day. We had not seen him since my father died. I felt so glad to see him again and; I started to smile as we approached each other. I went to shake his hand. I was shocked to see him pretend as if he didn't know me, and he walked right by me as if I didn't exist. That was the moment I realized I had become invisible - as if my existence in this world did not matter anymore. This idea devastated me and I wanted to hide myself where no one would see me. I walked back home, down that long, dusty road, feeling very lost and alone.

Soon, I realized, I had a responsibility to help myself and my family. Since in my village there was no job opportunities, I moved to the Dominican Republic to look for a better life. In this new country, things were not easy. There were occasions when I would spend up to three days without food, and I became so skinny and ugly, all my friends started to ignore me. It is tough to be ugly, even worse to be ugly and sick and the ultimate is to be ugly, sick and, broke. I had to get a good job, but to get a good job in the Dominican Republic, I had to learn to speak English. I didn't have money to pay for classes, there was no internet, no smart, or even a stupid phone. One morning, I found a lifeline: a VHS cassette of a movie (in English) about a huge tornado in Oklahoma. "Twister." I didn't have a TV in the small room where I lived, but my neighbor did, and I took this VHS cassette, my dear VHS cassette, and inserted it into the very old VHS player at my neighbor's. I saw people speaking English and I said to myself, this is my chance to learn to speak English. So, every day for weeks, I sat down on my neighbor's bed, since there was no couch or recline chairs, to watch the movie.

I tried to understand one word at a time, watching very closely how the actors moved their lips to pronounce the words, I found myself a piece of a broken mirror, to look at my mouth to see if I could do the same. It was not easy, I encouraged myself to keep trying when no one was around, and my hard work eventually paid off and I learned how to speak English! As a result of this learning process, I was raised from the misery of being broke and unrecognized to being hired as a supervisor at a Boost Mobile call center, having on my team, lawyers, teachers and even a doctor. My life changed, I got married.

Fast forward. I had lived in the Dominican Republic for 15 years, and knew that my biggest chance of making a successful and happy life was to move to America (the U.S.). So, on the 20th of August 2014 we landed at Fort Lauderdale Airport. My two kids, my pregnant wife and I arrived at the richest country in the world, ready to start over. Maybe I had watched too many movies, but as we talked (walked) out of the airport terminal I expected to see streets filled with Ferraris, all the kids wearing Louis Vuitton clothing, and everybody smiling and happy. My brother in law had come to the airport and took us in his car for a ride around Miami.

I was thrilled – what a beautiful skyline! Look at those buildings, those luxury hotels and expensive restaurants! Then, we got off I-95 in downtown Miami, Florida and as we turned off the exit ramped, I was surprised to see American kids lining the sidewalks asking for money, men with their dogs sleeping on the ground, women with long hair begging on the street and people passing by as if the existence of these homeless people did not matter. Was this the paradise I had dreamed of for so long? Where was the hope?

My first job in this new country was cutting grass for $50 a day. I have a family to feed and $50 was not enough. Things became so bad that I started to doubt myself, I started to think that I am not going to make it.

One day, I was watching a YouTube video and I saw this man who started to speak, saying that you have greatness in you. It was hard for me to believe that I had greatness in me. I started to investigate more and more. I started to listen to Les Brown the whole day, every day I was not cutting grass. The message and the story of this great man, has changed my life. Here I am now, a Certified Coach, Speaker, and Trainer. I have spoken to many people in 4 different languages.

Thank you, Mr. Brown.

CHAPTER 20: SUCCESS

Journey to your success

As I looked through my past emails, I found email sent to me by Les Brown on 25th August 2017. As I introduce this Chapter, I would like to share part of this email with you.

*All successful people have one thing in common, '**Successful people invest in themselves without fail**'. When I started investing in myself, I took a Greyhound bus from Miami to Dallas to attend a motivational workshop. My momma made me frog legs, sandwiches, and sweet potato pie that were supposed to last the entire 24 hour trip. When I arrived at this massive seminar, **I was hungry**…I ate the frog legs within the first two hours of the trip! But more importantly, I was hungry for information. I sat in every seminar. Asked questions and studied every presenter's walk, pace, and tone. No one understood why I would take a 24 hour drive for self-development when I had a good paying job as a garbage man. And when I arrived back to Miami still as a garbage man, I was taunted by friends… **"Ok Mr. Big Shot, motivate me!"** Don't worry I thought, I was **determined** to make something of myself. After years of study, networking, and working as a disc jockey, **my big investment was paying off.** I was voted as **#1 speaker in the WORLD!** I'm thankful to still stand tall in the industry today. Here's what I know about you without even knowing you…You are cut from a different cloth and **destined to succeed.** I only attract OQP, **Only Quality People** and you are one of them. **You have greatness in you! -Les***

Les Brown Changed Our Lives

Like Les Brown, I attribute most of my success to education. I have always had a hunger for education. It is because of this hunger that invested a lot of money to the point of gaining 7 university qualifications from 7 universities. In this chapter, you will encounter 5 examples of people who have been hungry for knowledge and how their hunger led them to success. If they have been successful against all odds, why not you? At the end of this chapter, my wish for you is that you gain all the knowledge you need to make the rest of your life the best of your life.

Dr Patrick Businge

Les Brown Changed Our Lives

Life On The Other Side

England, UK

Life On The Other Side

I was a police officer from over 8 years in the UK. In 2010, I was married with 2 older girls and twin boys that were 2. At this time, I was wrongly accused of a crime of (fraudulently signing a caution form) after interviewing a taxi driver that had assaulted an elderly gentleman. I was found guilty in the crown court and sentenced to 12 months custodial sentence. I mean prison!!!

As a consequence, I lost the job that I had done and loved for over 8 years. I had my beloved family with two young children taken away from me. I found myself in prison: in a place all alone with people that wanted to kill me. I was at my lowest point. I had no one to turn to and felt like giving up on life. Though there were other people like Nelson Mandela who had been accused of crimes they did not commit, it never crossed my mind to make links with them.

While in prison, one day I heard a piece of music on TV with a voice over from a guy doing motivational quotes. I really enjoyed it and did some digging to find out who it was. It was Les Brown. I asked my wife to download me some of his shows on an MP3 player so that I could listen to him while I sat alone in my prison cell. For 3 whole months and each night, I listened to Les Brown. He motivated me each day to keep going and to never give up. Here is one of his messages that had a big impact in my life:

> That it's necessary for us to begin to look at the future, know that it's possible that we can have our dream. Yes, it is. Other people have done it, then we can do it. We failed a lot of times. Well,

a lot of other folks failed and eventually they came back and they succeeded. So it's possible we can have what we want. And we know that we want to get it, it's necessary that we align ourselves with people that think like we do. It's necessary we get negative-do-nothing-people out of our lives. It's necessary we never stop learning and growing and developing ourselves. It's necessary that we never give up. We know that it's you, it's me, it's being responsible for our stuff and deciding that we're going to keep on keeping on, that we're going to find a way to win or to find a way to make it happen. And we know it's hard, it's not going to be a picnic. Yes, it's hard, it's hard and we will do it hard. And once we do it hard and we go through, we realize it was worth it and once you discover it was worth it, it is done, it's done.

When I was released from prison, I had the motivation to build on his message. My mindset had changed. It is because of Les Brown that I had the power to say to myself like Nelson Mandela that, 'As I walked out the door toward the gate that would lead to my freedom, I knew if I didn't leave my bitterness and hatred behind, I'd still be in prison'. Effectively, it is because of Les Brown that I walked out of prison with a new mindset. I was hungry for success. I used this mindset to start my own business.

I have now pursued other opportunities like magazine and TV deals. I now work on several shows and have a huge following in the UK on social media. I work with lots of celebrities and I'm still growing, learning and most of all happy. Les Brown literally saved and changed my life for the better and it is still to this day changing and bettering my life. I still listen to Les Brown whenever I can: when picking the kids up from school, on a run or just relaxing. Eight years on, I am still hungry. So, thank you Les Brown.

Fighting For My Dreams
Neil Huntley
England, UK

Fighting For My Dreams

We are now going to travel to Nottingham, England. Here we meet Neil Huntley. Neil has been in combat sports for over 25 years. He is an inspiring person who, with his martial arts background, has gone on to fight for his dreams. His story is about losing, learning, failure, persistence, triumph and creating a legacy for future generations. He firmly believes that no matter what happens to us, we have to keep fighting for our dreams.

In November 2010 while I was out with friends, I was attacked and stabbed with 9 injuries in total including internal bleeding and a punctured lung. In my fighting career, I was always knocked down but I would always get back up. At this point in my life, I could not get back up and my worst nightmares sank in. However, I had someone greater watching over me.

I was rushed to the hospital where I received 5 hours of operation in the theatre to save my life. This was a miracle as the medical professionals thought I wouldn't make it. After recovering, I suffered depression and anxiety for nearly 2 years. I started to drink a lot. I tried counseling and visited various doctors but nothing worked as I refused to take anti-depressants. I couldn't sleep but after watching motivational videos and listening to Les Brown, I started to sleep at night with ear phones on. His words and listening to him every night changed my life. I got motivated by messages like these.

It's hard. Easy is not an option. It's hard living.
Life is hard...So if it's hard then, do it hard. Now
what are you — how do you hang in there doing

the hard difficult times, Les? You must have faith. You've got to believe in yourself. You've got to believe in your abilities. You've got to believe in your service, your company, your ideas unquestionably. You've got to have faith and that faith gives you patience. That it's not going to happen as quickly as you want it to happen. A lot of things are going to happen that will catch you off guard. And so therefore you've got to deal with and handle it as it comes. And not only that, but that faith and patience drives you into action.

So ladies and gentlemen, if you want to make your dream become reality, the people that are running at that dream know that it's possible that you can live your dream. That it's necessary that you are relentless, that you have a plan of action, that you are creative. The people that are living that dream are fighting winners, to attach themselves to. The people that are living their dreams, are the people that know that, if it's going to happen, it's up to them and they are resolving within themselves it's not over until I win. The people that are running after that dream know they're going to have hard times, they keep on running because they're saying within themselves: I'm the one, I'm the one. No matter how bad it is or how bad it gets I am going to make it. The people that are running after their dreams are the people that are hungry.

These messages gave me hope and courage. As I was a professional fighter, I managed to fight again and win both in life and in boxing. I have become a champion in different weight categories. I now run my own gym. I have helped so many people over the past 3 years now and I genuinely think that is why I'm here. I am constantly raising money for charity and through the gym I have changed people's lives in health and happiness. So, I am very humbled to be in the position I'm in. My biggest, goal one day, is to meet Les Brown, shake his hand and thank him as he put me on the right track with the right mind set of never giving up.

Chasing Greatness
Benjamin Hinton
Pennsylvania, USA

Chasing Greatness

I sustained a traumatic brain injury January 9th, 2013. In my experience I have learned that the farthest distance in life we will have to travel is the 18 inches from the head to the heart. In our lifetime and in the society we live in, we must lead with the heart and the mind will follow. I started running full marathons in 2015. I started out running in the Pittsburgh Marathon. I was in good shape but I wasn't in marathon shape heading into my first one. I ended up with a finishing time of 5 hours and 49 minutes. The hardest physical experience and mental experience I have ever put myself through.

In 2016, I started listening to Les Brown on his YouTube channel. It was winter treadmill training heading into my second full marathon. Heading into the Pittsburgh Marathon, I knew it was going to be more of a mental game than anything. We must remember they say life is 90% mental and 10% physical. I started listening to Les Brown in particular on those early or late training runs. His principles helped form some of my life philosophies. Les says, "You have something special, you have greatness within you". Those words have taught me to "Chase Greatness". Everyone has greatness but not everyone chases greatness. They don't have the tools within to defeat their Goliaths.

The second thing Les taught me was that we are either running away from, running towards or stuck in a problem. This thinking changed my life philosophy as well. It reminded me to live in the solutions not the problem. In those early days of my personal development Les reminded me that 80% of our conversations are with ourselves. After a traumatic brain injury those early conversations with myself were not good! Thanks to Les, I learned how to change my inner dialogue. With these new skills I gained from Les Brown I have been able to understand the importance of self-management in time management. Your life management is yourself management.

We only have so much time on God's green earth to figure this stuff out. Some people live just to die a slow death. We only have so much time to serve others while serving our purpose. Thanks to Les Brown, I have now run 6 marathons since 2015. In September of 2017 I was able to achieve another marathon PR finishing time of 3:11.15. My current philosophy is "Be Encouraged Everyday! To encourage others is to encourage ourselves, to love others is to love ourselves". If I can chase my greatness like Les has chased his, so can you.

Father In The Skies
Benjovi Benson
Turkey

423

Father In The Skies

We now move to Istanbul, Turkey. Here we meet a man whose history and story have been shaped by Turkey. Turkey is blessed with clear waters, high mountains, small idyllic villages, and beautiful culture. It is among the birth places of ancient biblical history and has great food. Although living in Turkey is not easy not only for foreigners but also nationals, this man says that he has managed to go through tough times because of the motivation from Les Brown. His name is Benjovi Benson and here is his story.

Les Brown's words pierce my heart every time I hear them. I am able to influence everyone around me with my positive attitude while facing difficulties. I have never met Les Brown, but I watch and follow his videos on YouTube and Spotify. There have been a lot of down times in my life but Les Brown's words refresh me every day.

Thanks to Les Brown I now think positively about life. I never feel broke because, in my heart, I am always rich and grateful. Les Brown's words inspire my effort in my work place. Lots of things have changed ever since. I hear his encouragement and I believe without these videos from Les Brown and my belief in God, I would not be this successful in my life. Les Brown is the father in the skies for me.

It's Possible to be Successful
Anonymous
Zambia

I was born in a rural village in Zambia. I come from a family of 8 and I am the 6th born child. My Mother died when I was 7 years from unknown disease. Before my mother died, my father got married to the person who used to be the friend of my mother. I was left with my eldest sister who took care of me and helped me start school. I used to sell flutes and boiled eggs on the road for me to get money and continue schooling. As time went by, I started selling fertilizer on the market with the help of my elder brother. When I reached Grade 8, I moved out of my sister's house and started staying alone. I did this and became responsible for my life at the age of 15. Through my business of selling fertilizer, I managed to complete Grade 12. I then moved to Lusaka where I currently live.

It is when I moved to the capital city Lusaka that I bought a mobile phone and I was able to go on Facebook. In the city, I met a man who was a pastor. He helped me learn life in the city and through him, I was introduced to the networking marketing business. During the network marketing meetings, I met a man who advised me to listen to Les Brown.

When I started listening to Les Brown, my mind started changing. I learnt about positive thinking and learnt that it was possible for me to become successful, despite my background. I made it a routine that every day I listen to this powerful mentor. I tell myself every day that I am a winner and I will do everything possible to make my family change the way they think too. And this is what I am doing now. So, every day I make sure that I learn something from Mr. Les Brown. I follow him whenever he is online. I have never met Les Brown but I believe in him. I know that one day I will be with him chatting with him the chair.

CHAPTER 21:
TRANSFORMATION

Metamorphosis?

Reading the word transformation, led me straight to the life of a butterflies who go through a complete metamorphosis. To grow into an adult, they go through 4 major stages: egg, larva, pupa and adult. Each stage has a different goal and depending on the type of butterfly, it can take a month to a year to go through this stage. When we look at butterflies, we can hardly tell the challenging stages they have gone through to become beautiful.

Like butterflies, we too undergo visible and invisible transformation in our lifetime. While we look towards some of the transformations, we hate to think about or go through some others. We consider them to be tough times in our lives. Thanks to people like the American televangelist, motivational speaker, and author Robert Schuller who encourages us by his words, 'Tough times never last, but tough people do!'

The 5 stories you will read in this chapter are examples of people who have gone through profound moments of transformation. Like the beautiful butterflies, you can hardly tell the tough times they have gone through. While some have been able to move from homeless to millionaires, from crime to commitment, from drugs to dreams, others have confidently marched to their destinies. They all testify that what has helped them to go through tough times and become the tough people they are today is Les Brown. I now invite you to discover these transformed people.

From Homeless to Multimillionaire by Planting Better
Antonio T. Smith, Jr
Texas, USA

Best-Selling Author, Les Brown Certified Speaker, Corporate Trainer and Coach
www.AntonioTSmithJr.com

From Homeless to Multimillionaire by Planting Better

Antonio T. Smith, Jr. is a prolific public speaker, delivering over 2,000 keynotes at various colleges including prestigious universities and colleges in the United States of America, and for The United States Army personnel. You can listen to his top-ranked business podcast that reaches over 70 countries and is translated in 60 different languages. Antonio is an internationally recognized trainer and speaker, and best-selling author in self-help and religious categories. He specializes in Cognitive Behaviour Therapy, Business and Strength Training, Leadership, Teleconference Presentations, Personal Breakthroughs, Prosperity Consciousness, Mindset Training, and all levels of effective marketing, as well as scholarship in the Old Testament. He owns one of the most successful education companies in Texas. In his journey from abandonment to homelessness and brokenness, Antonio has developed a "plant better" attitude that he teaches people to plant better seeds in order to have a better life. Here is his story and how Les Brown has helped him achieve this unstoppable success.

Homeless at the age of 6

My life did not need a drastic change. I had already done that a long time ago. I was born in Galveston, Texas. By the time I was 6, I was homeless and I would stay that way until I was 14. I would eventually age out of being a child of the State of Texas when I was 18. I spent the bulk of my childhood living in a trash-can-dumpster not too far from where my biological parents lived. Well, did live, because their drug addictions would leave them homeless, too. I failed the 5th and the 6th grade— honestly. I failed them both. I was putting myself through school and couldn't keep up with the homework because every night I would go back to live in this dumpster with no lights, no running water, no food, and tons of bugs. Just imagine that for a moment. I was assigned homework and had no home. Crazy. In fairness, my teachers didn't know until I repeated the 6th grade and I was picked up by police officers for being homeless. My teachers were just doing their jobs.

Today, I can say I graduated with honours, speech and debate honours from Galveston Ball High School because of the Speech and Debate Coach Mr. Michael Merritte. Mr. Merritte saved my life before I ever met Les Brown. I have also graduated with my Bachelors as the President of the Theological and Religious Studies Honour Society. I also have graduated with my Masters while being number one in my class. I'm a pretty successful businessman as I write my story. You might be asking: So, how did Les Brown change your life? Well, Les Brown changed my life in 4 different ways.

I am an introvert

First, I am an introvert by biological makeup. I have many extroverted skills which I had to develop in order to eat as a kid. If you are wondering if you are an introvert or an extrovert, just simply ask yourself this question: Am I completely drained after social interactions, even if with just two people, or am I charged up and ready for more after social interactions? If you are like me, I fall into the first category. I regularly speak to thousands of people, I take time for each one of them, but when I am finished and

I get to my room at night, I am dead. I need to recharge with a book and a beer.

Yet, Les Brown and The Les Brown Institute forces me to open up to the people within it. This is hard for me for two reasons. One, I am an introvert. Two, I'm extremely private. I have to be the weirdest motivational speaker and public figure alive. Yet, both of these are true. However, Mr. Brown and his friends and co-labourers will allow you to be who you are, but they won't let you do what you have always done, because they understand that what got you here, won't get you there. So, they snatch greatness out of me, whether I am an introvert or not. I think they also understand that introverts are the most successful of people- sorry, I couldn't resist taking a shot at extroverts. It's true, however. We run the world.

The First Family of Motivation

Secondly, Mr. Brown has a family! I know, not a mind-blowing concept to you, but it is for me. Let me explain. I HAVE NEVER BEEN RAISED IN MY ENTIRE LIFE. Never. By the time I started remembering my own memories I was permanently homeless. I never had a childhood. I have never been nurtured in my entire life. I had to deal with this as I grew older. So, to be in a room with Mr. Brown, his sons, his daughters, and his friends who have become family, a homeless kid like me from a small tourist-driven city, this would stand out in a major way.

I was with Mr. Brown and his family not too long ago. They were all on stage. While some were making sure he drank water, others were telling embarrassing yet hilarious stories about their dad, and every single time his children talked, he would stop talking and listen. I couldn't believe my eyes. Then he would talk, and they would listen. They talked about their ups and downs, and all of their funny stories and all I could think was, "Wow!" If I die today, I could honestly say, I have lived all of my dreams and got to see a family be much more than a family. They were actually friends. I have been through more than most in my life, I can tell you this for sure, just because you are family, does not mean you are friends.

He made me a millionaire for my team

Okay, wait a minute. I am not a millionaire- yet. Though, it is interesting that when I had the opportunity to work with Mr. Brown and partner with him, I immediately said to myself, 'There is no way that a man like this is going to tolerate me leaving my team behind'. So, I didn't. I took them all and plan to bring along the few more people we have hired recently. I cannot give this credit to myself. Sure, most people will point out my good character, and they have— and I am grateful. But that is not what happened. My image of Mr. Brown is what happened. And that image will make me a millionaire millions of times over.

I just figured that Mr. Brown and I have very similar stories. We both were labelled unable to learn in school. I failed two grades because I listened to what they said about me, he struggled because of the same. He was adopted, much younger than me, I think. I was adopted at 14. I simply figured that he and I understood that you don't leave your GOOD friends behind, for anything. Ever! Emphasis on "good". In my mind, Mr. Brown would have been mad at me if I didn't bring them along with me. How could I live with myself if I did? So, I didn't. Of course, Mr. Brown isn't judgmental, I just understand he has a high standard for himself and his character. I better have the same.

He taught me how to tell my story

Oh, dear reader, if I can't do anything else today, I know how to tell my story. Mr. Brown taught me how to tell my story in a manner that inspires others to believe that they have their own stories. He taught me that I have greatness in me when I was already living a life that displayed such greatness. It takes a powerful man to look in your greatness and then challenge you to be even greater! Only Mr. Brown and the Les Brown Institute can do that. I am convinced of it. Today, I meet so many people that said, 'Les Brown changed my life'. They come from all walks of life. Every time I hear people say that, I always say the same thing, 'Yeah, he has a habit of changing lives'. Yes, you do Mr. Brown. Yes. You. Do!

The Les Brown of Rhode Island
Hector Luiz Cruz
Rhode Island, USA

435

The Les Brown of Rhode Island

We now travel to the "Ocean State," Rhode Island. Though it is the smallest state in America, it has the largest concentration of historic sites. Its waters form the gorgeous coastline and makes it beautiful, unique and ripe with opportunity and history. Here we meet the 35 year old Hector Cruz, hungry to share his story. Reading his story and connecting the dots backwards and forwards, I am led to believe that he is The Les Brown of Rhode Island. Read on and discover why I think this way.

Special education

Les Brown

I was born in Miami, Florida, in an area called Liberty City in an abandoned building on a hard linoleum floor with my twin brother. We were six weeks of age when we were adopted. When I was in fifth grade, I was identified as EMR, labeled educable, mentally retarded, put back from the fifth grade into the fourth grade and stayed in that category until I got out of high school. I don't have any college training. But I met a high school teacher who one day changed my life. I was waiting on another student and when he came in, he said to me, *'Young man, go to the board and write what I'm about to tell you.'* And I said, *'I can't do that, sir.'* He said, *'Why not?'* I said, *'I'm not one of your students.'* He said, *'It doesn't matter. Follow my directions now.'* I said, *'I can't do that, sir.'* He said, *'Why not?'* I said, *'Because I am educable mentally retarded.'* And he came from behind his desk and he looked at me, he said, *'Don't ever say that again. Someone's opinion of you does not have to become your reality.'*

Hector Luis

I was born in 1982 with respiratory issues and diagnosed with ADD and epilepsy in 1987. Throughout my years in school I took special education. Being in special education I was picked on every day. Because our class room was one room in the entire school. All my class subjects were in it. When I would go to lunch I would get picked on. I can't tell you how many times I was called a "retard". It hurt me to feel how I felt. And I believed them throughout all the years in school. From 1997 to 1998 I would sit on the stage steps at my high school, Blackstone Valley Tech in Upton, Mass. Being called retarded most of my life, it was enough with that. But not being able to learn like others did with my disorder, it was even more frustrating. Regardless of what people told me and knowing that my mother never graduated because she was a young mother at the age of 16, I had the courage to take on my studies, as I did not believe what other people said. I graduated and received my High School Diploma in 2000.

Adopted

Les Brown

And she looked at me, she said, 'Leslie, and you caused me so much problems as a boy, you were always into stuff.' She said, "No one could have convinced me that day when I walked in that house and this lady was holding you and your brother and she said, 'Ma'am, I want you to promise me two things'. And she said what is it? She says, 'One, promise me that you won't separate them'. She said 'I want them raised together. We're going to know each other. I got pregnant while my husband was away in the war and I can't keep him. Promise me that you won't separate them'. She said I promise I won't. I've never had children. I promise I won't separate them. And she said, 'Promise me that you'll never tell them about who I am because if my husband ever found out he would kill me'. She said I promise. And she said that she gave them to us and, and she kind of cried and she was walking out the door and she looked at my adopted mother, she said, 'Remember don't you separate them'. She said I swear to God, I won't. I won't separate them, I'll keep them together. And she said, as I held you all in my arms I never had any children my own. I didn't know how I was going to do it but I knew with the help of God I will do it''.

Hector Luis

In my twenties my mother and I didn't have the greatest relationship and I left home. Most of my life I was on medicine to help me, and I felt that life became more troubling than beneficial. I became cynical with my parents, with society and I felt I lost all hope. Knowing I could never go back home, I was adopted by the streets.

Being on the street opened up my eyes to all different kinds of people. I had to steal food because I had no money. I couldn't get a job because I had no documentation. During the winters I would store my food in the snow because it was the only way I could keep it from going bad.

Never give up

Les Brown

And I went over to a radio station, asked a guy that and told him that I was interested in broadcasting. He looked at me and maestro had his overalls. He said, *'Do you have any broadcasting background'*. I said, *'No sir, I don't'. 'What do you do?' I cut grass'*. Young ladies asked me what kind of work I do and I was working on a garbage truck. I say, *'Well, I'm a sanitary technician'*. He said, *'We don't have any job for you'*.

I decided that that was something that I was going to do. I decided I'm unstoppable. I'm going to go up and here, I'm going to do this. I started going to the radio station every day developing a relationship with the people that were doing what I wanted to do. And that's what I encourage you to do. Whatever area, you want to go and find people that are doing it the way you want to do it and develop a relationship with them.

Hector Luis

I never gave up, I walked all over, miles to find a job. It was difficult. But I did. In 2004 I got a job as a cook at a local pizza place in my area. I would go to work and when I was done I would find places to sleep. At times I would sleep at the police station because it was so cold outside. Some friends and family did help me along the way, but only for a short period of time. After a while I saved enough money to buy a car. And funny thing about it- it was the Chief of Police's daughter's car, which I saw at the police station that I was sleeping at. It was a 1993 Ford Escort. So, I got my car and kept working on finding more work.

In 2008, I met the love of my life. We ended up having 3 beautiful children. After my 2nd child was born in 2015, I kept stretching myself. I became a bouncer at 140 Pub and Club in Bellingham, Mass. I then got an opportunity to become a chef. Within that year I was certified and competing with 20-year chef veterans who had more education than I did. I never stopped growing. From there I went from kitchen to kitchen to learn from the best high end chefs.

Personal development

Les Brown

It's very important for you to believe that you are the one to make this happen. I remember this high school teacher Mr. Leroy Washington, at the end of school one June, it was just a few days before we were supposed to leave. And I just got my report card and it indicated that I had failed history and I failed English and I would have to go to summer school. And I was feeling within myself that I was a failure that I'm slower than most people in getting paperwork. And I was feeling down on myself and very negative. And Mr. Washington was giving a speech to the graduating seniors and I was in the 11th grade. And even though I wasn't supposed to be in there, I went in there because the speech he was giving, that speech was for me. And as he talked my heart began to beat fast, tears began to run by my eyes and I was in the back just listening to him, because he said — and he was a very dramatic man. I still talk to him to this day.

He said, *'As graduating seniors of Booker T. Washington High School, I want you to know that you are blessed and highly favored and that as you go toward the future, begin to know that you have greatness within you. And if just one of you here begin to envision yourselves as being blessed and highly favored to reach your goals, if just one of you capture the essence of what that means that you have greatness within you and responsibility to manifest that greatness, that you can make your parents proud, you can make your school proud, you can touch millions of people's lives and the world will never be the same again, because you came this way.'*

And the students gave him a rousing standing ovation. And as he left the auditorium, I ran down the steps and I caught him in a parking lot and said, 'Mr. Washington?' He said, 'Yes.' I said, 'Do you remember me, sir? He said, 'No.' I said, 'My name is Leslie brown. My mother — she works in the cafeteria. I am one of the twins: Leslie and Wesley'. I said, 'Mr. Washington, but you know I've got these big dreams and I like talking to people, I love people', and I said, 'I want to work with people and I've got this dream of buying my mama a home. Could I do that, Mr. Washington?' He said, 'It's possible, Mr. Brown.' And as he walked away I called him again, I said, 'Mr. Washington?' He said, 'What do you want now?' I said, 'I'm the one, sir'. I said, 'I'm the one — you remember me, I am Mrs. Mamie Brown's boy. I am the one, I am the one.' And you must feel that that's why you're here, because you are the one.

And I remember when PBS first played one of my specials called You Deserve, one Sunday afternoon in Miami, Florida, I had some friends call him to tell him to tune in. And he watched the program, he called me in Detroit and I answered the phone. I said, 'Hello?' He said, 'May I speak to Les Brown, please?' I said, 'Who's calling?' He said, 'You know who this is.' I said, 'Oh, Mr. Washington, it's you.' He said, 'You were the one; weren't you?' I said, 'Yes sir.' He said, 'And you were so crazy.' I said, 'I know but I'm rich now.'

Hector Luis

One day I was home and was listening to YouTube. And Les Brown's YouTube video came on. I had no clue who he was. It was titled Les Brown "You gotta be hungry!" That was the day my life unfolded all into one video. Hearing him say he was labelled EMR. It spoke to me. So I studied into what personal development was and how it works. My grandmother who passed away said to me. 'You are special. You are going to change the world'. So I did everything I could to learn ways to digest information. As I kept watching more of Les Brown's videos, I could relate to it in so many ways.

My eagerness to learn more become greater. I started looking into the pioneers who he wanted to learn from. It started with Earl Nightingale (you don't get in life what you want you get what you are). Then moved on to Wayne Dyer, Jim Rohn, Napoleon Hill, and Winston Churchill. I studied any and every book I could get my hands on. From that point on it was official that I dedicated my life to personal development.

Now I own a Facebook page with my own company name, Dynamic Minds. I'm in school for personal training and looking into becoming a certified speaker like he was. That's how Les Brown changed my life. I can't say I'm very successful, but I think I have found my purpose thanks to that one video I watched from Les Brown. It spoke to me all of my life. Thank you Patrick for giving me this wonderful opportunity. I hope one day I can shake Les Brown's hand and personally say thank you.

Marching Forth To My Destiny
Inna Joy Martin-Carter
Alabama, USA

Marching Forth to My Destiny

I am humbled to share my story with you. I am forever grateful for the opportunity to be a part of this inspiring book. I will start by narrating the story that has always touched me since I came to know Mr. Les Brown and I have decided to use it as a title of my story. This story is at the end of Mr. Les Brown's speech titled 'It's Possible'. It is about Jack and Les Brown says,

'And one of the things Jack always talked about is that he wanted to have his funeral while he lived. And so he invited a few friends, Wayne Dyer and myself and a few other speakers. He didn't tell us why we were there. But once we gathered there, the church they told us in the room, that Jack is going to announce the congregation, he's bringing his doctor up. The doctor is going to say that we felt we could keep it in remission it's out of remission and he doesn't have much time left. And whatever words you want to say to Jack that you would say if he had made his transition, speak those words now. We were shocked and we were somewhat stunned until Jack got there.

They brought him in a wheelchair and boy, was he courageous and he had a strong smile and they helped him up the steps. And he said behind the podium and each of us got up, and we said a few things about Jack and the impact that he made on our lives. And he said, the doctor after announcing that Jack didn't have long, he said, 'Doctor, I accept what you say but it's possible, that that does not have to be the case. But if it is, I will enjoy life to the very last breath I take, even the chemotherapy I will enjoy that'. And Jack did, ladies and gentlemen. And when they said that all of his vital organs were failing, they called his family and his whole church staff to the hospital and said he's dying. And so they came and they all gathered in the room. And Jack at that time was unconscious. And he gained consciousness and he looked at them and he said with what strength he had, he said, 'I want to thank you all for being here. You've been a great staff to me'. He looked at his sons, his daughters, he said, 'You've been a great family. So don't feel sorry for me, I'm ready to go. I'm looking forward to the next adventure'. And he sat there for a while, lay there and he closed his eyes and he lost consciousness.

About an hour and a half later he opened his eyes and he looked at them and said, 'This is embarrassing. I'm not dead yet'. They were laughing through their tears. They said, 'Jack, you are a character'. He said, 'Hey, I hate giving up this kind of control'. So they predicted that Jack would die at the end of February and then on the second, they said he won't see the light of day, he will be dead by morning. Ladies and gentlemen, Jack died on March 4. And we believe that even in his dying Jack sent his congregation a message that I want to give to you with his permission. March 4 is the day he died and we believe Jack was saying 'March forth'.

I began following Les Brown on 10th January 2018. This remarkable speaker has travelled from the United States to London, England for an engagement and had returned to the United States. He had been hospitalized and had gone through a surgical procedure. And not one day did he fail to encourage, inspire and educate me and others. In spite of his own challenges, he remained focused with a great sense of humour and humility. He was living the message of Jack: March forth in spite of your circumstances. That is greatness. I was witnessing his greatness unfold in my eyes. I stood in awe of this wonderful and gifted man of God.

I never dreamed of being a student of world renowned motivational speaker of all time; Mr. Les Brown. In his stories and using his life as an example, I have come to know that Mr. Les Brown feeds the soul, encourages the spirit and energizes the body. The diction and positivity of his words are so inspiring, that I could not ignore them. I had to start matching forth.

Through his life and stories, Les Brown has motivated me to 'keep on fighting' for I have something special, there is greatness in me! And I believe this! Mr. Brown has moved me from a state of hoping to action. He has inspired me from thinking that one day I will achieve my goals to marching towards my goals every day. With Mr. Les Brown and his words, I have embarked on the journey of transformation. Listening to positive messages, reading personal development books and making positive affirmations, has become my ritual. I'm making radical changes to my lifestyle. Here are a few of his quotes that inspire me that I have turned into my personal affirmations

- "Inna, it is possible to unleash my full potential"

- "Inna, you must separate truth from fear"
- "Inna, you must make the rest of my life the best of your life"
- "Inna, life is a fight for territory. If you stop fighting, what you don't want will take over. Keep fighting."
- "Inna, commit thy way unto the Lord; trust also in him, and He shall bring it to pass" from Psalm 37:5.

Indeed, Mr. Les Brown has inspired me and enriched my faith in God.

I am currently reading a book, suggested by Mr. Les Brown titled 'The Road to Your Best Stuff' by Mike Williams. In Chapter 2, Mr. Williams gives key insights into Les Brown's unique styles of speaking. One of the insights is that Les Brown finds elusive connecting points, creates connections with people, and invites them into his vulnerability with humour. There's an artistry to his great gift for speaking. I agree with Mr. Williams for whenever I hear Mr. Les Brown say, "You are a Masterpiece, because, you have a piece of the Master in you". I believe this!

Thank you, Mr. Les Brown, for recognising that your life is a gift. I can testify that how you have lived your life is a gift back to God. I am a testament of your gift and my life is forever changed! You have told me, 'as you look into the future, while other people are giving up feeling like victims, feeling powerless, becoming negative, turning on each other rather than to each other, feeling that they can't make it, "be ye not conformed to this world but be ye transformed by the renewing of your mind" with the mindset of that it's possible, that we can save this generation…So I say to you whatever your dreams are, whatever you want to do, do it in the spirit of Jack: March forth'. Les Brown, I am matching forth and I have become unstoppable because of you. It is not over until I win. Thank you.

From Crime to Commitment
PJ Douglas
Florida

From Crime to Commitment

Well, back in 2009 I got into some trouble and spent 4 years under house arrest. Upon getting off house arrest, my daughter was born. Four months after having her, my daughter's mother left for good to Miami, Florida. I was left with my daughter as a single father. With a criminal record, this wasn't the most promising title.

So, I figured if I work harder than everybody else, I would break through to financial stability. However, this never materialized. It never dawned upon me that my mindset was still affecting me. One day, I decided to watch a motivational video to try to get me out of a little bit of the slump I was in. This is when I heard Les Brown's voice for the first time. In his speech, *It's Not Over Until You Win!*, Les Brown said:

> It's very important for you to believe that you are the one to make this happen. I remember this high school teacher, Mr. Leroy Washington, at the end of school 1 June, it was just a few days before we were supposed to leave. And I just got my report card and it indicated that I had failed history and I failed English and I would have to go to summer school. And I was feeling within myself that I was a failure, that I'm slower than most people in getting paperwork. And I was feeling down on myself and very negative. And Mr. Washington was giving a speech to the graduating seniors and I was in the 11th grade. And even though I wasn't supposed to be in there, I went in there because the speech he was giving, that speech was for me. And as he talked

my heart began to beat fast, tears began to run by my eyes and I was in the back just listening to him, because he said — and he was a very dramatic man. I still talk to him to this day. He said,

'As graduating seniors of Booker T. Washington High School, I want you to know that you are blessed and highly favored and that as you go toward the future, begin to know that you have greatness within you. And if just one of you here begin to envision yourselves as being blessed and highly favored to reach your goals, if just one of you capture the essence of what that means that you have greatness within you and responsibility to manifest that greatness, that you can make your parents proud, you can make your school proud, you can touch millions of people's lives and the world will never be the same again, because you came this way.'

And the students gave him a rousing standing ovation. And as he left the auditorium, I ran down the steps and I caught him in a parking lot and said, 'Mr. Washington?' He said, 'Yes.' I said, 'Do you remember me, sir? He said, 'No.' I said, 'My name is Leslie brown. My mother - she works in the cafeteria. I am one of the twins: Leslie and Wesley'. I said, 'Mr. Washington, but you know I've got these big dreams and I like talking to people, I love people', and I said, 'I want to work with people and I've got this dream of buying my mama a home. Could I do that, Mr. Washington?' He said, 'It's possible, Mr. Brown.' And as he walked away I called him again, I said, 'Mr. Washington?' He said, 'What do you want now?' I said, 'I'm the one, sir'. I said, 'I'm the one — you remember me? I am Mrs. Mamie Brown's boy. I am the one, I am the one.'

And you must feel that but that's why you're here, because you are the one. And I remember when PBS first played one of my Specials called *You Deserve*, one Sunday afternoon in Miami, Florida, I had some friends call him to tell him to tune in. And he watched the program, he called me in Detroit and I answered the phone. I said, 'Hello?' He said, 'May I speak to Les Brown, please?' I said, 'Who's calling?' He said, 'You know who this is.' I said, 'Oh, Mr. Washington, it's you.' He said, 'You were the one; weren't you?' I said, 'Yes sir.' He said, 'And you were so crazy.' I said, 'I know but I'm rich now.'

It felt as if he was speaking to me and only me. As Mr. Washington told Mr. Brown "You have greatness within you", these words sparked the WANT to change in me. This process has been difficult. Cutting off friends, even some negative family members from my life was one of the hardest parts.

Since then the progress, not only financially but with all my relationships is completely amazing. Those who thought they knew me now don't even recognize me. My family sees an immense change in my behavior as a father and business owner. How did this change start? It all started by me listening Les Brown's speech *It's Not Over Until You Win!* in the Georgia Dome.

Then in February 2017 I finally got to see him in person in Orlando, Florida. And ever since then my hunger to succeed has been insatiable. If there is ever a chance to thank him or express my gratitude for him being who he is I will take it 100 percent. Les Brown, Mrs. Mammie Brown's baby boy, I am thankful for your existence. You made your mark on many but I thank you for the mark you put on me. Listening to you has allowed life to open doors for me and as you say, 'If your dream is too big, the odds don't matter'. Your life's lessons have changed my life. And thank you Patrick Businge for reaching out. This is more than I've ever expected from Les Brown's Team.

From Drugs to Dreams
Anonymous

From Drugs to Dreams

I would like to express how Mr. Les Brown has helped me to make a difference in my life. I was home alone, flipping through channels on TV. On this boring evening, I was just looking for something to pass time on. I then came to PBS where I began listening to someone that I had never heard of before. However, his talk grabbed my interest. This man was talking about how he came up from being left in a shoebox. Then being raised by Miss Mammie Brown. In his story, I realized that he was blessed and I knew that this was not a mistake. It was a divine word from GOD through Mr. Les Brown.

Next, I heard him talk about the graveyard. He said, 'The graveyard is the richest place on earth, because it is here that you will find all the hopes and dreams that were never fulfilled, the books that were never written, the songs that were never sung, the inventions that were never shared, the cures that were never discovered, all because someone was too afraid to take that first step, keep with the problem, or determined to carry out their dream'.

At this point, he had my full attention as he talked about great minds going to waste. At that point in my life, I was a drug addict with a job. My job was my hustle. I was trying to figure out just how I was going to get out of a drug infested marriage and an insane life style. Listening to Mr. Les Brown helped me do just that. Les Brown helped me make a transition from a life of drugs to a life of dreams.

CHAPTER 22: UBUNTU

Dr Patrick Businge

A manifestation of Ubuntu?

You might be wondering and asking, what is *Ubuntu*? Ubuntu is an African word that is difficult to render into any other language. Despite this being the case, Ubuntu is Africa's greatest gift to the world. It refers to the African belief that our humanity is intricately linked and we all belong to a bundle of life. About *Ubuntu*, the Nobel Peace Prize winner Desmond Tutu says,

> When you want to give high praise to someone we say "Yu, u nobuntu"; he or she has *Ubuntu*. This means they are generous, hospitable, friendly, caring and compassionate. They share what they have. It also means that my humanity is caught up, is inextricably bound up, in theirs. We belong in a bundle of life…I am human because I belong, I participate, and I share.

The stories in this book are a clear evidence of Les Brown as a man with *Ubuntu*. Through these stories, Les Brown is seen as a father, brother and a close family member who is open to give and share his life. After having a house fire and still wearing the same clothes after the fire, Les Brown took Wishum Gregory, aka King Twitty, from New York to the Beltway Plaza Mall and went into a Webster's Menswear store. Talking to the manager, Les Brown said, 'This is my friend, King Twitty and he's had a character-building experience. Tell them your sizes, Twitty…After that he said give my friend 7 suits, 10 shirts and 14 ties'. As he went through marital problems, Samuel Gerson Andrisse from Belgium discovered Les Brown and came to the conclusion that Les Brown was like my brother telling me what to do.

In now invite you to read the rest of this chapter and discover how Les Brown has manifested his *Ubuntu* in the words of the people who have experienced these life defining moments.

Dr Patrick Businge

Touched by the Fire...
Awakened by the Flame
Wishum Gregory King Twitty
New York, USA

Celebrity Photographer and Digital Collagist
www.wishumgregoryart.com

Touched by the Fire...
Awakened by the Flame...

It was on Sunday, April, 21, 1996 that I assumed I was on the path to building my business and living my dreams. With a $200 investment with my last unemployment check two years earlier, I now have $10,000 worth of paid for inventory and $8,000 in cash to be deposited into the bank on Monday. Somewhere along my journey I had heard your life can change in a flicker of an intention, and April 22, 1996 at 2:16am it was the beginning of a truly life transforming experience.

While working on my computer in the front office of my condo, I detected smoke coming from my bedroom. Racing back to that area I discovered my bed was on fire and it was rapidly spreading. In a state of panic I ran out the front door to warn the neighbours above my terrace condo was on fire. Someone called the fire department but as luck would have it, it took almost 11 minutes for a single fire truck to arrive with two volunteer firemen who had trouble with their hose and water pressure. By the time backup arrived my condo was totally destroyed. Escaping in only a t-shirt and my underwear, some kind lady gave me some clothing. Now I find myself angry, confused and wearing size 9 ladies' jeans and size 12 tennis shoes (I wear 9-1/2). After sleeping in my van the first night, I called a friend, Sheryl Douglas who had been working sales for me and she invited me to stay at her house around the corner. Something my father said to me as a teenager was now becoming a reality. He said son, you have to able to handle two basic experiences, life transforming and character building. And this was definitely a life transforming experience.

The following day me and a neighbour, Chonda Swann, went back to the condo to try and salvage anything not destroyed by the fire. After hours of going through the rubble, everything I now owned would fit on a 4' x 6' table. The most memorable of those things were $30 in Susan B. Anthony dollar coins and two dozen embroidered "Protected by Jesus" t-shirts. When Chonda found the t-shirts in a burned out room, she marvelled that not only weren't they damaged but had no smell of smoke. Maybe this was a sign of something good was about to happen to me. That feeling was short lived when the third day after the fire my insurance company told me my policy had lapsed and I had no coverage. At 48 years of age, now behind on my bills and dreams, I concluded it's over and I've failed. I was too embarrassed to ask my parents for help and had accepted the fate God was punishing me for my years of walking on the wild side of the dark side and dancing with the devil, along with all the lies and emotional hurt many women in my orbit experienced, including two ex-wives.

It was now Friday, April 26, 1996 around noon. After a few days drowning in pools of self-pity and with the few dollars left, the demons in the Tanqueray bottle were calling me. Walking about ¼ mile to the liquor store, I was determined to pickle my mind and body with alcohol until I was in a world of unconscious bliss. Approximately ten feet from the entrance I get a number I didn't recognize on my pager. Fortunately there was a pay phone right outside the liquor store and a voice in my head said make the call. I called the number and a voice I hadn't spoken with in over 21 years since leaving Columbus, Ohio in disgrace, was on the phone. It was Les Brown. How he got my pager number is still unclear. He said 'King Twitty, I heard you had a fire and I need to see you. I'm at the Greenbelt Marriott so meet me there tomorrow at 11am.' Now I'm filled with excitement and also real fear.

After graduating from Capital University and opening my photography business, I first met the man about town Les Brown during his heyday as a disc jockey and promoter at WVKO radio station in Columbus, Ohio. Over the next few months we became extremely close friends and eventually formed a company called Three Tuff Guys Entertainment with another jock at the station, Bill Moon. It was Les Brown who paid my legal fees for my first divorce and aided in the purchase of my new Cadillac Eldorado. We were like brothers, Les Brown and King Twitty. Over time the fast life twisted and blinded my life perspective. Hanging out with big name entertainers and unsavoury players in the life, I became addicted to this new lifestyle of chills, thrills, and dollar bills. Instead of pursuing dreams and visions I was now seeking thrills and fantasies.

My lifestyle was not in alignment with Les Brown's goals and we started to drift apart. And after years of trusted friendship, my faulty moral compass took over and I ended up embezzling thousands and I mean thousands from my best friend Les Brown. When Les found out he was furious and in those days Les was a force to deal with if you crossed him. On occasion I had witnessed the Liberty City side of Les, especially when money was involved. Word on the street was Les is looking for you and he's going to kick your ass, he's really hurt and mad because he trusted you like a brother. With Les Brown looking for me along with a few other enemies, I decided it's best to leave Columbus. I packed up everything I could in a 6' trailer, kissed my girlfriend Leslie J. good bye, and proceeded to move back to Washington, DC with my parents and make a fresh start.

Now 21 years later Les Brown is telling me to meet him at 11:00 am at the Greenbelt Marriott. At the time I didn't know he was in town for a major speaking engagement. Still wearing the same clothes after the fire, I washed up in a gas station restroom and called my friend Margie B. to give me a ride to meet him. During the 3 plus mile ride I was thinking what I would say to a man I had double crossed and embezzled money from 21 years earlier? Is this going to finally be my day of reckoning with Les or what? Do I tell him how I have become an integrity based person now and have been transformed by a renewing of my mind? Do I tell him I'm God-awful sorry for my past actions or what? Right before arriving at the hotel I remembered a passage from one of his books and decided to greet him with "If I wouldn't do it today, don't convict for my past."

Looking like a homeless crackhead, I sauntered up to the desk at the Marriott and asked the sister behind the counter for Les Brown's room. Giving me the side eye while looking me up and down, I determined she wasn't about to give me that information so she asked my name and I said tell him it's King Twitty. She called and said he'll be down shortly. Nervously waiting in the lobby for 20 minutes Les finally appeared and hollered across the lobby, 'King Twitty!'. I felt a little at ease thinking he's not going to knock me out in the lobby. I greeted him with my "If I wouldn't do it today, please don't convict for my past life." To my surprise he hugged me and asked me how I was. I repeated about how devastating the fire was. He asked again, "how are you?" Hoping he might give me a few dollars, I told him how I had a few burns on my hip and feet trying to get the $8,000 I had lost in the fire. Again he looked me straight in my face and asked again "but how are you?" I answered, outside of being broke and homeless I'm ok. His next reply bewildered and confused me. He said, "This is only a character-building experience, but boy you look homely" and we laughed. Next thing out of his mouth was "Let's go shopping."

We proceeded to go to Beltway Plaza Mall and went into a Webster's Menswear store. The manager, Versandra Kinnebrew and others recognized Les and were excited to see the master motivator in person. He next said, 'This is my friend, King Twitty and he's had a character-building experience. Tell them your sizes, Twitty.' I replied 40R and 15-1/2 x 34 shirts. After that he said give my friend 7 suits, 10 shirts and 14 ties. As the clerks started bring suits out for my approval, I became overwhelmed by the moment and tears of joy began flowing down my cheeks. Emotionally overwhelmed I asked to use their phone to make a collect call to my parents. My father answered and accepted the call and told me he hadn't had time yet to ship me some of his old suits and shirts. I said 'Dad, Les Brown the motivational speaker is buying me 7 suits, 10 shirts and 14 ties.' My dad's first response was 'Why are you taking advantage of him, whoever he is?' I said 'Dad it is Les Brown, the millionaire married to Gladys Knight.' Evidently not impressed, my dad closed by saying 'Make sure he buys you some underwear.'

After that mind-blowing experience, Margie B. and I drove Les to various radio promotions, the last one being with

Joe Madison the Black Eagle. Because of my appearance I offered to stay in the car. He said 'Come on Twitty, let's go.' Madison was very courteous and gracious during Les' interview, probably thinking I was some homeless guy Les was helping. After hours of interviews at local stations, we took him back to the hotel and he said he would be right back. Ten minutes later he returns to the car with a check made out to King Twitty for a $1000 and asked for a number he could reach me on later. Wow, it's been over 6 hours and no mention of my past sins. As he left the car his last reply was 'Remember Twitty, "Honesty is the fashion that never goes out of style" and "It's not over until you win." At the time I didn't realize that last statement would be the title of one of his best-selling books.

Now you might say Les Brown has already changed my life but two weeks later he super-sized it. Les always stressed that an opportunity of a lifetime must be seized during the lifetime of the opportunity. And my opportunity was about to come calling. He had called and asked if I was available to work with him at a big national Amway Diamond in a week. Of course I said yes without checking schedules or anything. He was flying me to Hershey Pennsylvania to help coordinate sales at his booth and paying me $500 a day plus expenses. Talk about my life changing in a flicker of an intention, my life was back on fast forward. When I arrived at the rally Les said he wanted me to handle the cash sales of his books and cassettes and help his sons Patrick and Calvin with a marketing strategy. He knew I had a strong background in those areas. Wait a minute, our friendship dissolved over my mismanagement of thousands of dollars and you're putting me in charge of money?

After setting up for the venue and preparing for sales, like a Las Vegas dealer I took off my jacket and partially rolled up my sleeves to make sure everything was visible. Les came out for his session with over 18,000 screaming Les Brown with the sound system blasting "Eye of the Tiger" waving 2 American flags and the crowd went wild. That night we took in over $50,000 with $35,000 in cash. After his autograph session after his performance, we went back to his room as I stacked his cash in piles of a thousand dollars. And still no word of my past as we continued the tour.

My experience with Les Brown truly changed my life and not only was it life transforming and character building, but also life sustaining. After being temporarily homeless and experiencing catastrophic financial fluctuations in 1996, thanks to Mamie Brown's Baby Boy, I've gone on to live my dreams and have become the ultimate possibility thinker. I've learned to honour the past, imagine the future but live my todays. No matter what you're experiencing in life always strive to be intention driven, purpose based while maintaining a proactive mindset, a bias for action and a commitment for excellence. I can truly say my 46 year relationship with Les Brown has been one I will always cherish and respect. I continued to wish my brother a faith-filled and blessed life. Les Brown changed my life and I'm alive, I'm alert, and I feel good.

Hold the Vision
Samuel Gerson Andrisse
Belgium, EU

Founder of Kensyle Recruitment
www.kensyle-recrutement.com

Hold the Vison

We now travel to Brussels in Belgium where we meet Samuel, a native of Mozambique. Here is his story. I got married to a Belgium woman while in Mozambique. When my wife got pregnant, she came to Belgium to have our baby. While we were living in Mozambique, my wife always said that she had depression. I spent a lot of time trying to help her. However, it came to a point when I realized that she was not fine in her mind. For example, when she was pregnant with our second baby, she did not tell me till she was 6 months. When I asked her, she said that she did not know.

When we came to Belgium, she asked for divorce. This was at a time when I was trying to learn French and get a job. I come from Mozambique and we speak Portuguese. I was thinking of what I was going to do. My wife started telling people of things that I did not do. She told them that I was abusing her physically and sexually. All these things she was telling people while I was trying to help her see her doctor and contact her mother so that she helps her with her depression. Because of these things, I was crying.

I was crying

A man saw me crying and I told him my story. I told him that I was working in Human Resources in Mozambique and I was managing people in my department. I loved my job in Mozambique and everything was going well for me until I left my job for this woman. This man gave me a book from Zig Ziglar called *Born to Win*. In this book, I was advised to read lots of books and listen to lots of cassettes. One day, I was looking and I found Les Brown, who told me one important thing, 'It's possible'. I started believing that it is possible.

Les Brown was telling me that whatever I was doing was possible. From this day forward, I decided to listen to Les Brown every day. I learnt a lot things from his speeches like *You Gotta Be Hungry*. For example, in this speech I learnt how to fight for my dreams.

> When would a baby walk? It will walk when it walks. That's when it will walk. Les, when will you be known nationally as the motivator? I will be known when I am known. That's when I'll be known. Don't get caught up in — well, I've tried it four or five times and things didn't work out. If there's something that you want and you're hungry for it, you've got to do whatever is necessary until and when you give the best you can and that's not enough, you must do what is required. And don't give up on yourself. Don't throw the towel in so quickly. Many people give up on the one yard line. What if they have the determination just to keep on knocking, there is a funny thing about life. If you are home one day and someone is knocking on the door and you say I don't want to be bothered today. And if that person just keeps on knocking, can you believe that the fool is still knocking? Pretty soon you say what is it? What do you want? And that's how you got to be about your dream.

My brother telling me what to do

Les Brown was like somebody talking to me. He was like my brother telling me what to do. Whatever he was saying was feeding into my own life. One day, I was cooking for my children, he said that I have to go and read books and pay for conferences. He told me that the only thing I have to do in my life is to hold my vision. If I held my vision, the how was none of my business. Now, after 5 years, I believe that great things are happening to me. After my wife telling people that I was abusing her while I was working hard, I can say that it's possible. Today on a Saturday night at 9pm, I am seating here writing this story and there are people outside driving my taxis.

Les Brown says that if everything works well, I won't have the opportunity to grow. Life has given me these opportunities to grow, to learn more, and to become someone I was not. I thank God and Les Brown for helping me hold my vision. I have now learnt French in less than 3 years. My wife who should have helped me never told me what to do. Les Brown told me to dream big and I continue to dream big. I am starting a big project and I know I will do this because of Les Brown. While attending a big conference, I have met a vice president of a company with over 220 million euros and he would like to partner with me. If it was not for Les Brown, I would be in a depression. I would be here in Belgium like a homeless person. Today I have my kids with me and I have the judge on my side in the divorce with my wife. I would like to shout out and say, 'I won…I won'. For me winning is to see that it's possible and you can win too.

Fired up After the Tunisian Revolution
Selsabil Hamrouni
Tunisia

Dr Patrick Businge

Fired up After the Tunisian Revolution

We are going to travel to Tunisia in North Africa. Situated on a large Mediterranean Sea coast is its capital, Tunis. This beautiful white city extends along the coastal plain and the hills that surround it. We are going to go through its narrow streets and admire the ancient city popularly called Medina. Here we will recreate the life the 28-year-old Selsabil lived just before the Tunisian revolution. We will then journey with her to Dubai in the Middle East where she will tell us the rest of her story after the revolution.

I am the oldest daughter of my parents and I have 4 sisters. Our life was happy and perfect and my dad was successful in his professional life, until one day he lost everything after the crises of revolution in my country, Tunisia. The same year I finished my studies and started working for my parents and sisters. After some time it became hard sponsoring the 6 people of my family. I then decided to leave the country to Dubai to start again and become stronger. I felt responsible yet alone all the time. Then I started listening to motivational speakers and reading books for the same reason. I felt I needed that or else I couldn't progress.

As I listened to motivational speakers, I felt Les Brown was the best!!! I started listening to his speech every day on my way to the work. Sometimes I could listen to the same speech for many times and I would find myself saying, without knowing, what he was saying. For example, I would find myself saying "It is not over until I win". This became my daily affirmation as I have a lot of goals that I am sure I am going to achieve. "Shoot for the moon and if you miss you will land among the stars" is my favorite quote from Les Brown because I always feel it is true every time I achieve something.

Today, I feel stronger and Les Brown has allowed me to discover another part of life. I have started seeing life differently only because of Les Brown. I have been inspired by this quote 'You gotta be hungry'. Whenever I am making plans for my goals and I remember 'You gotta be hungry', I quickly realize that I must be hungry for what I want in life. It is now 4 years I have been living in Dubai. I am one of the leaders in my company. I sometimes give training to my staff and in my training I use quotes from Les Brown to start or end my training sessions.

One of my sisters recently finished her studies as an architect. She has started helping me and I feel proud now that I have supported her to succeed with her studies. We are planning to restart our father's business that had collapsed during the Tunisian revolution. Restarting this business will take time. It will not be easy. However we are inspired by Les Brown and we are hungry. We know that easy is not an option. We will do it and it is worth it.

So what can I say? I used to work only for my family and sometimes I did not have anything for myself at the end of the month! While working hard for a purpose and keeping positive and powerful, I succeeded in my own career as well. Even now, after my morning prayers I have to listen to Les Brown's speech, although I know all of it now, but I can't stop.

I don't know if Les Brown is aware of the changes he is making in people's lives. That is why I have decided to share my story in your book. I would like to thank him for changing my life. I wish to meet him one day and say 'Thank you' while he is looking at my eyes. He is the closest person to me that I never met or spoke to. He will surely feel and see the impact he has had in my life.

Easy is Not an Option
Simone Tessari
Guatemala

Easy is not an Option

We travel to Guatemala: a country with over 15 million people and with a lot of rain. Here we meet Simone who now tells her story.

What led me to start listening to Mr. Les Brown was a motivational video I got from my dad on New Year's Day. At that time, I didn't know who was talking on the video. It went something like this: 'It's not going to be easy, easy is not an option!' That video change my life. I haven't been the same since I heard it.

I had looked on YouTube for more motivation videos and listened to many motivational speakers. When I heard Mr. Les Brown I was amazed. I heard him with my heart. I heard the human side of him: all that he has been through and how he has overcome so many obstacles. I just wanted to hear more of him. Les Brown told me that I have greatness within me. His message has helped me in every area of my life. It has motivated me to be more thankful for what I have and to have faith in my future. It has made me disciplined to accomplish my goal which is to lose weight and be able to run in a marathon and also to become an Iron Man. I now listen to Les Brown every day in the morning when I go to run. It motivates me to change my life and pushes me to do more and become more.

CHAPTER 23: VISION

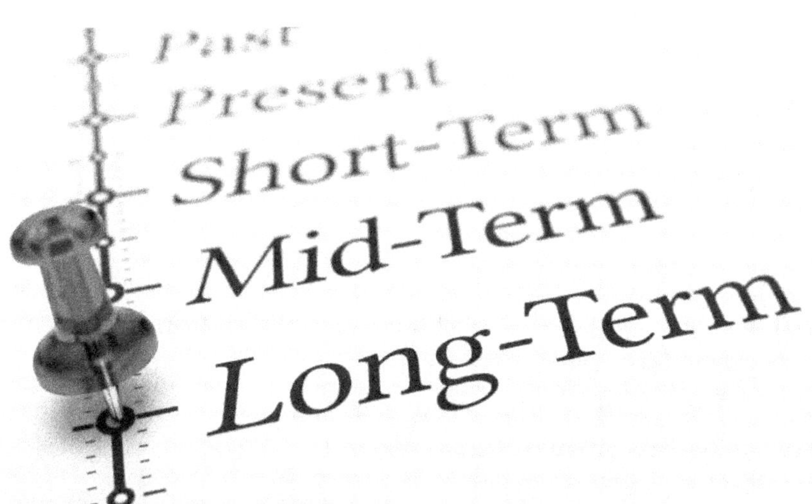

V.I.S.I.O.N©

In Proverbs 29: 18, it is written, 'Where there is no vision, the people perish'. For me this means that if you don't have a vision for your life, you are at risk of having a premature death. Having vision is essential to having a long and fulfilled life. In my book '7 Steps to Greatness', I consider **V.I.S.I.O.N** to be the 5th step to greatness. The acronym **V.I.S.I.O.N** stands for:

- Visualise
- Inside the mind
- Senses
- Imagine
- Overcome obstacles
- No fear

To help you remember this V.I.S.I.O.N©, I urge you to learn this sentence: I Visualise Inside my mind with my Senses and I Imagine Overcoming obstacles with No fear. Let us now read stories from visionaries who have been inspired by Les Brown to get more from life.

A Visionary Inspired by Les Brown
Lynnette Richardson
Virginia, USA

Candace Jamila Richardson Avents RIP
www.cjafoundation.com

Candace Jamila Richardson Avents RIP

My daughter died in 2013 at the age of 30 after a 15 month battle with Triple-Negative Breast Cancer (TNBC). She was motivated and inspired by Les Brown as she lived her life. She was a wife and mother of 2. She was also a business owner and director of a school. She used Les Brown's quotes, books and videos to train her staff and encourage everyone she met along the way. It is because of Les Brown that she achieved more in 30 years than most people do in a lifetime up until she took her last breath.

Candace was born on December 6, 1982 to Ralph and Lynnette Richardson. A native of Portsmouth, VA she graduated from I.C. Norcom High School. She received a BS degree from Liberty University, Lynchburg VA and was an entrepreneur and published author. As a loving wife and mother of two talented children, she was a devoted follower of Christ. She led numerous volunteer and mentoring events across the Hampton Roads area. She led Youth Ministries at Little Grove Baptist Church and served as Director of the Foundation Learning Center. Foundation Learning Center (FLC) was started as an after-school program that grew into a school that provides a Christian foundation and quality education for students.

CJA Foundation

In September of 2005, Ms. Candace, as she was affectionately called by her students, introduced the Learn Though Play curriculum. Children learn Bible verses, foreign languages, sign language, phonics, and math among other subjects. FLC remains committed to the original ideals of setting a Christian foundation for all students.

Prior to Candace being called home to be with the Lord in 2013, she established the CJA Foundation to lead efforts around education and enrichment in the community.

It was her desire to establish a lifelong legacy that inspires young people to achieve personal goals. Her legacy indeed lives on among the 75+ current students and 20 staff members of FLC. There are several projects that we are trying to solve including building a space that will meet the needs of our growing community population.

We need your support. With your charitable donation, we will be able to carry out and fulfil the mission of FLC, Changing our Community one Christian scholar at a time". You've met the VISIONARY who was inspired by Les Brown...please help fulfil the VISION! You can read more about the CJA Foundation she started at www.cjafoundation.com. Thank you for your support.

Lynnette Richardson
Loving mother of Candace Jamila Richardson Avents.

From War to Blessed Hill Children's Centre
Lucy Sabiiti
Uganda

www.facebook.com/blessedhillcentre/

Children of war

We now travel to Uganda: a country that has had a turbulent history of war. Here we meet Mrs. Lucy Sabiiti who has been taking care of children orphaned by war and disease since 1998. This has come with a lot of challenges including being accused of child trafficking and put in prison. Mrs. Sabiiti is an example of a person who believes that if your dream is too big, the odds do not matter. Here is her story and how, of recent, her mindset and that of the children at Blessed Hill Orphanage is changing because of Les Brown.

Fighting for education

After losing my brothers and sisters to HIV/AIDS in 1998, my husband and I found ourselves looking after 9 orphaned children. We had to ensure that these children were fed, clothed and got formal education. Having to look after a family of 15 children including ours meant we had to search for additional resources which were scarce. Thinking about the cost of education in Uganda, which was not free, my husband suggested that we hire teachers so that we home-school these children. This was the cheapest option.

Using my savings from my salary, I rented a house in Makindye in Kampala where we were able to take care of my brothers and my sisters' children and other orphans. We had about 30 children. But in 2007, the cruel hand of death, snatched my husband, a sales manager at Gulf Air. This left me the burden of paying the teachers single-handedly, feeding and clothing the orphans. But I had to carry on. However, more problems were yet to come. My landlady also died, leaving behind children who were not interested in the extension of the rent contract of the house we used for the children. In early 2008, we were thrown out of the house and I had no choice but to send back some of the orphans to the communities where I had picked from.

Towards the end of the same year, I rented a piece of land in Wakiso District in Uganda where I constructed a simple shelter to accommodate the orphans who were now numbering 170. But in 2013, the landlord evicted us because he wanted to develop his piece of land. As I tried to find a place for them, I was arrested by police on accusations that I was dealing in child trafficking. I cried. I knew I was doing the right thing. When I was released, I continued building my capacity. God was on our side as a visiting pastor known as Mark said he could get some sponsors for the orphans. Indeed, Pastor Adrian from England was among our first sponsors who bought land to build a permanent home in Mityana in Uganda where we now have over 200 orphaned children.

The war inside of children

Most of these children have lived in war especially by the Allied Defence Forces (ADF) and tribal clashes in the Rwenzori region and DR Congo. They have witnessed their parents die either by war, disease or natural disasters such as landslides. Most of these orphans ran from their home villages and escaped to Kampala, the city where they hope to begin a new life through approaching voluntary organisations, relatives and well-wishers. Not all of them are lucky to get to Blessed Hill Orphanage.

Dr Patrick Businge

In January 2018, I read a book called '7 Steps to Greatness' written by Patrick Businge. In this book, he narrated how he too had lived in war but did not let war live in him. He wrote, 'though I was living in war during those years, I did not let war live in me. The belief that war was not permanent allowed me to dream while I was awake. During the one year while I was out of school, I dreamt of going back to school and completing my education. I dreamt of completing my education in a world class university. I dreamt of teaching about peace and writing stories that restored hope in people'.

I was touched by his story and his dreams. As he shared a similar experience of war, it made me think of the 200 orphanages I had at Blessed Hill and the dreams they had. As I thought about this, I realised that, though Blessed Hill was a safe zone for the orphans, there was still a lot of war inside them. This was manifest in the way they treated each other, the nightmares they had at night in their dormitories and in the fighting among themselves they got involved in. Though physical war had stopped for them, they were still experiencing a lot emotional and psychological war inside them. I got in touch with Patrick Businge and asked him to propose me a solution. He suggested that I should listen to Les Brown and he would change their lives.

I started listening to Les Brown's videos and they have really inspired me to think about the education programme that I would like to give these children to get rid of the war that is inside of them. Here are some of the powerful messages I have heard from Les Brown:

> When you've got an idea you want to move on.
> You might not have the money, you might not

have the education, you might not have the support or the resources you need. What is that something that can keep us going, that will enable us to act on our dream? What's one of those keys that will begin to help us to discover the secrets to our dream? Here's what I want you to repeat after me please with power and conviction, say: 'It's Possible'. It's all I want you do when you look at your dream, just say to yourself every day: It's possible. Just say that every day to yourself: it's possible. Because what does that do? See, it begins to change your belief system…

So I say as you look into the future, while other people are giving up feeling like victims, feeling powerless, becoming negative, turning on each other rather than to each other, feeling that they can't make it, 'be ye not conformed to this world but be ye transformed by the renewing of your mind' with the mindset of that it's possible, that we can save this generation. It's possible that we can create new industries, a new economy. It's possible that I can find a new profession, a new job. It's possible I can create a new life. And it's necessary that I become actively involved in becoming a positive force in my life and on the planet. And it's me, yes it's you. It's all of us pulling together, working together, to create this brand new future and it's going to be hard, easy is not an option. But if it's hard, we will do it hard. Whatever is required to snatch victory from the jaws of defeat and it's worth it, yes. It's worth whatever we have to do and once we know that it is done, it is done, it is done.

Messages like these are very powerful for our children. I have asked some my teachers to use them as affirmations at the start of the lesson to motivate children. Affirmations like: It's possible; It's not over until I win; Easy is not an option; My condition is not permanent; I will persist until I succeed; There is greatness within me; have started making a difference.

Unlike many other primary schools and orphanages in Uganda, Blessed Hill Orphanage offers these children life skills. So, getting such messages from Les Brown and integrating them in what we do will surely equip children with a positive mindset so that they are ready to win against all odds. This is a key skill for them to have in a country where there is a lot of bad things happening. My dream is to have lessons that integrate these messages to help children get rid of the war inside them and prepare them for success. If I get funding, I will be able to hire someone to help me look at our curriculum and see how we can integrate some of the resources from Les Brown to make a greater impact. This will help our children have a positive outlook on life and aspire to achieve more despite their circumstances. Thank you for reading my story and if you are in Uganda, come and visit us at Blessed Hill Orphanage.

Create The Life Of Your Dreams
Ronnette Hopgood
Wisconsin, USA

Create the Life of Your Dreams

We are now going to Milwaukee, Wisconsin 'The Dairy State'. Here we will meet Ronnette Hopgood: a certified Les Brown speaker and teacher. It is her passion to help you go beyond your circumstances by taking control of your life. Before she tells you her story, she would like you to answer a couple of questions: What dreams and passions do you envision for yourself? Are you living out your passion or are they buried away by your own ridicules, insecurities and limited belief system? Now that you have pondered on the answers to these questions, she is ready to share with you the path to creating the life of your dreams.

I came to know Mr. Les Brown at a time when I was feeling 'stuck' in my life. I wasn't where I wanted to be with my life. I have always heard about Les Brown as the powerful speaker and great force that he is in communities and world around us. I have always wanted to help since I was a young girl. I used to play pretend and put out tables and chairs and envisioned a whole audience of people, my family was happy to participate.

My story - On this particular Saturday, I knew that there was more to life than working a 9-5 job that left me unfulfilled. I couldn't see myself beyond my circumstances. Growing up, my mother worked 2 jobs to take care of her 4 children including my 'twin' sister. As an adult, I still see the 'struggle' in my family and in my own life and where I was economically. I wanted to fill this void and get out of this undesired place.

One morning, my husband gave me a CD of Mr. Les Brown on my commute to and from work. I would listen to him every day and feel so 'empowered' to do great and more with my life. When I heard Mr. Brown say, "It's possible and you can change the direction of your life, no-one else can live your dream, your dream was only given to you". I've never heard anyone say this before with such power and conviction. It felt as if Mr. Les Brown was talking to me. I remembered the tears flowing down my face. This is when I started to believe in myself and see that my life could be changed. I was really stuck in that 'unlimited belief system'.

Les Brown helped me to see that I could create the life that I want for myself and for my family. It was through Les Brown's story and his words that changed my life forever. What touched me with Mr. Brown's story was that determination. He lived in an office he worked in and no one knew this for two weeks, until janitors and the security guard saw what was happening. Les Brown said, 'you don't have to be great to get started, but you have to get started to be great'. Also, when Les Brown believed the ridicule about not 'being smart enough' to solve a problem and Les Brown said, 'I can't do that'. Mr. Washington, Les Brown's teacher, said, 'Don't let someone's opinion of you become your reality'. Mr. Brown was labelled 'educable mentally retarded'. So what if we continue to believe the opinions of others? Where would we be with ourselves and in life?

Mr. Brown, I personally want to say thank you for impacting my life and the lives of others. I'm honoured to say and carry out your legacy for others. I don't know where my life would be right now if you, Mr. Brown, hadn't given me courage and inspiration to go out there and make a difference in the lives of others with my dreams. I'm now able to see my life beyond my circumstances. I've broken the generational curse from the family line.

My dream is to leave a legacy, which is to inspire and transform my children, family, and generations to come. I want people to know that they can be more, have more and become more, live their dreams and really be their authentic selves. Les Brown, thank you for your vision of the 'Les Brown Institute' where many dreams are really becoming a reality.

Thank you, ~ Ronnette Hopgood

CHAPTER 24: VOICE OF HOPE

497

What is the size of your hope?

In my bestselling book '7 Steps to Greatness', I write about the shortage of hope as one of the biggest challenges facing our world today. I remember being told a story about a town in Europe. Whereas people in the Western part of this town were affluent, those in the East were poor. Whereas people in the Western part of this town lived longer, those in the East had shorter lives. The main reason people in the Western part were affluent and lived longer was because they had unlimited hope. The main reason people in the Eastern part were poor and lived shorter lives was because they had a shortage of hope.

In this final chapter, you will discover how Les Brown's voice gave hope to people. By increasing the size of her hope, Vi Nedd-Jackman from Illinois was able to move from the valley to the mountain top. As he faced life's challenges, Les Brown's voice woke up Richard Shokane from Brunei from the deep sleep of helplessness, depression and came to the conclusion that Les Brown's voice is God's voice. As he tuned in on Les Brown for the first time, Jayson Gerald Nenis from Michigan heard, "Most people have done all that they are ever going to do. They raise a family, they earn a living, and then they die!" These words led him to the realisation that so many lives that have no drive, no direction, and people who are not really living in their life! As he did not want to be like them, Les Brown's voice set him on the journey of looking for more from life. Listening from The Sunshine State of Florida, Terrance Stafford had a great epiphany when he heard Les Brown talk about changing your mindset and using all that is inside of you. This allowed him to see that the sky is not the limit but just the beginning.

As you read this final and powerful chapter, be open to the possibility that you might be failing to reach your greatness not because of the place you are born and not because of your career, gender or race. You might be failing because of the size of your hope. My question to you is - what is the size of your hope? Are you ready to measure the size of your hope? Are you willing to increase the size of your hope? What are you willing to do or change after reading this book so that you increase your hope? I leave you with the words I heard from Pope Francis while in Rome in 2017, 'Hope does not disappoint. Hope is sure. Be men and women of hope'.

The Voice That Gave Me Life
Jayson Gerald Nenis
Michigan, USA

Founder/CEO
www.biglakevisions.com

The Voice That Gave Me Life

The area in and around Muskegon, Michigan is surrounded by creeks, wooded areas, rivers, marshes, ponds, lakes and the mighty Lake Michigan, one of the largest bodies of fresh water in the world. The eastern shore of Lake Michigan boasts some of the most visually magnificent sand dunes in the world, as well as being the largest freshwater dune system in the world. Commonly referred to as the 'Big Lake', Lake Michigan is a local and tourist destination year-round with its inspirational beauty and recreational opportunities. It is here where Jayson Gerald Nenis has lived most of his life and is considered his 'forever home'. He is a Director of Food Safety in the food manufacturing industry, as well as the founder/CEO of Big Lake Visions (www.biglakevisions.com), where the mantra is #haveavisionformore. Big Lake Visions offers life coaching, leadership training, and speaking engagements for those who wish to have more in their lives.

In the late summer of 2017 I made yet another flimsy attempt to improve my health by going for long walks. Occasionally, this included some jogging. Usually, I would listen to music to get me through it but this time I decided to give motivational speech compilations a try. I would play these YouTube videos in my headphones as I pushed my flabby 250-pound body down the street. These videos were great. I picked up a plethora of wisdom from the various speakers and celebrities. There was, however, a particular speaker that stood out from the rest. One that literally sent chills down my spine whenever I heard him speak; like an audible artist, a master of vocalization. The sound of his voice was so powerful, so mesmerizing. The words that left his mouth absolutely captivated me.

One of the very first things I heard this voice say that really struck me was, "Most people have done all that they are ever going to do. They raise a family, they earn a living, and then they die!" As I thought about those words, my jog turned into a walk, and then my walk turned into a standstill. I literally started to tear up on the side of the road. You see, there is so much truth in those words. I began realizing how many friends and family I had that fit that exact description. So many lives that have no drive, no direction, and people who are not really living in their life! I didn't want to be them. I wanted more than raising a family and earning a living. Les Brown went on to say,

> When you know within yourself that there's something you want to do and I believe that all of us was born with a purpose, that all of us have something that we are supposed to do, that all of us have some goodness within us and that goodness gives us a responsibility to manifest our greatness. And when you know that you could feel it in your guts and you know that you are deliberately operating below your potential, you've gotten comfortable, you stop expanding, you stop stretching, you stop challenging yourself, let me share something else with you. Not only is it possible for you to have your dream, but it's necessary. It's necessary that you have it, that you work on it, that you develop yourself, that you go for what is yours in the universe.

I said to myself, there is more to my life than this. Now, don't get me wrong. My family is the most important thing in my life. I am a full-time single father of 3 beautiful and intelligent little girls. There is no question that my life revolves around them. I also have a wonderful career for which I am grateful for, every single day. However, I have realized that there is much more out there. Why should I limit myself to only a few of life's simple pleasures? Why shouldn't I pursue my passion? The first thing I had to do was to find out who that amazing voice belonged to. I listened to the video a few times and started to Google some of the quotes. It turns out, that magnificent voice belonged to none other than The Great Les Brown.

Once I discovered the name that went with the voice, I started looking up his speeches on YouTube. The greatest speech I have ever seen or heard by Mr. Les Brown was his speech at the Georgia Dome. I am actually listening to that speech (for the 1,000th time) as I write my story now. If you've never seen or heard it, I would suggest you watch or listen to it in its entirety. It is life-changing. As a result of this newfound interest in Mr. Brown I have now read all of his books. I am also a member of the Les Brown Institute where I am training to be a motivational speaker, trainer and coach. You see, I have a story to tell.

I may not have grown up in poverty, but I certainly made some misguided choices in my young adult life that sent me to rock bottom by the time I was in my mid-twenties. I was well versed in the area of depression, as well as drug and alcohol abuse. I was trying to survive on minimum wage jobs and food stamps. I was a loser. I was losing at life. Eventually I got myself out of the hole and onto stable ground, and I'll tell that story someday when I write a book of my own. As for now, I have reached a point in my life where people can look at me and say "Yeah, he's successful". I suppose maybe I am, according to everyone else's standard, and I AM proud of what I have accomplished and overcome. However, Mr. Brown has made me realize that this is only the tip of the iceberg, and that I am DESTINED to do great things.

My destiny lies in helping others overcome their challenges with depression and drug abuse. To help others realize their true worth, their true potential. To realize that they owe it to themselves to push to their limits, and to also understand that it is going to be hard. It is incredibly hard, but I am here to tell you it is worth it! There is no better high than successfully achieving your goals. I only wish I had realized this in my twenties. My 'roaring twenties', as I now refer to them.

I'd love to end this and say I've lost 30 pounds because of Les Brown, but that's not the story. I'm still a flabby 250 pounds, but my mind and spirit are stronger than they have ever been. I have a successful career and I am in the beginning stages of getting my own business off the ground. I owe a bit of that to Les Brown. Les Brown is the mentor I never had. His voice and words of wisdom guide me every single day. In April of 2018 I will have the chance to meet my mentor. I will do my best to avoid tearing up when I shake his hand and say "Thank you, Mr. Brown. Thank you for your guidance. Thank you for helping me find my greatness."

Dr Patrick Businge

'Les Brown's voice is God's voice'
Richard Shokane
Brunei, Island of Borneo

'Les Brown's Voice is God's Voice'

We travel to Brunei to meet a man who believes 'Les Brown's voice is God's voice'. He is none other than Moshe Richard Shokane, son of Judy Shokane. Born and raised in Johannesburg in South Africa, he has travelled to many places including Dubai, and Saudi Arabia. He is currently living in Brunei and working as a teacher. From the tiny nation on the Island of Borneo which is surrounded by lovely beaches and the biodiverse rainforest, Richard tells how Les Brown changed his life.

In 2012 I lost my car, an Audi A4, which I had driven for only 2 months. I was tricked into a wrong deal by a Nigerian gentleman. From that time onwards, I started taking loans to make up for the loss of the car to an extent that I couldn't repay the money. This forced me to move to Saudi and then Dubai. During my difficult days, I used to listen to Les Brown daily.

As I listened to his videos and tapes, I could hear Les Brown telling me:

- 'If you stop fighting for what you want, what you want don't will automatically take over'.
- 'Too many of us are not living our dreams because we are living our fears'.
- 'Our ability to handle life's challenges is a measure of our strength of character'.

Les Brown's voice woke me up from the deep sleep of helplessness and depression. Though I would go to church, I was never touched like I was with Les Brown. I would like to let him know that his voice is God's voice. I love him and he is doing a great job. I thank God that Les Brown was born into this universe and he is alive today. While he's still alive I would like him to know that he himself has greatness within him. Listening to his story, I know how hard he worked to achieve his dreams.

There is a lot happening in the world right now. However, Mr. Brown chose to be the voice of hope. He speaks from the heart, hence he is heard by the hearts. His voice is heard all over the world. It is the voice that woke me up when I was down and deep asleep. He talked to me when I had no one to talk to. Les Brown spoke to my heart. He speaks with his heart. I know that minds can be captured but I also know that the heart is free and he has had the courage to follow it.   It's only God that can give Les Brown words with so much power to enter the hearts of many people and transform them. Les Brown, you speak with God's voice.

I am currently working in Brunei as a teacher. I know Mr. Les Brown wants to train more than 2,000 speakers. I know he wants to do more for humanity. Mr. Les Brown has changed lives of many people. My dream is to be part of the team that is already taking his works forward. I get joy in seeing someone succeed because of my effort. I want to reach out to people. I want to help them achieve their dreams. I want to be part of the driven people helping the people in need. As I come from South Africa, I know that South Africa and Africa at large would appreciate having the Les Brown Institute, too. The more voices of hope, the better for the world. I am willing to make this happen. Thank you, Dr. Patrick Businge, who has allowed me to express my message to Les Brown.   I believe this is the beginning of collaboration with the Les Brown Team to bring his institute to Africa.

From the Valley to the Mountain Top
Vi Nedd-Jackman
Illinois, USA

Speaker, Wellness Coach and Author
www.vineddconsulting.com

Dr Patrick Businge

From the Valley to the Mountain Top

We now travel to Chicago where we meet Vi: author of the upcoming book *The Healthier Youer You* and CEO of Vi Nedd Consulting Corp. that helps people design their lives and achieve total well-being. Vi is passionate about Forest Park: the town where she lives. She says: It is indeed an honor to reside in Forest Park, a suburb 20 minutes away from the historic city of Chicago, home to the tallest building in America. The Willis Tower, formerly called Sears Tower, stands 110-stories high and was the tallest building in the world for almost 25 years. Chicago is the birth place of the famous Walt Disney and also former residence of the 44th US President Barack Hussein Obama II. Chicago is the 3rd most populated city in the US, after New York and Los Angeles. The highlight of Chicago is the Cloud Gate Sculpture famously called the "Bean" which is the main attraction of Millennium Park. What is so special about the Bean? It is made of 168 plates of highly polished stainless steel which gives an illusion of liquid mercury. When you come to Chicago make sure the Bean is on your bucket list.

It was in this great city that I was at a point in my life where being in the valley was my regular place of abode. I couldn't seem to make it to the mountain top and if I did, it wasn't for long before I would find myself down in the valley again. It took me more than half my life to put everything into words of what I went through: chronic fear, the desire to end it all, verbal, emotional, and physical abuse.

As I sat and pondered on what this great city had to offer, I began a quest to discover territories beyond my circle because after feeling stuck for more than half of my life I said to myself, 'there has to be more in life than just this'. In my desperation while surfing the internet, I came across a video that gave me hope. This video was by Les Brown. In this video, he said, 'You have greatness within you'. This message touched my heart and challenged me to believe in myself.

After listening to this video, I was able to move from the valley with fears to the hill top with my dreams. I said to myself, if Les Brown who was born in an abandoned building, adopted, and did not have a college education was able to live his dreams, I can too. I never knew Les Brown before nor did anyone introduce me to him. After this encounter through video, I went to bed every night with him in my ears saying, 'You have greatness in you'. Les Brown was my virtual mentor for almost 2 years until May 2017 when I stumbled upon a Facebook invitation to partner with Les Brown. Immediately I contacted the Les Brown Institute and became a member. The most valuable advice he gave me was to surround myself with likeminded people. That is what the Les Brown Institute is there for.

I thank God for my great mentor Sir Les Brown. When everyone had given up on me, he gave me hope. He said there is something special inside of you, there is greatness within you. He helped me to move from the valley and strive to the mountain top. Since then, my life was never the same again.

Finding My Voice
Terrance Stafford
Florida, USA

Finding my voice

I found myself in a cycle of entanglement and caught up in mediocrity. One day, I came to the realization that I am the man in the family, I have a university degree and I should not be struggling. For sure I was committed and hardworking. However, I was committed to someone else's vision. I then began to listen to Dr. Myles Monroe and to Les Brown. I listened to Les Brown and how he talked about being Mammie Brown's baby boy and how things were not easy for him. I identified with what he was saying. My mother was a single mother who raised me with my brother. She too was committed to providing for us but life was not easy.

One day I was listening to Les Brown and I had a great epiphany when he talked about changing your mindset and using all that is inside of you to manifest it to your reality. It wasn't until I heard Les Brown talking about how he had to be hungry when others were able to go home and he stayed selling TVs that I too started walking the extra mile. So even now, I find myself where I am at because I stay up late. I work as a funeral director in a Caucasian funeral home where I embalm over 90 percent of the bodies that come here. Many people don't know that as a Black American I can work in a Caucasian funeral home. Les Brown gave me the confidence in being secure with who I am. I carry great value so I don't diminish my value for anyone. I carry great value and I am not intimidated when I go into a place where people don't look or talk like me. I control the change that I want to see. I control what I want to manifest.

Les Brown allowed me to see that the sky is not the limit but just the beginning. I am listening to him now calmly battling with cancer and I hear him saying, 'God don't take my voice'. For such a long time, I was in a state where I had a voice but did not have my voice. Les Brown gave me the confidence to find my voice and speak up against injustices. I stand against what is popular and contrary to what people think. When I am doing this, Les Brown is by my side. If I am going to fail, Les Brown tells me that if I fail, I must fail big.

Last year, I made a conscious decision that I was going to meet Les Brown in 2018. It was on my vision board. I said I have to manifest this because I understand that my words frame my world. If I don't ever say anything or if I don't ever see it, I wouldn't believe it. If I don't believe it I would never manifest what I don't believe. Les brown gave me the confidence that if I can believe it, I can see it, and if I can see it, I can achieve it. Les Brown gave me the confidence in understanding that the sky is not the limit but the beginning. He gave me the power to understand my character.

So, one of the things I did was to transcend where I was working. I had to leave the business I was outgrowing. I had been there for about 5 years. They considered me a family member but yet I had a cap on my income. I had all these big things I wanted to do for my family but I couldn't. Les Brown gave me the ability to go in there and challenge the norm and walk away. I didn't have the 5 point exit strategy while living. All I understood was that my value was more and they were not adding to my value. Now I understand that my dream is just a dream if I don't do anything about it. It's just a dream until I act upon it.

Now I am getting ready to open up my own business which is a funeral home.

Recently, Les Brown has given me the ability to work on my ministry. I am getting ready to do my empowerment sessions with various groups of people because of Les Brown's voice and encouragement to do what I want. I now understand that what I have been through is a foundation for me to go to the next level. If it was not because of Les Brown and his ministry (some people look at it as a business but I see it as a ministry), I wouldn't be where I am today. Les Brown was anointed to do what he does and he said, 'Preachers preach the Gospel about Jesus Christ. I preach the message Jesus Christ preached'. That is empowering because we have lots of people with talents who die without using them. He says, these people could have been great but they were afraid to be great. Les Brown has given me the ability to go beyond my fears and do what makes me happy. I now plan to go sky diving this year. People say I am crazy. This is amazing to be able to hear the voice of Les Brown and know that he has the ability to empower me. Once again he says, God don't take my voice. I can coincide with him and my fear is that if I ever call upon God and he doesn't respond, it's because I don't hear his voice. I want to thank Les Brown for who he is and the impact he has had on my life. I pray that in the near future I have the ability to sit face to face with him and eat at his feet because I don't deserve to eat at the top. God bless you.

CONCLUSION

Than You

Congratulations you have completed reading 77 stories on how Les Brown changed people's lives. What a journey you have had in reading these stories. Now that you have read all the stories, you do not have to stop here. It is time for you to create your greatest life with all that you have learnt.

You know you are gifted with greatness. You are in this universe for a purpose. You have lots of dreams within you. You have the power to use all that you have learnt to live the rest of your life as the best of your life. Step into action now. Walk with faith and show the world that you are unstoppable. Manifest your gifts and demonstrate to your community that you are an asset and not a liability to them. Live full and die empty.

I believe in you. I believe in your dreams. Go and live your life as a masterpiece because you are a piece of the master. If you want more information, please read the next pages where you will find discover more about Les Brown Unlimited and Greatness University.

Les Brown Unlimited

From humble beginnings to being recognized as one of the world's most renowned motivational speaker, Les Brown has a way with words that will motivate you to take action like no one else.

In Les Brown Unlimited, you have around the clock access to his life altering lessons that will bring lasting results. Les' straight-from-the-heart passion and high-energy will help motivate you to step beyond your limitations and into your personal and professional greatness.

Les is there to help you face your challenges and adversities. He's there to help you find true happiness and success. He's there to help you gain skills that will benefit both your personal and professional life. He's there … always … with his big smile and tireless energy to help you maximize the greatness within you.

A master of the science of achievement, Les Brown helps you commit to building and maintaining relationships, as well as helps you plan, measure, and execute goals. Learn how to be hungry for success and how to achieve beyond your horizons. Remember, it's not over until YOU win!

Master motivator Les Brown brings you daily motivation, inspiration, insights, knowledge, and stories to help you live the life you desire. You'll learn how to pursue your greatness and rise above your circumstances. You'll also tap into your full potential and learn how to say "Yes" to your life, "Yes" to your dreams, "Yes" to your unfolding future, and "Yes" to your potential.

Legendary speaker Les Brown teaches you how to tell your story, deliver a public speech, combat stage fright and even earn money as a public speaker. You will earn a personalized Certificate of Completion when you finish this powerful program on how to share your greatness with the world through better communication. For more information, visit **www.lesbrownunlimited.com.**

Greatness University

We are the world's first institution dedicated to discovering, unlocking, and monetising greatness in individuals and businesses. Our goal is to help you tap into your greatness faster and easier than you ever imagined. At Greatness University, we are always looking to partner with like-minded people from all corners of the world.

We offer online courses, run face to face training, offer one to one mentoring, and organise boot camps in various countries in the world.

As world leaders, our faculty members are always learning, being inspired and mentored by great people to continually unlock their greatness. One of our mentors, the world's number one motivational speaker Les Brown says, 'You have something special. There is greatness within you'. Allow us to help you tap into your greatness faster than you ever imagined in any area of your life. our courses include:

- Goal Setting
- Live Your Dreams
- Walking in Greatness
- The Millionaire in You
- Speak and Change the World
- Discover the Book in You

To discover more about our work, visit us at **www.greatness-university.com** where you will also be **register** and access our free course on **'Step into your Greatness'** now. We look forward to working with you and walking the path to greatness together.

About the Author

Dr Patrick Businge

Born in a small village in Uganda, Dr Patrick Businge did not let his circumstances characterised by war and abject poverty become his standard. Following his dreams while believing that no condition was permanent, he took steps to raise above his circumstances and made greatness his benchmark.

Dr Patrick Businge has gone on to become the Founder of Greatness University: the world's first institution dedicated to discovering, unlocking, and monetising greatness in individuals and businesses. His main goal is to help you tap into your greatness faster and easily than you can ever imagine.

Dr Patrick Businge is an educator. He has taught over 50,000 people in classrooms, churches, orphanages, villages, community centres, and boardrooms throughout the United Kingdom of Great Britain, Europe, Africa, and the Americas.

Dr Patrick Businge is also a strong believer in lifelong learning and personal development. He has studied in over 7 universities and acquired over 10 postgraduate qualifications. He has researched, written and spoken for approximately 20 years in the fields of ethics, philosophy, religion, education, armed conflict, disability, and greatness. Living in a world characterised by war, plagued by a shortage of hope and marred with average performance, his ultimate vision is to inspire one million people become instruments of peace, messengers of hope and channels of greatness. It is because of his vision and insight that he has recently got an Authentic Leadership Award.

Dr Patrick Businge is a bestselling author. He has written various books including:

- 7 Steps to Greatness: The **Masterplan** to Take Your Life, Studies, Career and Business to the Next Level
- 7 Steps to Greatness: The **Workbook** to Take Your Life, Studies, Career and Business to the Next Level
- 7 Steps to Greatness: The **Journal** to Take Your Life, Studies, Career and Business to the Next Level

He is a Book Creation coach and runs a retreat on how to discover, write, publish and monetise the book in you.

Dr Patrick Businge speaks to various audiences on Personal and Professional Development. His exciting talks, transformational seminars and life changing boot camps on 7 Steps to Greatness, Book Writing, Self-Esteem, STAR Goals, Success Mindset, and Finding Your Best Self bring about immediate change and long-term results.

Dr Patrick Businge has travelled and worked in over 10 countries on 3 continents. He speaks four languages: English, French, Swahili and some Arabic. Patrick is happily married and has 2 children. He is active in community and national affairs. To learn more about his programs, seminars and services, please visit **www.greatness-university.com**. If you have any personal questions email him directly at info@greatness-university.com or meet him on Facebook, Twitter, LinkedIn and Instagram.

Changed My Life Series

Change is a fact of life and to live is have changed often. As we go through life, there are a lot of people, places and circumstances that have changed our life. Why not share your story in my upcoming books? In sharing your story in 'Changed My Life' series, you will automatically become a co-author and get 100% royalties from the sales of the whole book. You will gain instant credibility in your field, widen your global presence, and leave a legacy for future generations. Here is a sample of the titles I am working on:

- My Mother Changed My Life
- My Father Changed My Life
- My Teacher Changed My Life
- My Children Changed My Life
- Jesus Changed Our Lives
- Les Brown Changed Our Lives
- America Changed My Life
- Britain Changed My Life
- Africa Changed My Life.

To discover more about my work, email me at info@greatness-university.com or visit **www.greatness-university.com** where you will also be able to get my bestselling book **'7 Steps to Greatness'** for free. I look forward to publishing your story and walking the path to greatness with you. You might also be interested in my other books on the next pages.

The Road To Your
BEST SELF
Discover the Miracle Power,
Uncommon Nature and Greatness in You
DR PATRICK BUSINGE

PATRICK BUSINGE
'This first moving book is full of great ideas that will inspire and motivate you to achieve all your goals'.
- Brian Tracy, Bestselling Author.
7 STEPS TO GREATNESS
The Masterplan to Take Your Life, Studies, Career and Business to the Next Level

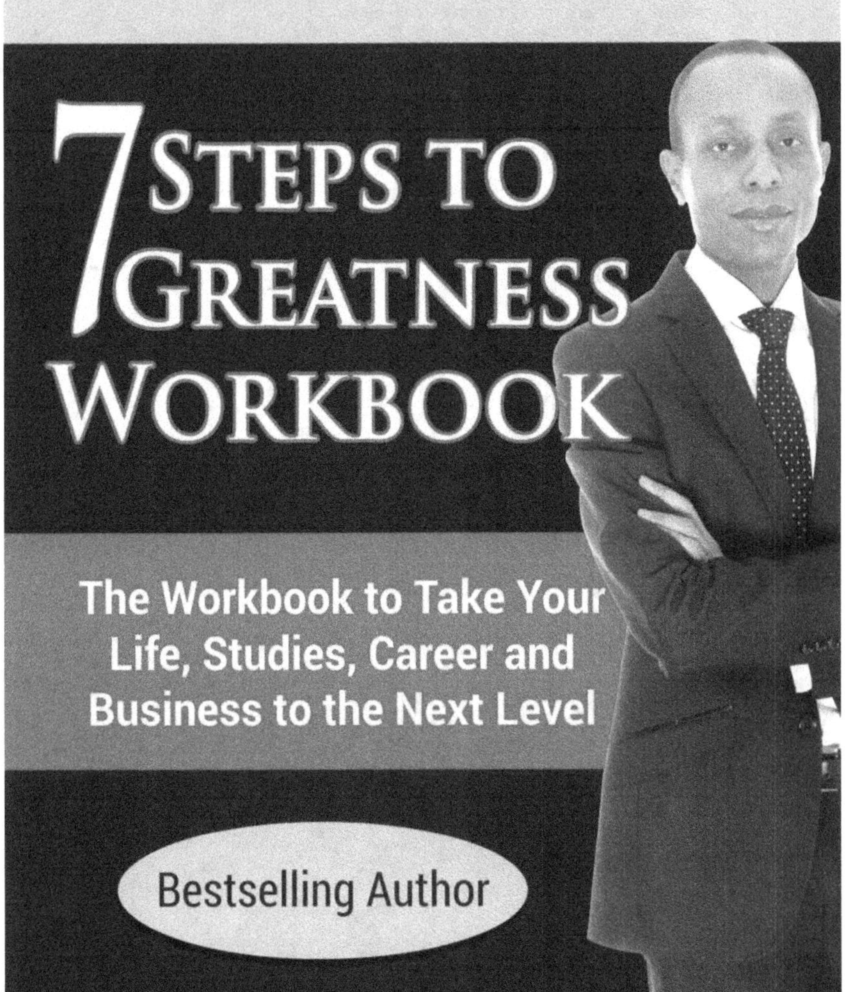

PATRICK BUSINGE
7 STEPS TO GREATNESS WORKBOOK
The Workbook to Take Your Life, Studies, Career and Business to the Next Level
Bestselling Author

7 STEPS TO GREATNESS JOURNAL

DR. PATRICK BUSINGE

Les Brown Changed Our Lives

INDEX BY CONTRIBUTOR

Les Brown Changed Our Lives